Organisation Development

STANDARD LOAN

Organisation Development

Metaphorical Explorations

edited by

Cliff Oswick and David Grant

PITMAN
PUBLISHING

PITMAN PUBLISHING
128 Long Acre, London WC2E 9AN

A Division of Pearson Professional Limited

First published in Great Britain in 1996

© Pearson Professional Limited 1996

ISBN 0 273 61451 7

British Library Cataloguing in Publication Data
A CIP catalogue record for this book can be obtained from the British Library

10 9 8 7 6 5 4 3 2 1

Typeset by Pantek Arts, Maidstone, Kent
Printed and bound in Great Britain by Bell and Bain, Glasgow

The Publishers' policy is to use paper manufactured from sustainable forests.

CONTENTS

LIST OF TABLES AND FIGURES

Tables

Figures

ABBREVIATIONS

BA	British Airways	NVQ	National Vocational Qualification
BITC	Business In The Community	OD	Organisation Development
BPR	Business Process Re-engineering	OMD	Outdoor Management Development
CEO	Chief Executive Officer	QC	Quality Circle
DNA	Deoxyribonucleic Acid	R & D	Research and Development
FA	Football Association	RDT	Resource Dependency Theory
HRM	Human Resource Management	SIT	Social Identity Theory
IBM	International Business Machines	SME	Small Manufacturing Enterprise
IIP	Investors In People	SPC	Statistical Process Control
MBO	Management By Objectives	SWOT	Strengths, Weaknesses, Opportunities and Threats
MBWA	Management By Wandering About	TQM	Total Quality Management
NASA	North American Space Agency		

PREFACE

Much of the literature available on Organisation Development (OD) is geared towards meeting the needs of practising OD consultants rather than those of students. This predisposition reflects the action-based origins of OD and the essence of the discipline as an applied area of behavioural science knowledge. Although aimed at students, most OD textbooks have perpetuated the imbalance between practitioner and academic needs. This is reflected in the content of these texts which tends to be broad, descriptive and heavily biased towards success. This book adopts a contrasting position by focusing upon analysis rather than description and depth rather than breadth. The positivist stance commonly found in OD texts is rejected in favour of a more critical perspective.

The essays contained in this book seek to provide insights into the nature and complexity of OD by using metaphor as a vehicle for analysis. Here, OD is treated as a process of planned change which draws upon behavioural science knowledge as a means of enhancing an organisation's efficiency and effectiveness. The incorporation of metaphor is intended to operate at two levels. First, as an aid to learning and a mechanism for enhancing the reader's understanding of previously unfamiliar aspects of OD. Secondly, to act as a basis for analysing the appropriateness of the metaphor and the nature of the target area. To this end, readers are encouraged to challenge the metaphors offered and generate ones of their own in order to stimulate a deeper understanding of OD.

The term 'explorations' in the title reflects the philosophy underpinning the book. It attempts to take the reader on a journey of discovery – a form of metaphorical expedition. In doing so metaphors are applied to a number of key themes, namely: the nature of organisations and organisational analysis, key elements of the OD process, planned organisational change, aspects of organisational culture, and management initiatives. Within the 'expedition' framework, these themes are either concerned with stages of the journey or represent differing routes towards the common destination of improved organisational effectiveness.

ACKNOWLEDGEMENTS

Our thanks go to Penelope Woolf, Annette McFadyen and their colleagues at Pitman Publishing for the encouragement and helpful advice they have provided. We would also like to thank Paul Strinati and Paul Suff for their enthusiasm and administrative support during the formative stages of this project.

Cliff Oswick and David Grant

CONTRIBUTORS

Nic Beech Lecturer in Organisational Behaviour, Strathclyde Business School, University of Strathclyde.

Mike Broussine Principal Lecturer in Management Development, Bristol Business School, University of the West of England.

Adrian Carr Senior Lecturer in Organisational Studies and Change, Department of Management and Administration, University of Western Australia.

Timothy Clark Research Fellow in International Management, School of Management, The Open University.

Graeme Currie Senior Lecturer in Human Resource Management, School of Business, University of Derby.

Richard Dunford Professor of Management, The Management Group, Faculty of Commerce and Administration, Victoria University of Wellington, New Zealand.

David Grant Lecturer in Human Resource Management and Industrial Relations, The Management Centre, King's College, University of London.

Joy Hocking Lecturer in Organisation Theory and Industrial Relations, School of Management and Law, Edith Cowan University, Australia.

Dawn Inns Lecturer in Organisational Behaviour, School of Business and Management at Harrow, Faculty of Business Management and Social Studies, University of Westminster.

Philip Jones Senior Lecturer in Organisational Behaviour, School of Business and Management at Harrow, Faculty of Business Management and Social Studies, University of Westminster.

Jimme Keizer Senior Lecturer in Organisation Theory and Management Consulting, Graduate School of Industrial Engineering and Management Science, Eindhoven University of Technology, The Netherlands.

Maire Kerrin Researcher, School of Business, University of Derby.

Savita Kumra Senior Lecturer in Human Resource Management, School of Management and Professional Studies, University of Greenwich.

Sidney Lowe Lecturer in Marketing and Strategic Management, The Management Centre, King's College, University of London.

Cliff Oswick Head of Department and Lecturer in Organisation Development, The Management Centre, King's College, University of London.

Ian Palmer Associate Professor in Management, School of Management, University of Technology, Sydney, Australia.

Lew Perren Principal Lecturer in Business Analysis, The Centre for Management Development, University of Brighton.

Ger Post Senior Lecturer in Organisation Theory and Management Consulting, Faculty of Industrial Engineering and Management Science, Eindhoven University of Technology, The Netherlands.

Graeme Salaman Reader in Sociology, Social Science Faculty, The Open University.

Russ Vince Principal Lecturer in Management Development, Bristol Business School, University of the West of England.

Organisation Development and metaphor – mapping the territory

Cliff Oswick and David Grant

Metaphors are firmly embedded within the Organisation Development (OD) literature; indeed, the use of metaphor in OD appears to be almost as old as the field itself. To elaborate, the roots of OD can be traced back almost half a century to Kurt Lewin's work in 1946. His pioneering research into group dynamics, inter-personal relations and survey feedback has laid the foundations on which modern OD approaches have been built. Lewin framed much of his research in metaphorical terms. In particular, two examples are found in his most widely cited and enduring models (Lewin, 1951). First, the use of 'unfreezing–change–refreezing' to convey a particular approach to instigating major organisational change relies on metaphor. Second, the development of 'force-field analysis' – a technique for plotting the tension between the *driving* and *restraining* forces for organisational change – has definite metaphorical connotations.

As the reader moves through this book, the extent to which the literature has enlisted metaphor to describe and illuminate a number of facets of OD will become increasingly apparent. Organisations have been described as analogous to: machines and organisms (Burns and Stalker, 1961), garbage cans (Cohen et al, 1972), icebergs (Selfridge and Sokolik, 1975), brains and psychic prisons (Morgan, 1986), theatres (Mangham and Overington, 1987) and soap bubbles (Tsoukas, 1993). A proliferation of metaphors for OD consulting styles have also been provided, including among others: the court judge (Block, 1981), the reflector (Tilles, 1961), the doctor (Schein, 1969), the collaborator (Lippitt and Lippitt, 1978), the detective (Steele, 1975), the pathfinder (Leavitt, 1986), and the friendly co-pilot (Nees and Greiner, 1985). We even find metaphors being applied to the process of OD, e.g. 'red flags' in diagnosis (Harvey and Brown, 1992) and the 'organisation mirror' as an intervention strategy (French and Bell, 1990).

It has been argued that metaphor merely represents a fanciful literary device (Pinder and Bourgeois, 1982). Conversely, and in support of metaphor, it has been posited that their role extends beyond acting as a form of figurative embellishment. In effect, they help to make the complex simple and aid our understanding. They also provide *ways of seeing and thinking* about organisations (Morgan, 1986). We would hope that this book conveys the essence of this debate. The contributors are all aware that its primary purpose is not simply to add to the array of colourful metaphors which pervade organisational language and OD. Nor is it an attempt to eulogise the use of metaphor. Instead, the volume brings together a collection of critical essays which draw on metaphor as a means of exploring and analysing OD. In doing so, each chapter encourages the reader not only to think about the value of metaphors in relation to particular OD subject areas, but also to consider the limitations, and on occasion dangers, of applying metaphors to organisational analysis. The intention is then to look beyond the surface application of metaphors to organisational problems and interventions.

For example, readers are encouraged to challenge and question the metaphors provided. Both the aspects of similarity (the *ground*) and dissimilarity (the *tension*) between the metaphor and the target domain should be critically examined. Readers should also seek to formulate metaphors of their own. Using the text in this way enables an approach similar to that used with case study material to be developed and this process, whether undertaken using group discussion or individually via reflection, should help to generate a deeper understanding of OD issues.

The use of the term 'exploration' in the title of this book encapsulates the way in which it approaches the study of OD: as a form of *metaphorical journey*. It is the equivalent of a 'reconnaissance', in the military sense of a focused journey of discovery aimed at mapping some key features of unfamiliar or uncharted terrain. The key features, or what might more aptly be described as 'strategic targets', surveyed in the book are divided into four main sections: organisational analysis, organisational culture and change, the intervention process, and management strategies and development. The rationale underpinning the centrality and relevance of each of the topics, and further details of the content of specific chapters, can be found in the short introductions provided at the start of each part.

Much of the discourse on OD has been couched in a consultant-friendly way. In particular, the discipline has been beset by prescriptive stage models and step-by-step guides. These treatments of OD issues tend to adopt a highly descriptive, and largely optimistic, stance. They often fail to consider the limitations and shortcomings of the techniques they espouse. Arguably, insufficient attention has been given to questioning some of the underlying assumptions on which this dominant OD paradigm is built. At least in partial response to this problem, this volume is primarily aimed at an academic audience rather than at OD practitioners – although we would expect that practitioners will find it of some assistance when tackling organisational problems. The work takes a phenomenological viewpoint, and in doing so it seeks to use metaphor as a tool with which to address 'why' questions as opposed to simply prescribing solutions to the more positivist, practitioner-oriented 'how' questions. The concentration on *analytical depth* in providing an exploration of key OD issues means that this book can be used to counterbalance, or at the very least complement, the *descriptive breadth* offered in most mainstream OD textbooks. To stay with the theme of an 'exploratory journey', the book requires the reader to embark on a *cerebral expedition*.

REFERENCES

Block, P. (1981) *Flawless Consulting*. San Diego, CA: Pfeiffer.

Burns, T. and Stalker, G.M. (1961) *The Management of Innovation*. London: Tavistock.

Cohen, M.D., March, J.G. and Olsen, J.P. (1972) 'A garbage can model of organizational choice', *Administrative Science Quarterly*, Vol. 17.

French, W.L. and Bell, C.H. (1990) *Organisation Development: Behavioural Science Interventions for Organisational Improvement*. 4th Edition, London: Prentice-Hall.

Harvey, D.F. and Brown, D.R. (1992) *An Experiential Approach to Organisation Development*. 4th Edition, London: Prentice-Hall.

Leavitt, H.J. (1986) *Corporate Pathfinders*. Illinois: Dow Jones-Irwin.

Lewin, K. (1951) *Field Theory in Social Science*. New York: Harper and Row.

Lippitt, G. and Lippitt, R. (1978) *The Consulting Process in Action*. La Jolla, CA: University Associates.

Mangham, I. and Overington, M. (1987) *Organisations as Theatres: A Social Psychology of Dramatic Appearances*. Chichester: Wiley.

Morgan, G. (1986) *Images of Organization*. Newbury Park, CA: Sage.

Nees, D.B. and Greiner, L.E. (1985) 'Seeing behind the look-alike management consultants', *Organization Dynamics*, Vol. 14, No. 1.

Pinder, C.C. and Bourgeois, V.M. (1982) 'Controlling tropes in administrative science', *Administrative Science Quarterly*, Vol. 27.

Schein, E.H. (1969) *Process Consultation: Its Role in Organization Development*. Reading, Mass.: Addison-Wesley.

Selfridge, R.J. and Sokolik, S.L. (1975) 'A comprehensive view of organizational development', *M.S.U. Business Topics*, Winter.

Steele, F. (1975) *Consulting for Organizational Change*. Amherst, Mass.: University of Massachusetts Press.

Tilles, S. (1961) 'Understanding the consultant's role', *Harvard Business Review*, November–December.

Tsoukas, H. (1993) 'Organisations as soap bubbles: an evolutionary perspective on organisation design', *Systems Practice*, Vol. 6, No. 5.

PART I

Metaphors and organisational analysis

INTRODUCTION

Our metaphorical journey commences with a discussion of two key questions. First, how central are metaphors to our everyday understanding of organisations – i.e. how do they affect our interpretation of what organisations are and do? Second, what is the relationship between metaphor and Organisation Development? The three chapters in this opening section of the book all address these questions, demonstrating how and why the authors of subsequent chapters have chosen to adopt metaphor as a medium by which to analyse organisational change.

It is hoped that, for those readers not familiar with the concepts and issues surrounding metaphor and organisation, these opening chapters will provide a useful introduction to the existing literature in this area. That said, the importance of these chapters is that each takes the reader beyond the established literature. Using their own theories and concepts, they demonstrate the power, the value, and equally important the limitations, of metaphor when applied to an organisational setting.

In Chapter 1 Palmer and Dunford demonstrate the role of metaphor in organisational analysis by inviting the reader to carry out a simple exercise. The value of this exercise is that it highlights the pervasiveness of particular metaphors in relation to organisations, and also shows the way in which people use metaphors to make sense of their organisational experiences. The exercise can easily be applied in either an organisational or learning environment. Participants are asked to describe an organisation in which they are in some way involved. The results tend to display a high degree of consistency both within groups of participants and among groups as a whole.

We have suggested that this book represents a metaphorical journey through OD. It is this point on which Inns homes in. She argues in Chapter 2 that humans tend to experience the world via sets of culturally based beliefs, values and concepts, all of which are expressed or reaffirmed using a number of dominant or root metaphors. Inns goes on to demonstrate how the root metaphor of a journey has in fact formed the basis of our understanding and interpretation of the field of OD. Her analysis of changes in Western culture and of OD literature, combined with a discussion of the history of OD, leads her to conclude that OD has moved away from a position where it believed that if it could simply take an organisation on a journey from point A to point B it would therefore have solved the organisation's problems. Instead, we now see Organisation Development's role as taking an organisation on an explorative journey – an expedition where the destination is unclear and the outcomes unknown. We therefore pay more attention to the OD processes in use while the journey is under way, for it is these processes that have an impact on organisational effectiveness and not arrival at some predetermined destination.

Kumra examines the contribution of human metaphors to organisational analysis. Her chapter demonstrates how the organisation is regularly perceived in terms of it being a human entity (a point emphasised in Palmer and Dunford's chapter) and that this perception pervades the field of OD. Such a perception often leads us to assign human attributes to organisations. These include physical, behavioural and mental attributes. As Kumra points out, given that this process has a number of limitations as well as benefits, this has considerable implications for OD. If, for example, the human metaphor impacts on the way an OD consultant thinks of organisations, it may well be that it shapes the way in which the consultant perceives organisational problems and then goes about remedying them.

CHAPTER 1

Understanding organisations through metaphor

Ian Palmer and Richard Dunford

WHY METAPHORS MATTER

Metaphors matter because language matters. As a central constitutive element of language, metaphors often play an important part in determining how we think and act in the world. They provide mental pictures that are highly graphic, enabling the transformation of words from a context in which their use is literal to a context in which they provide an analogy. This involves making a link between something which is familiar and something which is less familiar in order to make sense of it (Boland and Greenberg, 1988). For example, consider the following discussions of organisational restructuring:

> What do donuts and corporations have in common? The answer: a hole in the middle. . . The widening gap in the organisation is its mid-section, once rotund, even portly. Some call the reductions 'tummy tucks'. . . As companies retrench, layoff casualties come increasingly from deep cuts in mid-level management. (Skagen, 1992: 1)

> Corporate America is on a crash diet, sloughing off a bulge of white-collar employees. . . A wave of big mergers has left many companies with bloated staffs. . . There can be a lot of advantages to making a company leaner. . . Over the past 18 months, nearly 300 companies have slimmed down. . . Others. . .are just beginning to sharpen the knife. (Nussbaum, 1986: 52–53)

The imagery in the above sections of text is not hard to identify. The state of organisations is presented as akin to that of an overweight individual. These images, taken largely from terms that have a literal meaning in the context of a discussion of the human body and medical interventions, are used 'out of context'. That is precisely where their seductive power resides. The reader is invited to see the situation of the organisation as akin to that of a sick or overweight person.

The power of the metaphor comes from being able to take us beyond the limits of literal language and, by so doing, implying that a connection in context A also applies in context B. To remain with our example of the organisation as an overweight person, the connection is that overweight people are often required to take remedial action in order to become slimmer. Therefore, when transferred to the organisational context, an explicit or implicit implication is that similar action is warranted. This linkage to action is an important characteristic of metaphors. Metaphors 'do not simply describe an external reality; they also help constitute that reality and prescribe [both] how it ought to be viewed. . .and a mode of behaviour' (Tsoukas, 1991: 570). That is, metaphors help name a state ('This is fat'), often communicate an attitude to that state ('Fat is undesirable'), and often specify or imply the appropriate course of action ('Fat must be removed').

It has been argued that metaphors are part of our cognitive structure (Lakoff and Johnson, 1980; Morgan, 1986) and that they 'are so deeply embedded in our daily language that we become blind to the important ways in which they shape our thought and influence our behaviour' (Kendall and Kendall, 1993: 149). Following Weaver (1967), Kendall and Kendall (1993: 150) argue that metaphors function to make abstract ideas concrete, to help clarify ambiguity, to assist in thought and to facilitate expression of the subjective. Ortony (1975) describes the utility of metaphors in terms of three 'theses'. The 'compactness thesis' presents metaphors as 'quick, concise and effective'. The 'inexpressibility thesis' builds on the fact that for any given language there are certain things which are inexpressible, so that metaphors become the way of saying something for which literal terms do not exist. The 'vividness thesis' argues that metaphors are effective because they are able to build on experiences and thus have enhanced cognitive and emotional impact. Metaphors 'allow the transfer of coherent chunks of characteristics – perceptual, cognitive, emotional and experiential – from a vehicle which is known to a topic which is less so' (Ortony, 1975: 53).

Metaphors may reinforce existing interpretations. As a core component of language they may be key contributors to the establishment of the orthodox view. Metaphors are not necessarily disruptive of established views. However, they do have the potential to open up new ways of 'seeing' situations. They can 'give new meaning to our pasts, to our daily activity, and to what we know and believe' (Lakoff and Johnson, 1980: 139). Using a metaphor to characterise metaphors, Morgan (1993: 5) describes them as 'lenses'; changing metaphors is akin to changing lenses and thereby getting a new perspective on a phenomenon. Sometimes, through metaphors providing a different conceptualisation of a situation, alternative courses of action may be generated that may otherwise not have emerged. However, it is important to recognise that any metaphor can only provide a partial insight. Two situations cannot be perfectly analogous without becoming one and the same, therefore understanding a situation via a transferred image must always be less than comprehensive. A metaphor, no matter how 'revealing', cannot help but alert us to some features and draw our attention away from others (Linstead, 1993: 56; Tsoukas, 1991).

The idea that metaphors do not just describe reality but also are involved in the creation of reality is based on the view that what is real is not wholly external to, and independent of, how human beings conceptualise the world (Lakoff and Johnson, 1980: 145–146; Morgan, 1993: 272–276). That is, the meanings that we attribute to what is going on around us influence the actions that we take. Reality is not some totally given, unambiguous 'thing' that is revealed remorselessly, independent of human agency. What we think affects how we act, and by acting we influence the construction of 'reality'. For this reason, reality and the part metaphors can play in its construction have stimulated considerable debate – especially where metaphors are applied to the analysis of organisations. Issues raised in these debates include: whether metaphors facilitate or mitigate against the production of scientific knowledge; whether particular metaphors are compatible; why some metaphors gain prominence over others; and whether single or multiple metaphors should be used in order best to comprehend particular organisational situations (see, for example, Alvesson, 1993; Bourgeois and Pinder, 1983; Morgan, 1983; Palmer and Dunford, 1995; Pinder and Bourgeois, 1982; Reed, 1990; Tinker, 1986; Tsoukas, 1991, 1993a).

METAPHORS IN ORGANISATIONAL ANALYSIS

There is now a substantial body of literature in the field of organisational theory which deals with the use of metaphors in organisational analysis, much of it building on the work of Gareth Morgan. In his seminal text, *Images of Organization*, Morgan (1986) argues that many of our conventional ideas about organisation and management build on a small number of taken-for-granted images, especially mechanical and biological ones. When we think of an organisation as if it were a machine we treat it as a purpose-driven device whereby various inputs are transformed into outputs. At the core of this image is the idea that a common goal or purpose exists and that this will be achieved primarily through ensuring that the organisation is correctly designed. The reference to a biological metaphor picks up the heavy reliance in management language on the idea that an organisation comprises a number of functionally differentiated and interdependent parts and that it operates in an environment to which it must adapt if it is to survive. In short, the organisation is often spoken of as if it were an organism – a point developed in Chapter 3 by Kumra, who discusses how the biological metaphor has been used to portray the organisation 'as a human entity'.

There has been a proliferation in the range of metaphors applied to organisations. Morgan (1986), following his identification of the dominance of mechanical and biological metaphors, suggests that we can usefully think of organisations in a number of other ways. These include brains, cultures, political systems and psychic prisons; Gergen (1992) encourages us to think of organisations as clouds and songs, and Tsoukas (1993b) identifies organisations with soap bubbles. Analogies have been drawn from a variety of disciplines external to the field of management. For example, metaphorical insights into either the practice or the teaching of management have been drawn from the arts, including literature and storytelling (Boje, 1991; Cowden, 1989–90; Harris, 1991; Shaw and Locke, 1993), music (Sommers, 1993; Zimmerman, 1985–86), film (Baker, 1993; Gallos, 1993; Gartner, 1993; Powell and Veiga, 1985–86; Serey, 1992), drama/theatre (Golden-Biddle, 1993; Greenberg and Miller, 1991; Rueschhoff, 1989–90) and art (Cowan, 1992).

Metaphors have been used to characterise not just organisations as a whole but also fields of organisational practice, including strategic planning (Morgan, 1993), structure (Peters, 1992; Morgan, 1993), organisation development (Akin and Schultheiss, 1990), information technology (Kendall and Kendall, 1993), organisational culture (Brink, 1993), organisational change (Lundberg, 1990; Marshak, 1993; Morgan, 1993), policy (Doubuzinskis, 1992), human resource development (Marx and Hamilton, 1991), leadership (Bensimon, 1989), entrepreneurship (Stewart, 1990), problem solving (Boland and Greenberg, 1988; Proctor, 1989), and production systems (Garud and Kotha, 1994).

A METAPHOR EXERCISE

With a few exceptions (for example, Broussine and Vince's work in Chapter 4), most applications of metaphor-based analysis to organisations involve a deductive approach, in that the emphasis is on illustrating how particular metaphors can be applied to organisational situations. By comparison, the exercise outlined in this chapter employs an inductive approach. It does not impose specific metaphors or seek to demonstrate the relevance or worthiness of specific metaphors. Rather, it seeks to highlight the metaphors with which people already operate as a result of their experience of organisations. It can be used with people of both very limited and extensive organisational experience. The objectives of this exercise are:

1 To identify metaphors-in-use through which people make sense of their organisational experiences.
2 To demonstrate that people experience organisations differently, as reflected in the variety of metaphors which are used to describe organisations.

3 To illustrate how metaphors both illuminate and blind us to ways of seeing organisations.

To carry out the exercise it is necessary to get the co-operation of a number of people such as friends or associates, fellow students or work-mates. Those who agree to participate will only be required to spend 5–10 minutes answering the question(s), as discussed in the following section. When this is complete you can carry out the remaining stages yourself if you wish. However, for reasons explained below, it would be useful if some of the participants could also be part of a group discussion concerning the responses received.

Step 1

Table 1.1 contains the details of two ways of asking people to address the issue of the nature of organisations (Sheets A and B). Give the instructions on Sheet A to approximately one-third of the participants, Sheet B to the remainder. Sheet A requires participants to provide a formal definition, while Sheet B requires them to use a metaphor drawing directly on their experience of a particular organisation. This exercise can be used with people of both limited and extensive organisational experience. You should give Sheet A to those with the more limited experience, as it is not dependent on any experiential base.

Table 1.1 Definitions and metaphors

Sheet A: Please write a brief definition (one or two sentences) of an organisation.
Sheet B: One way of describing an organisation and how it operates is by using a *metaphor*, e.g. 'My organisation is like a well-oiled machine – it runs smoothly and without squeaks'; or 'My organisation is like a butterfly: it flits from one idea to another without any seeming logic or connection.' 1. In relation to an organisation in which you work, or have worked, what metaphor best describes what it is really like and how it operates?   My organisation is like …   2. What is it about your organisation that you are trying to convey through this image?

There are two key features associated with the wording of Sheet B's questions. First, examples of both positive and negative organisational metaphors are provided prior to the request to provide a metaphor. This is intended to legitimise either response, so that participants do not assume that they are expected to provide a particular (for example, negative/critical) response. Second, because metaphors may be ambiguous or paradoxical (Kendall and Kendall, 1993) clarification of their meaning is required. For example, if an organisation is described as a circus, this could be either a positive image (well co-ordinated, efficiently run) or a negative image (lots of acts, all competing for attention and lacking overall co-ordination). Hence, as well as providing a metaphor, respondents are asked to explain what it is about the organisation that they are trying to convey through their metaphors. This is important in enabling a contextually meaningful interpretation of the metaphors that emerge. According to Lakoff and Johnson (1980: 19) 'no metaphor can ever be comprehended or even adequately represented independently of its experiential basis'.

Step 2

Collect the responses to Step 1. First look at the definitions of organisation that your participants have provided on Sheet A. Having run this exercise over a number of years it is our experience that the answers overwhelmingly represent the mechanistic metaphor, with its emphasis on order, planning, structure and common goals. Responses from a recent group that we worked with included:

> **An organisation is a body of people who work or co-operate within set parameters to achieve a common goal.**

> **An organisation is a collection of knowledge, skills and attributes co-ordinated to work towards a common objective by providing services and/or products to some other defined body or bodies.**

> **The organisation is a collection of people with specific objectives and goals and clearly defined roles and responsibilities for each person.**

> **An organisation is a group of people, either large or small, who can interact in pursuit of a common purpose or goal.**

The responses to Sheet A are usually so similar that we jokingly ask the participants who have provided them whether they have all read and memorised the same book!

Sheet B requires the respondent to describe the organisation in terms of a metaphor. Table 1.2 provides some examples with which we have been presented.

Table 1.2 Organisational metaphors and the meaning their originators seek to convey

Metaphor	Meaning
An excited impatient child	The organisation is growing, rather uncontrolled, getting stronger, focused on being different, not yet mature.
Family	The organisation has a senior manager who is benevolent, tolerant but not always approachable ('Dad'); there is a feeling of caring ('Mum'), but sometimes there is a child–adult relationship between management and staff.
A coffee plunger	The organisation looks good, 'smells good', but there is pressure coming down from the top.
A chameleon	The organisation has an ability to rapidly change its appearance in response to threats and opportunities in its business environment.
Keystone cops	People race from one crisis situation to another without any overall plan.
A car with a flat tyre	The organisation knows how and why to progress but because of its tradition-bound practices it can only move erratically and slowly.
A circus	The original appearance of the organisation may be one of disorganisation, but it is actually carefully organised and orchestrated.
A leaking boat from which the rats are fleeing	Restructuring is breaking up the organisation leading to a reduction in performance. Anyone who can is leaving because of the feeling of doom and gloom.
A misunderstood teenager	People in the organisation have an at times confused, but overall reasonably solid idea of what they are doing and why, even if from the outside they appear to act irrationally.
A river	The organisation moves at a fairly slow pace, but it is consistent and it gets things done.
A winning racehorse with weights on its back	The organisation has shown the ability to perform well and has great potential to do even better, but it is being held back by internal dissension.
A cluster of cyclones rampaging independently of each other	The organisation lacks leadership and direction. It is structured in such a way that too many independent parts are operating independently without any general co-ordination or accountability. There is no drawing together of the various divisions to achieve a common goal.
A dinosaur	The organisation is old, awkward, out of its time, place, doing things the same old way it's always done – unable to adapt/unaware of its environment, slow to respond – headed for extinction.
A new-born baby. It has no teeth to bite, no muscles to flex, it can hardly crawl, let alone walk or run, but it screams very loud and it grows	The organisation is young, unstructured but dynamic.
A roller-coaster	There are great peaks and troughs of activity. The organisation rapidly fluctuates from being very busy and pushed to its limit to being very quiet and slow.

As can be gauged from the responses listed in Table 1.2, a variety of creative metaphors are likely to emerge, ranging from those which portray an organisation in a positive light through to those which present a very negative image (the latter usually predominate). The metaphors invariably create a great deal of humour when reported in a group setting. It is the experience of the authors that the humour associated with the exercise has a positive outcome in terms of facilitating discussion of the utility of metaphors.

Step 3

Focus on the divergence between the answers to the two questions. The majority of metaphors arising from Sheet B are likely to contrast sharply with the machine metaphor-focused definitions that Sheet A typically produces. Consider – or if you are in a group, discuss – why this is the case. The metaphors provided by participants will provide insights into the way in which organisational participants view organisations. This is likely to reveal a much more complex, ambiguous, paradoxical and messy reality than that revealed by standard definitions such as those typically provided in response to Sheet A. As Morgan (1989: 30) has noted, the conventional definition of organisation 'eliminates almost all the interesting features of organisations in practice'. What features of organisations are indicated by your participants' metaphors that are not indicated in the Sheet A definitions? Note also that the metaphors are likely to vary in terms of their utility. A useful metaphor is one that provides a new insight. For example, if someone describes an organisation as a 'mountain' on the grounds that both are 'big', the value of applying the metaphor is virtually nil.

The variation in metaphors that participants provide may also be used to highlight the divergent experiences that people have of organisations. Explore a range of possible explanations for this divergence, including the different characteristics of different organisations, the effect of a person's position in the organisation (for example, variation by department and level of seniority), stage in career, ethnicity and gender.

Step 4

The next stage in the exercise is to categorise the metaphors provided by the participants. This can be used to provide a quantifiable picture of the experience of participants along two dimensions (see Table 1.3). One dimension concerns which organisational practices the metaphors focus on. Palmer and Lundberg (1995), in a study of over 400 North American hospitality students' use of organisational metaphors, found that the metaphors clustered around seven organisational practices. These were:

Table 1.3 Categorising metaphors

Organisational practice	Positive image	Negative image
Managerial skills		
Organisational structure		
Operations		
Organisational life cycle		
Strategic orientation		
People orientation		
Power orientation		

managerial skills, organisational structure, operations, organisational life cycle, strategic orientation, people orientation and power orientation. However, this particular categorisation should be used flexibly and adjusted, either to exclude some areas or to include new ones, depending on the nature of the particular sample of metaphors being categorised. If a group has been formed to discuss the data, use it to distribute individual metaphors into categories. The objective of this categorisation is to demonstrate the way in which specific metaphors are partial in their focus. Consequently, they alert us to some organisational practices (for example, people orientation), but may well be silent in relation to others (for example, effectiveness of structure).

A second dimension can be added by categorising the metaphors according to whether these practices were experienced negatively or positively. If metaphors can be used 'to chart morale and gauge the organisation's health' (Brink, 1993: 370), then this dimension provides some insight into participants' perceptions of 'how well their organisation is doing'. If the participants are present for a group discussion, ask them how typical they think their response is compared to that of others within their respective organisations.

CONCLUSIONS

Metaphors are 'one of the few tools to create compact descriptions of complex phenomena' such as organisations (Weick, 1989: 529). As organisations struggle to operate in increasingly complex and fluid environments, metaphors will help people find meaning and convenient reference points

(Morgan, 1993). On the basis of this view, Morgan (1993: 12) argues that the 'ability to invent evocative images or stories that can resonate with the challenges at hand and help people to achieve desired goals, or to cope with the unknown, is becoming a key managerial skill'. Similarly, Bolman and Deal (1991) assert that effective managers are those who are able to make use of multiple metaphors, rather than being locked into one way of understanding and responding to situations that they experience within organisations.

Creatively reflecting on the nature of an organisation through metaphors can provide some therapeutic/cathartic value for the people involved (Brink, 1993). For people who are in some way uncomfortable with a current or past experience as a member of an organisation, seeing that organisation through the perspective provided by metaphor may make sense of a situation that was previously a source of confusion. Using metaphors to describe a situation may also enable some individuals to express views that otherwise would have remained latent, even suppressed. Metaphors can provide useful vehicles for organisational change interventions (Marshak, 1993; Morgan, 1993).

Clearly then, metaphors matter in an organisational setting, but where managers acknowledge their value they are faced with two key issues. First, where a plethora of negative images is used to describe their organisation, managers are faced with the task of identifying appropriate actions which they might take to alter people's perceptions. But, since metaphors are experientially based, it is unlikely that simply proposing a new metaphor will significantly alter those perceptions unless this is accompanied by a series of changes to management and organisational practices. Certainly, metaphors that express a future desired state may be visionary, but whether they are transformational depends on their becoming embedded through some perceived consistency with organisational practice.

It is important not to underestimate what is involved in getting people to adopt new metaphors in a way that significantly affects their actions. As Lakoff and Johnson (1980: 145) have argued, much of our everyday activity is based on firmly established metaphors that operate at a largely unconscious level. Therefore one's behaviour is not altered simply through a conscious decision to adopt a new metaphor. Nonetheless, it is precisely because of the subtle influence of embedded metaphors that the conscious application of new metaphors can serve as a means of bringing to the surface this 'taken-for-grantedness'. One proviso is that the metaphor must resonate with the experience of the person trying to apply it. Otherwise the new insight and comprehension that metaphors can bring may instead be replaced by 'confusion and despair' (Ortony, 1975: 52).

Second, managers are also likely to be confronted by the limits on their actions within organisational settings. In their study of managers' use of multiple metaphors to 'reframe' organisational situations, Dunford and Palmer (1995) found that structural and political factors inside organisations were commonly cited as material constraints on the actions that can be taken. Thus, even where a particular metaphor is adopted because it resonates with the experience of organisational members, this can be insufficient to bridge the cognition–action gap. Such problems mean that creativity through the use of metaphors requires those managers using the process to display a degree of astuteness about the patterns of power and influence at work in their organisation.

REFERENCES

Akin, G. and Schultheiss, E. (1990) 'Jazz bands and missionaries: OD through stories and metaphor', *Journal of Managerial Psychology*, Vol. 5, No. 4.

Alvesson, M. (1993) 'The play of metaphors', in Hassard, J. and Parker, M. (eds) *Postmodernism and Organizations*. London: Sage.

Baker, H.E. (1993) 'Wax on–wax off: French and Raven at the movies', *Journal of Management Education*, Vol. 17, No. 4.

Bensimon, E.A. (1989) 'The meaning of "good presidential leadership": a frame analysis', *Review of Higher Education*, Vol. 12, No. 1.

Boje, D.K. (1991) 'Learning storytelling: storytelling to learn management skills', *Journal of Management Education*, Vol. 15, No. 3.

Boland, R.D. and Greenberg, R.H. (1988) 'Metaphorical structuring of organisational ambiguity', in Pondy, L.R., Boland, R.J. and Thomas, H. (eds) *Managing Ambiguity and Change*. New York: Wiley.

Bolman, L. and Deal, T.E. (1991) *Reframing Organizations: Artistry, Choice and Leadership*. San Francisco: Jossey-Bass.

Bourgeois, V.W. and Pinder, C.C. (1983) 'Contrasting philosophical perspectives in administrative science: a reply to Morgan', *Administrative Science Quarterly*, Vol. 28.

Brink, T.L. (1993) 'Metaphor as data in the study of organizations', *Journal of Management Inquiry*, Vol. 2, No. 4.

Cowan, D.A. (1992) 'Understanding leadership through art, history and arts administration', *Journal of Management Studies*, Vol. 16, No. 3.

Cowden, A.C. (1989–90) 'Mystery novels as organizational context', *Organizational Behavior Teaching Review*, Vol. 14, No. 2.

Doubuzinskis, L. (1992) 'Modernist and postmodernist metaphors of the policy process: control and stability vs. chaos and reflexive understanding', *Policy Sciences*, Vol. 25, No. 4.

Dounford, R. and Palmer, I. (1995) 'Claims about frames: practitioners' assessments of the utility of reframing', *Journal of Management Education* (forthcoming).

Gallos, J. (1993) 'Teaching about reframing with films and videos', *Journal of Management Education*, Vol. 17, No. 1.

Gartner, W. (1993), 'Can't see the trees for the forest', *Journal of Management Education*, Vol. 17, No. 2.

Garud, R. and Kotha, S. (1994) 'Using the brain as a metaphor to model flexible production systems', *Academy of Management Review*, Vol. 19, No. 4.

Gergen, K.J. (1992) 'Organization theory in the postmodern era', in Reed, M. and Hughes, M. (eds) *Rethinking Organization: New Directions in Organization Theory and Analysis*. London: Sage.

Golden-Biddle, K. (1993) 'Organisational dynamics and dramatic stagings about them', *Journal of Management Education*, Vol. 17, No. 1.

Greenberg, E. and Miller, P. (1991) 'The player and the professor: theatrical techniques in teaching', *Journal of Management Education*, Vol. 15, No. 4.

Harris, C. (1991) 'Using short stories to teach international management', *Journal of Management Education*, Vol. 15, No. 3.

Kendall, J.E. and Kendall, K.E. (1993) 'Metaphors and methodologies: living beyond the systems machine', *MIS Quarterly*, Vol. 17, No. 2.

Lakoff, G. and Johnson, M. (1980) *Metaphors We Live By*. Chicago: University of Chicago Press.

Linstead, S. (1993) 'Deconstruction in the study of organisations', in Hassard, J. and Parker, M. (eds) *Postmodernism and Organisations*. London: Sage.

Lundberg, C.C. (1990) 'Towards mapping the communication targets of organisational change', *Journal of Organisational Change Management*, Vol. 3, No. 1.

Marshak, R.J. (1993) 'Managing the metaphors of change', *Organisational Dynamics*, Vol. 22, No.1.

Marx, R.D. and Hamilton, E.E. (1991) 'Beyond skill building: a multiple perspectives view of personnel', *Issues and Trends in Business and Economics*, Vol. 3, No. 1.

Morgan, G. (1983) 'More on metaphor: why we cannot control tropes in administrative science', *Administrative Science Quarterly*, Vol. 28.

Morgan, G. (1986) *Images of Organization*. Newbury Park, CA: Sage.

Morgan, G. (1989) *Creative Organization Theory: A Resource Book*. Newbury Park, CA: Sage.

Morgan, G. (1993) *Imaginization: The Art of Creative Management*. Newbury Park, CA: Sage.

Nussbaum, B. (1986) 'The end of corporate loyalty', *Business Week*, August 4th.

Ortony, A. (1975) 'Why metaphors are necessary and not just nice', *Educational Theory*, Vol. 25, No. 1.

Palmer, I. and Dunford, R. (1995) 'Interrogating reframing: evaluating metaphor-based analyses of organisations', in Clegg, S. and Palmer, G. (eds) *The Production of Management Recipes: Critical Perspectives*. London: Sage.

Palmer, I. and Lundberg, C. (1995) 'Metaphors of hospitality organizations: an exploratory study', *Cornell Quarterly Research Forum* (forthcoming).

Peters, T. (1992) *Liberation Management*. London: Macmillan.

Pinder, C.C. and Bourgeois, V.W. (1982) 'Controlling tropes in administrative science', *Administrative Science Quarterly*, Vol. 27.

Powell, G.N. and Veiga, J.F. (1985–86) 'Using popular music to examine management and OB concepts: a rejoinder to Springsteen's thesis', *Organizational Behavior Teaching Review*, Vol. 10, No. 1.

Proctor, R.A. (1989) 'The use of metaphors to aid the process of creative problem solving', *Personnel Review*, Vol. 18, No. 4.

Reed, M. (1990) 'From paradigms to images: the paradigm warrior turns postmodernist guru', *Personnel Review*, Vol. 19, No. 3.

Rueschhoff, M.S. (1989–90) 'Theatre in the OB classroom: to role play or not to role play – that is the question', *Organizational Behavior Teaching Review*, Vol. 14, No. 3.

Serey, T.T. (1992) 'Carpe Diem: lessons about life and management from *Dead Poets Society*', *Journal of Management Education*, Vol. 17, No. 3.

Shaw, G. and Locke, K. (1993) 'Using fiction to develop judgement', *Journal of Management Education*, Vol. 17, No. 3.

Skagen, A. (1992) 'The incredible shrinking organisation: what does it mean for middle managers?', *Supervisory Management*, Vol. 37, No. 1.

Sommers, D.I. (1993) 'Team building in the classroom through rhythm', *Journal of Management Education*, Vol. 17, No. 2.

Stewart, A. (1990) 'The bigman metaphor for entrepreneurship: a "library tale" with morals on alternatives for further research', *Organisation Science*, Vol. 1, No. 2.

Tinker, T. (1986) 'Metaphor or reification: are radical humanists really libertarian anarchists?', *Journal of Management Studies*, Vol. 23, No. 4.

Tsoukas, H. (1991) 'The missing link: a transformational view of metaphors in organizational science', *Academy of Management Review*, Vol. 16, No. 3.

Tsoukas, H. (1993a) 'Analogical reasoning and knowledge generation in organization theory', *Organization Studies*, Vol. 14, No. 3.

Tsoukas, H. (1993b) 'Organisations as soap bubbles: an evolutionary perspective on organisation design', *Systems Practice*, Vol. 6, No. 5.

Weaver, R.M. (1967) *A Rhetoric and Handbook*. New York: Holt, Rinehart and Winston.

Weick, K. (1989) 'Theory construction as disciplined imagination', *Academy of Management Review*, Vol. 14, No. 4.

Zimmerman, D.K. (1985–86) 'Using country music in the classroom', *Organizational Behavior Teaching Review*, Vol. 10, No. 1.

CHAPTER 2

Organisation Development as a journey

Dawn Inns

INTRODUCTION

The role of metaphor in shaping the way we think, perceive the world and approach problems has been well described (Lakoff and Johnson, 1980; Morgan, 1986). This chapter builds on Lakoff and Johnson's (1980) central thesis that humans experience the world through a set of cultural beliefs, values and concepts that are expressed and reaffirmed through a variety of dominant or root metaphors. It seems important, therefore, to examine closely some of the root metaphors in a given culture and how these may shape perceptions of reality and reveal underlying cultural assumptions and values, particularly when these metaphors appear for the most part to escape questioning, being accepted as the normal way to experience phenomena.

In what follows we shall consider the 'journey' metaphor and how this metaphor seems to have underpinned and shaped the field of OD. Lakoff and Johnson believe that the journey metaphor is one of the central metaphors of Western culture, embodying notions of progress, direction and purpose (1980: 92). The 'journey' metaphor is at the heart of the Enlightenment view that humanity and Western civilisation are propelled by a dynamic of continual improvement.

Lakoff and Johnson argue that there is a 'metaphorical coherence' in Western culture (1980: 88). Such coherence is evidenced by the way in which many aspects of human life are interpreted using the journey metaphor: life itself is seen as a journey, with career development and self-development part of an attempt at continuous improvement. This then is a metaphor that gives purpose and meaning to our lives and encourages us to measure how far we have come and how much distance remains to be covered. In this way metaphor can act as a form of control, determining how we interpret and give meaning to our existence.

When applied to the field of OD, the journey metaphor needs to be examined for subtle variations. There appear to be two main interpretations of a journey, and these have been highlighted by Marshak (1993). First, a journey can be seen as a departure from a known place, with the intention to cover a fixed distance and arrive at a clearly defined destination, measuring steps and progress on the way. This may be termed the 'destination-oriented' journey (Marshak, 1993: 400). Furthermore, it appears to have dominated the field of OD until quite recently.

In contrast, a very different vision of a journey is possible where the journey is essentially an explorative process. The outcome may be unknown, and the exploration and trying out of new behaviours and incremental improvements are important, rather than arrival at a goal fixed prior to departure. This interpretation may be termed a 'process-oriented' journey and it is beginning to filter into the field of OD and organisational change. For example, it may well be that the journey towards human resource management which Grant discusses in Chapter 12 fits this interpretation.

The distinction between 'destination'- and 'process'- oriented journeys is significant, because it represents contrasting philosophical approaches to organisational improvement and change. This chapter looks at the two different approaches and how they have characterised OD at different stages of its life. It begins by briefly outlining the field of OD, its aims and background. It goes on to review examples of the 'destination-oriented' journey metaphor used consciously or unconsciously in Organisation Development texts. The alternative, 'process-oriented' approach to a journey is then explored via more recent literature on organisational change. Finally, various contextual influences are examined which may have fed into this progression and necessitated a changing journey perspective.

Exploring how OD theory and practices are working within the conceptual framework of a journey, and particularly a certain interpretation of a journey, is useful for three main reasons. First, it reveals to us central assumptions and beliefs that have structured OD interventions. Second, we are able to trace a progression in the literature on OD in terms of an emerging new philosophical approach to change. This is revealed via differences in the use of the metaphor, which allow us to trace Organisation Development's own journey, as much as is possible within a highly diversified field. Third, recent years have seen mounting criticism against OD and 'planned change' attempts, and a fear about how OD will survive. As Palmer and Dunford argue in Chapter 1, an examination of dominant metaphors in use can often help us to understand and break free from the restrictive effects of a particular framework. Therefore, conducting a metaphorical exploration of OD may suggest alternative possibilities for organisational interventions.

ORGANISATION DEVELOPMENT: AIMS AND BACKGROUND

OD refers to planned attempts at change which draw on the behavioural sciences to help an organisation become more effective (Harvey and Brown, 1992). French and Bell, for example, define it in the following way:

> **Organisation Development is a top-management supported, long-range effort to improve an organisation's problem-solving and renewal processes.** (1990: 17)

This improvement to the way an organisation functions is carried out with the help of a 'change agent' (internal or external consultant) who assists the organisation in defining a given problem, gathering data, discussing the implications of the data, and recommending action. Interventions may focus on the interpersonal behaviour of individuals, groups and/or wider structural and technical improvements (see, for example, Harvey and Brown, 1992).

In order to uncover the roots of the dominant metaphor of OD as a destination-oriented journey, it is necessary briefly to trace the subject's origins. It is also important to examine the underlying values which have shaped the field and ensured the dominance of this metaphor.

In *Interactions and Interventions in Organizations*, Mangham (1978) narrows down the chief influences on OD to humanism and systems theory. OD in the United States grew out of laboratory training methods which concentrated on interpersonal behaviour, and also from the humanistic theories of Lewin, Maslow and Rogers (Harvey and Brown, 1992). In the United Kingdom, early development was strongly influenced by the work of the Tavistock Institute which adopted a psychoanalytic focus and also a socio-technical or systems approach (French and Bell, 1990). One can therefore see that, given the specific origins of OD, the two dominant threads of humanism and systems theory are in many ways an inevitable feature of the subject area.

Relating these two threads to their wider social context, it is possible to identify broader cultural influences on OD. Gergen (1992) believes that organisation theory in general has been guided by two discourses which have structured Western society at large: the 'Romantic' and the 'Modernist' discourse. The 'Romantic' discourse sees humans as deep, rich and complex and suggests the importance of openness and understanding in interpersonal relations. The 'Modernist' discourse emphasises reason, progress and scientific rigour. Inevitably, then, OD has absorbed the values and assumptions from organisation theory in general, which has in turn absorbed them from the wider Western cultural context.

Returning to the notion of OD as a journey, these two discourses are evident in two respects. First, OD places emphasis on individual and group development as the road to greater self-understanding and awareness. Second, it encourages an organisation to improve its efficiency through rational planning and a review of the interdependence of the different component parts. Having explained the aims and background of OD, it is now necessary to look more closely at the nature of its relationship with the journey metaphor. It is changes in the interpretation of the journey metaphor that have recently led to significant changes in Organisation Development's theory and practice.

ORGANISATION DEVELOPMENT AS A DESTINATION-ORIENTED JOURNEY

When OD is presented and interpreted via the metaphor of a journey, a clear framework for understanding organisational change is provided. The journey metaphor provides rationale for a change process, offering a positive perspective which focuses on arrival at a goal. This focus on a clear goal offers participants reassurance that the road to organisational improvement may be long but arrival at the desired destination will be worth the effort. As Marshak states: 'The reward is not in the journey but in reaching the pot of gold at the end of the rainbow' (1993: 404).

Lewin's (1951) three-stage model of change – unfreeze, change, refreeze – clearly reveals the influence of the destination-oriented journey metaphor in OD. The model describes organisational change as a process which first creates an awareness in an organisation of the need for change. This initial 'unfreeze' stage can be likened to the mental preparation before a journey and awareness of the necessity of undertaking a journey, through to the first steps. For the change process to be successful it must have a clear goal or end state in view which is communicated to the organisation's members, and the change involves moving towards these goals by setting clear targets. Arrival at the desired destination is signalled by the final stage of change, 'refreeze', and an attempt to ensure that the new behaviours are absorbed into the organisation's culture and practices. Marshak (1993) argues that this is a very linear model of change. Moreover, it views change as relatively unproblematic.

It is not suggested that this model of organisational change is entirely inaccurate for the reality experienced by companies. However, by presenting a change process in terms of this metaphor we may unconsciously be selecting and structuring information to fit in with a preconceived conceptual framework of what change should be like. In effect, the danger is of omitting 'untidy' parts of the process that do not fit neatly into Lewin's framework.

Further examples of the journey metaphor are to be found in OD accounts of the consultant's or change agent's role. This is conceptualised in many texts through the metaphor of a journey. Leavitt (1986), for example, talks of 'corporate pathfinders' who supply the vision and direction necessary to give an organisation the momentum it requires to change. A change project triggers anxiety. Therefore the ability of the consultant to provide support to senior management and an indication that they have 'been there' before, seems crucial (McLean et al, 1982). Harvey and Brown (1992: 207) refer, for example, to the use of 'war stories' by consultants who recount tales of similar experiences, thereby emphasising their wide travels and acquired expertise.

McLean et al argue that there is considerable pressure on a consultant to give organisational members confidence to 'step into the dark' (1982: 31). They must be 'pioneers ... building and lighting beacons in various strategic and/or safe places' (1982: 32). The consultant, then, is presented as someone who can offer well-tried and tested routes to company success, such as programmes of empowerment, job enrichment and quality circles.

Nees and Greiner (1985) identify five main types of management consultants. The implicit metaphor of OD as a journey clearly underlies four of these, most blatantly in the 'strategic navigator' who offers the company expert guidance in planning long-term solutions to problems. It also underlies the 'friendly co-pilot', who is less concerned to give expert advice and is more a source of support during the journey. 'Mental adventurers' is also a journey-laden term, as is the description of the 'management physician'. Of course, the overall metaphor for 'management physician' is medical, but as Nees and Greiner themselves suggest, these consultants still see their role as a guide:

> **The client simply doesn't know how or won't face the problems of getting from A to Z. We can usually figure out what is blocking them and then hold their hands through rough waters.** (1985: 75)

The consultant or 'change agent' as a guide is a common theme in the literature. Their task is to lead the organisation through treacherous conditions, interpreting dangers and opportunities in the landscape along the way. They must watch out for 'red flags' in the process (Harvey and Brown, 1992: 142) which indicate that a temporary barrier to advancement has appeared. Consultants must also navigate around the 'organisation iceberg' (Harvey and Brown, 1992: 264), handling hidden cultural forces which are not apparent on the surface.

The implicit message in many accounts of the theory of OD is that the change process is a rational, structured and linear journey. The terminology in texts centres around notions of 'goal setting' (Harvey and Brown, 1992: 275) and progress and direction through techniques such as 'management by objectives', where measurable targets are defined collaboratively with employees.

The importance of progress towards goals in OD is also expressed in the technique of 'gap analysis'. This looks at the difference between 'where one is and where one wants to be' (French and Bell, 1990: 77), using OD techniques to move towards the desired place.

At a micro, individual level, goal setting takes the form of life and career planning and the pursuit of well-defined career paths. French and Bell talk of a 'career trajectory' (1990: 160) which captures the linking in Western culture of time with improvement, progression in time and space invariably being linked with a trajectory of improvement and progress.

Pettigrew, summarising the state of OD in 1985 and exploring the limitations of the field, states that a large amount of work has operated with models of change underpinned by 'highly rational and linear theories of process' (Pettigrew, 1985: 16). He argues that OD largely sees change as a clearly definable event. Change separated in time and space to the extent that it becomes 'an episode divorced from the immediate and more distant context in which it is embedded' (Pettigrew, 1985: 15).

The opening chapter of Pettigrew's *The Awakening Giant* (1985) is an insightful forage into some of the problems with the destination-oriented journey model of OD. As he argues, one of its central weaknesses is that it ignores, or at the very least substantially downplays, the importance of an organisation's political, cultural and historical context and the extent to which this will determine change opportunities and limitations.

Pettigrew describes why organisational interventions often do not achieve their goal: they are unrealistic about the extent to which an organisation can 'leave behind' a set of practices, beliefs and values and 'arrive' at an entirely new place. He concludes his report on ICI's attempts at cultural change with the caution: 'don't expect too much too soon' (1985: 513). In doing so he is exposing the naivety of some OD attempts which aim to cover too much 'distance' and underestimate how difficult it is to undertake large-scale organisational change.

Weick (1990) seems to support Pettigrew and challenges the journey metaphor by emphasising that a change process will involve keeping some of the 'old' alongside the 'new', and therefore it may not be a case of simply moving from one place to another. Both writers also state that there may be regression to previous behavioural patterns, thereby challenging the linear model of change.

So far it has been argued that a significant proportion of OD work has been dominated by the metaphor of a destination-oriented journey. As such this work looks at linear development towards a measurable goal and emphasises the central Western cultural values of rationality and progress. There appear to be three main reasons for the hegemony of this metaphor:

- pressures on management in organisations and on consultants to behave according to a set of preconceptions about managerial behaviour;
- the influence of the origins of organisation development which have determined its core values;
- the dominance of the journey metaphor in Western culture at large.

To take the first point, it is hardly surprising that consultants use the metaphor of a journey consciously or unconsciously when selling their skills and packages to organisations. Given the cost and considerable risk involved in change for an organisation, senior management needs to be convinced of the benefits of change and the competence of the 'change agents' – a factor discussed by Clark and Salaman in Chapter 10. One way in which these two elements can be convincingly presented is via the journey metaphor. Management are unlikely to embark on a project with a consultant who suggests that outcomes of change are uncertain and must to a large extent be discovered *en route*. They are more likely to be stirred by the presentation of a plan which uses well-tried paths, gives milestones to measure progress, and generally fits into the dominant framework of rationality and planning that is viewed as being at the heart of organisational life.

Secondly, it was argued at the start of the chapter that the origins of OD explain, to a large extent, the dominance of certain values within the subject – values which underlie the journey metaphor. Friedlander (1976) describes what he sees to be the three main influences on the subject: pragmatism, rationality and existentialism. These three influences, he argues, have been pulling OD in opposing directions. Pragmatism emphasises progress and productivity and is dominant in the practitioner perspective. Rationality looks at theoretical coherence and the placing of events within a broader perspective, and is emphasised in the academic interest in OD (Friedlander, 1976). Both of these influences are seen in the use of the destination-oriented journey metaphor. Existentialism – the third influence – represents a departure from this and as we shall see is gaining importance in more recent process-oriented approaches to organisational change.

Finally, it is not surprising to see the dominance of the journey metaphor in OD given its centrality in Western culture. Journey stories are well ingrained in Western society and are widespread in the arts and literature (Dunn, 1990). The presentation of a journey in the arts and literature may often have a different emphasis, however, and an examination of this via a brief example will provide the turning point for us to consider the second interpretation of a journey: as a process-oriented, explorative activity, where precise outcomes are unknown at the start.

Dunn (1990), discussing the use of the journey metaphor in fairy stories, myths and films, draws attention to two key aspects of these accounts. These are first, that a journey often symbolises the death of an immature self and the birth of a more self-aware being; second, that this process is triggered by leaving a known setting, encountering fear and danger, and returning with new insight. In these stories there is fear, uncertainty and the impossibility of knowing and determining outcomes at the start. There are no well-tried routes available; exploration often involves leaving the main paths and finding one's own way (Dunn, 1990).

A typical example of how the journey metaphor is used in literature is illustrated in the famous French novel *La Modification* by Butor (1957). In this novel a journey symbolically represents a process of self-discovery or, more precisely, a physical journey triggers and mirrors a psychological journey. A middle-aged man disrupts his regular routine of taking the rapid, overnight train from Paris to visit his Italian mistress in Rome and is instead obliged to take a daytime train to Rome. This journey, much longer than his habitual one, triggers a parallel journey of self-awareness which results in his realisation that the relationship with his mistress is significantly flawed, and his subsequent return to his wife in Paris.

Butor's novel is chosen here because it demonstrates very well a common use of the journey metaphor in the arts and literature: as an activity where the *process* is emphasised rather than the outcomes, and where the outcome cannot be known in advance. It also depicts how a relaxing of all that is usual and known can be a necessary precursor to a deepening understanding of one's situation and subsequent insight into new perspectives.

It could be argued that OD, in adopting the journey metaphor, has taken only some aspects and has omitted or downplayed some unavoidable features of a journey which are described in detail in the arts and literature. The reasons for doing so would stem from a desire to avoid situations which will necessitate going 'off piste'; for example, uncertainty, exploration and the need to find one's own individual route. Where an organisation takes such an approach, those such as Pettigrew (1985) might argue that this involves combining elements from its unique cultural and historical past with proven recipes, rather than a clear movement from one state to another; for example, from a hierarchical to an empowerment culture, as Lewin's three-stage model implies. This view of change represents a radically different philosophical approach which will now be examined.

ORGANISATION DEVELOPMENT AS A PROCESS-ORIENTED JOURNEY

In their preface to the fourth edition of *An Experiential Approach to Organization Development* (1992), Harvey and Brown highlight a number of additions made to previous editions. These largely relate to increased reference in the text to the themes of uncertainty, volatility, and the corresponding need for continual change and adaptation facing organisations in the 1990s. Comments on the instability caused by economic, social, political and technological fluctuations as the world becomes increasingly a meshed 'global village' (McLuhan and Powers, 1989) have become so commonplace that it seems banal to mention the topic. However, with regard to OD these strains on organisations will determine its future.

Writers such as Marshak (1993) have questioned the ability of OD to respond to these demands using its earlier 'destination-oriented' model which saw 'change' as an entity separated in time and space. Increasingly, such writers have recognised the need for a new approach to OD which emphasises the continuous nature of change and where 'arrival' triggers only another departure (Marshak, 1993). Early examples of commentators recognising this need might include McLean et al's (1982) work. Using the 'process-oriented' journey metaphor, they describe OD in the following terms:

> **The current emphasis is akin to the activities of early explorers who had a vague notion of their destination, based perhaps on rumours and stories of new territories across the water, but, with only very rudimentary maps, needing to draw on all their skills of seamanship to ensure their survival, whilst having to pioneer their own routes.** (1982: 125)

This quotation illustrates the clear shift that is occurring in conceptualising organisational change and the corresponding modification of the journey metaphor to encompass a view of organisational change as explorative. Change is seen as a process where the destination is unknown in advance and where 'well-trodden routes' or 'packages' offer only vague guidelines to help organisations make their own paths.

Two further aspects of change are emphasised in the process-oriented approach. First, change is usual, and tension and the potential for chaos are inherent in all systems (Smith, 1982; Wheatley, 1992; Marshak, 1993). Second, change draws attention to the interrelationships within systems, as change in one part of an organisation triggers the need for change in another part in an ongoing cycle (Wheatley, 1992; Marshak, 1993). Change, therefore, is not as programmable and predictable as Lewin-type models imply, since repercussions on different parts cannot always be accurately forecast. The development of the journey metaphor in relation to organisational change from a destination-oriented to a process-oriented model allows important, but previously hidden elements of the journey to come to the fore: uncertainty, circularity, exploration, unpredictability.

It is important to recognise that elements of this approach have existed in OD from the start, but they have been downplayed until relatively recently because of the prevalence of the rational, linear approach within the subject. In particular, Lewin's 'action research' model is clearly cyclical. The action research model, as described by French and Bell (1990), accepts that change is ongoing and involves a continual process of gathering and interpreting data, acting on it, reviewing progress, and starting the process of gathering data again. Although French and Bell see action research as the basic OD model, it is questionable to what extent action research has been used in a fully cyclical way, or has instead often been integrated within a basically linear change attempt.

McLean et al (1982) have also pointed out that the explorative, uncertain and process-oriented approach to change is probably closer to the reality of what many consultants have actually experienced during interventions. Unfortunately, they often fall prey to the belief that organisational life should be dominated by rationality and planning, causing them to interpret their experiences in terms of a linear model.

FROM DESTINATION- TO PROCESS-ORIENTED JOURNEY: THE CONTEXTUAL FACTORS

It was argued at the start of the chapter that there is coherence within a culture and that dominant root metaphors reflect values and assumptions in the wider cultural fabric of a particular society; hence the centrality of the destination-oriented journey metaphor related to wider values of modernism in organisation theory in general, and to faith in rationality and linear progress in Western society at large. If this is the case, any major alteration in the dominant metaphor in OD should also reflect developments in organisation theory in general and in Western culture as a whole. This is clearly so and this interrelationship will now be examined.

Three topics will be addressed to see how these contextual influences may have fed into the field of OD:

- the questioning of the rational model of Man and purposive organisational functioning in management theory;
- the emergence of different cultural models of change in organisation theory, in particular the Eastern model;
- developments in the natural sciences which are having an impact on the social sciences.

On the one hand, it seems unnecessary to emphasise the interconnectedness of these different influences. On the other, it is difficult fully to conceptualise the extent to which our thought processes are governed by the dominance of certain cultural perspectives, and how modifications to these in one domain have multiple and wide-ranging impacts. These changes are revealed through shifting root metaphors. Metaphorical explorations therefore offer a way into the 'webs of significance' (Geertz, 1975: 5) that we have constructed for ourselves, and also a way out of them.

The questioning of the rational, purposive model of Man in organisation theory has been convincingly presented by March (1988) who argues that the dominant perspective in management science is that of a 'technology of reason' (1988: 265). This view sees behaviour in organisations as rational. It is made in accordance with pre-existing goals and a knowledge of end destinations. It also creates an organisational environment where purpose and consistency dictate actions and where the most direct way of achieving goals is carefully evaluated.

This model of Man has been influential in organisation theory and March's attack on this perspective is an attack on a cornerstone of Western ideology. Yet his work aims not to destroy the idea of rational planning but to supplement it and question how appropriate it is for most decisions that have to be made. March questions the notion of 'pre-existence of purpose' (1988: 254), and knowledge in advance of goals and end-destinations. He argues that we often discover these *en route* and that choices cannot be rationally evaluated in the way often prescribed by management science because future preferences cannot be known, nor can the future consequences of different actions (1988: 269). March believes that this 'technology of reason' must therefore be supplemented by a 'technology of foolishness' where rules can be temporarily relaxed and intuition given scope. This he terms 'sensible foolishness' (1988: 259). It requires an openness to the unplanned, since the unplanned may hold the seeds of future preferences and goals. March's perspective on career planning, for example, would emphasise that individuals give importance to intuition and impulse, and would question the notion of 'career planning' as anything other than a set of hypothetical goals to be tested, rather than fixed, immovable milestones.

March's ideas have been influential in organisation theory. Brought into the debate on OD, they force reconceptualisation of the destination-oriented journey metaphor. Pettigrew, in 1985, suggested that OD could benefit from the application of March's ideas to its core assumptions. This needs to be done in a more extensive way than is possible here. Certainly his ideas seem relevant to the difficulty of assessing future goals and preferences in an uncertain and complex environment.

The model of Man presented by March is close to the picture of humans described in literature and the arts: of humans paralysed by indecision, and subject to shifting values and preferences discovered through (often unplanned) experience. Clearly, an organisation as distinct from an individual must have mechanisms for planning and goal setting in order to co-ordinate collective action, but perhaps the rigidity of these should be regularly reviewed and questioned.

March's ideas about the importance of openness to intuition and the unplanned appear to be influenced by Eastern values and particularly aspects of Taoism. They inherently seem to make reference to the notion of 'Wu-Wei' – the necessity of 'non-action' on occasions. This leads to the next contextual influence on OD: the emergence of alternative cultural models of change and particularly the Eastern or Confucian model. This is reviewed extensively and contrasted with the Lewinian model of change in Marshak (1993). This model, Marshak argues, may capture more accurately the nature of the evolutionary and continuous change facing many organisations in the 1990s, and may be a supplement to Lewin's model which is more appropriate to transformational change.

The Taoist model corresponds to the 'process-oriented journey' and is a cyclical model. Very different notions about change underpin this model. In particular, periods of calm and of change are not differentiated clearly but each leads on to the other in a perpetual motion. This is based on the yin–yang notion of opposites in the universe which are mutually dependent and fold into an underlying unity. Working with a mental picture of change and the universe defined in the above way will result in very different ideas about organisational change interventions, and these are explored in some detail by Marshak (1993).

March's ideas of 'sensible foolishness' and openness to the unplanned, and the Taoist model of the universe which argues for the importance of non-action and intuition, are also coherent with a wider 'paradigm shift' (Kuhn, 1970) which is occurring in the science fraternity and which has huge repercussions for the social sciences (Wheatley, 1992; Marshak, 1993). The social sciences have to a large extent modelled themselves on the natural sciences and it is to be expected that they will be influenced by changing paradigms in science.

In *Leadership and the New Science* (1992), Wheatley discusses some of the ideas behind the 'new sciences' (principally chaos theory and quantum physics) and integrates these ideas into organisational change theory. The 'new sciences' present a radical shift from the atomistic and mechanistic vision of the universe offered by Newtonian physics (Zohar, 1994) – a vision which has dominated the field of organisation theory (Goldstein, 1993). The 'new sciences' change the focus dramatically to look at how the universe is composed, not of separate parts, but of 'energy fields which only become substantial when they are in *relationship* to some other energy field' (Goldstein, 1993: 87). The interconnected and mutually dependent nature of the universe means then that change attempts must be aware of complex interactions and relationships. These are constantly changing and can be disturbed by movement in a distant part of the system.

Wheatley also argues that a period of 'constructive chaos' (Goldstein, 1993: 90), loss of direction or confusion is a necessary precursor to creative outcomes. He goes on to suggest that following a period of deliberately created confusion organisations may discover a more effective mode of 'self-organisation'. Pushing members of an organisation into 'chaos, emotional and intellectual confusion' (Goldstein, 1993: 88) is a very different technique for consultants than those prescribed by the goal setting of the 'destination-oriented' journey model, and Wheatley recognises that this demands sophisticated consultancy skills.

It is important to note that some of the ideas of the 'new sciences' which stress 'the creative importance of the indeterminate and the unpredictable'

(Zohar, 1994: 14) are not only consistent with both the Eastern approach to change and March's ideas, but also with the reality of human existence as it has been portrayed in the arts and literature. These media portray the journey as an activity which involves an initial openness to alternative directions. It is an activity which requires an acceptance of moments of crisis and the expectation of confusion as old values and rules are relaxed and no clear way out is perceived. Ultimately, it is a journey that enhances human understanding, while at the same time acknowledging that this will not be a permanent state. In an organisational context these are critical aspects of change, yet they are often obscured. It may be, then, that perception of change in organisation theory has all too often been hampered by a rational, linear straitjacket.

CONCLUSIONS

This chapter has undertaken a metaphorical exploration of the field of OD. It has identified the root metaphor within the subject – that of a journey – and has discussed contemporary modifications to this root metaphor and why they are occurring. In taking this approach it has placed the root metaphor of OD within a broader cultural framework, showing how the journey metaphor can be seen as one of the dominant Western cultural metaphors.

It was stated in the introduction that examination of the root metaphor of OD as a journey was important for three main reasons:

- to reveal core values and assumptions of the field;
- to trace the progression of OD and look at an emerging new philosophical approach to change;
- to help explore alternative frameworks for OD which may be more appropriate to the complex, volatile environment it now must operate in.

Let us briefly review the findings on each of these.

The dominant thread within OD until quite recently can be summarised as an approach to organisational change which sees change as a 'destination-oriented' journey. This, we argued, is consistent with the values of rationality and linear progress that are part of the wider cultural fabric of the Western world. Change is seen as a discrete entity, separate in time from the normal operations of an organisation and involving clearly defined steps towards a predetermined goal.

In contrast, an emerging new philosophical approach to change was reviewed. This is revealed via a change in the use of the journey metaphor. This new approach has been labelled 'process-oriented' and sees a journey as a primarily explorative process, where clear outcomes are not known in advance and where change involves leaving the familiar and deliberately creating confusion as a step in the process to greater order. In this model, change is cyclical and there is no arrival or final 'homecoming' (Dunn, 1990). There are only periods of stability and change constantly interspersed and each one triggered by the other in an endless cycle.

These changes in the metaphor and interpretations of a journey echo wider cultural developments. In particular, we have noted the questioning of the 'Rational Man' perspective in organisation theory, and developments in the 'new sciences' which necessitate a radical revisioning of OD and organisation theory as a whole. These latter approaches offer potentially enlightening insights.

This chapter has examined some of the conceptual developments and the background to emerging approaches in OD. The wider cultural changes feeding into these need to be understood at a conceptual level before they can be to some extent 'operationalised' and put into a form useful for OD practitioners. This seems to be what Wheatley (1992) is currently doing: translating complex conceptual ideas into workable models or techniques for OD interventions. Similarly, more investigation into the extent and effectiveness of attempts to secure organisational change using the process-oriented framework would be welcomed. The pressures on consultants mean that these are important areas of enquiry.

In addition, it may be useful to examine whether organisations, when choosing management consultants, are beginning to consider more seriously smaller firms of consultants which offer the flexibility and process-oriented, customised approach necessary to meet the above demands. Nees and Greiner (1985) categorise some of the largest management consultancy firms in terms of the standard approaches they prefer to use with clients, or the 'well-tried routes' they recommend. Perhaps the shift in the approach to change means that smaller consultancies may become more sought after. These may provide consultants with fewer preconceptions of the best approaches to change and who are keen to offer the less directive service of facilitator rather than navigator and pilot.

REFERENCES

Butor, M. (1957) *La Modification*. Paris: Les Éditions de Minuit.

Dunn, S. (1990) 'Root metaphor in the old and new industrial relations', *British Journal of Industrial Relations*, Vol. 28, No. 1.

French, W.L. and Bell, C.H. (1990) *Organization Development: Behavioural Science Interventions for Organization Improvement*. 4th Edition, London: Prentice-Hall.

Friedlander, F. (1976) 'OD reaches adolescence: an exploration of its underlying values', *Journal of Applied Behavioural Science*, Vol. 12, No. 1.

Geertz, C. (1975) *The Interpretation of Cultures*. London: Hutchinson.

Gergen, K.J. (1992) 'Organization theory in the postmodern era', in Reed, M. and Hughes, M. (eds) *Rethinking Organization: New Directions in Organization Theory and Analysis*. London: Sage.

Goldstein, J. (1993) 'Revisioning the organization: chaos, quantum physics, and OD – an interview with Margaret Wheatley, Ed.D.', *Organization Development Journal*, Vol. 11, No. 2.

Harvey, D.F. and Brown, D.R. (1992) *An Experiential Approach to Organisation Development*. 4th Edition, London: Prentice-Hall.

Kuhn, T.S. (1970) *The Structure of Scientific Revolutions*. 2nd Edition, Chicago: The University of Chicago Press.

Lakoff, G. and Johnson, M. (1980) *Metaphors We Live By*. Chicago: University of Chicago Press.

Leavitt, H.J. (1986) *Corporate Pathfinders*. Illinois: Dow Jones-Irwin.

Lewin, K. (1951) *Field Theory in Social Science*. New York: Harper and Row.

Mangham, I.L. (1978) *Interactions and Interventions in Organizations*. Chichester: Wiley.

March, J.G. (1988) *Decisions and Organizations*. Oxford: Basil Blackwell.

Marshak, R.J. (1993) 'Lewin meets Confucius: a re-view of the OD model of change', *Journal of Applied Behavioural Science*, Vol. 29, No. 4.

McLean, A.J., Sims, D.B.P., Mangham, I.L. and Tuffield, D. (1982) *Organization Development in Transition: Evidence of an Evolving Profession*. Chichester: Wiley.

McLuhan, M. and Powers, B.R. (1989) *The Global Village*. Oxford: Oxford University Press.

Morgan, G. (1986) *Images of Organization*. London: Sage.

Nees, D.B. and Greiner, L.E. (1985) 'Seeing behind the look-alike management consultants', *Organization Dynamics*, Vol. 14, No. 1.

Pettigrew, A. (1985) *The Awakening Giant: Continuity and Change in ICI*. O.. ʊ.d: Basil Blackwell.

Smith, K.K. (1982) 'Philosophical problems in thinking about organizational change', in Goodman, P.S. and Associates (eds) *Change in Organizations: New Perspectives on Theory, Research and Practice*. London: Jossey-Bass.

Weick, K.E. (1990) 'Fatigue of the spirit in organizational theory and organization development: reconnaissance man as remedy', *Journal of Applied Behavioural Science*, Vol. 26, No. 3.

Wheatley, M. (1992) *Leadership and the New Science*. San Francisco: Berrett-Koehler.

Zohar, D. (1994) 'Forces of reaction', *The Sunday Times*, 6th February.

CHAPTER 3

The organisation as a human entity

Savita Kumra

INTRODUCTION

> The . . . doctor should be regularly checking the health in order to establish just what condition it is in. Hopefully, preventative medicine can be used to save the patient from the awful trauma of. . . anorexia, but if the condition is well advanced, the doctor should be prescribing a programme of recovery aimed at focusing the patient's mind on getting well. (Pullinger, 1992: 330)

From the above paragraph, one might think the author is providing advice to physicians on the treatment of the condition 'anorexia nervosa', a wasting condition where a person continually reduces their body weight, until they are unable to regenerate themselves. However, what the author is actually writing about is a condition he terms 'organisational anorexia', in which he likens the practice of many organisations, near obsession with 'cutback after cutback until the very heart of the business is affected' to the human condition outlined above (Pullinger, 1992: 328).

Pullinger has used what amounts to an 'anthropomorphism' to describe an organisation, i.e. he has likened an organisational phenomenon to a human condition. According to the *Oxford Dictionary of Current English*, anthropomorphism is the 'attribution of human form to god, animal or thing'. This chapter seeks to examine the contribution of human metaphors to theories of OD. It commences with an assessment of the value of metaphors in helping us understand the nature of organisation. It goes on to discuss the concept of anthropomorphism, highlighting some of its useful properties, as well as some of the concept's attendant difficulties. It then analyses three of the most influential human metaphors used to describe OD, these being the organismic, population ecology and organisational life cycle metaphors. The use of two 'cognitive' metaphors is also explored, those of organisational learning and organisational memory. These are mechanisms which enhance the value of the organismic, population ecology and life cycle metaphors when applied to OD. The chapter concludes with a brief discussion about the utility of such metaphorical thinking to students of organisation, as well as those charged with making them function: the individuals within them.

THE METAPHORICAL IMPERATIVE

Proponents of the use of metaphor in administrative science argue: 'Organisational scientific discourse does not describe, explain or intervene in an independent reality, but essentially draws upon symbolic construc- tions helping to bring about such a reality' (Tsoukas, 1991: 566; *see also* Astley, 1984; Manning, 1979). They believe that organisational science has been constrained by functionalist assumptions which view society as having 'a concrete, real existence, and a systemic character oriented to pro- duce an ordered and regulated state of affairs. Behavior is always seen as being contextually bound in a real world of concrete and tangible social relationships' (Morgan, 1980: 608). In pointing out the constraints of the functionalist perspective, Morgan offers interpretative and radical perspec- tives as alternative ways of viewing society. The interpretative paradigm views social relationships as a product of social constructions, thus oppos- ing the functionalist position of 'concrete and tangible' social relationships. According to this view the contribution of metaphor lies in its ability to promote novel ways of thinking. This in turn allows those seeking to study complex organisational phenomena to begin to analyse the diversity of variables, and the interplay between them – factors which constitute much of organisational activity (Morgan, 1980, 1983, 1986; Weick, 1979). The opposing view highlights the imprecision and low conceptual content of metaphors; while inevitable at the early stages of theory development, they are not appropriate at the later stages of scientific enquiry, where they should be replaced with literal language (Bourgeois and Pinder, 1983; Pinder and Bourgeois, 1982).

Despite criticism, there does seem to be considerable evidence to suggest that metaphor pervades our way of thinking about the world, that it can be a useful educational device and that it aids mutual understanding between theoreticians and practitioners of OD. In terms of the pervasiveness of metaphor, take Lakoff and Johnson's work (1980). They view the use of metaphor in the following way:

> Metaphor is not just a matter of language, that is, of mere words. . . human thought processes are largely metaphorical. This is what we mean when we say that the human conceptual system is metaphorically structured and defined. Metaphors as linguistic expressions are possible precisely because there are metaphors in a person's conceptual system. (1980: 6)

Ortony (1975) emphasises the great educational utility of metaphor. He points to evidence which indicates that 'imagibility correlates very highly with learnability' (Ortony, 1975: 51). Rich and vivid detail provides an effective means of moving from something which is known to the beginning of an understanding of something which is less well known or unknown. However, the effectiveness of metaphor is not derived through visual aspects alone; depending on the metaphor, many of the senses can be engaged simultaneously, in addition to its emotive power.

Ortony (1975) sees the educational value of metaphor as twofold:

> The vivid imagery arising from metaphorical comprehension encourages memorability and generates of necessity a better, more insightful personal understanding. But also, it is a very effective device for moving from the well-known to the less well-known. (1975: 51)

In explaining why 'metaphors are necessary and not just nice', Ortony continues:

> Metaphors are necessary as a communicative device because they allow the transfer of coherent chunks of characteristics – perceptual, cognitive, emotional and experiential – from a vehicle which is known to a topic which is less so. In so doing, they circumvent the problem of specifying one by one each of the often unnameable and innumerable characteristics; they avoid discretizing the perceived continuity of experience and are thus closer to experience and consequently more vivid and memorable. (1975: 53)

So, if we agree with Ortony, there is a powerful educational utility to be gained from the use of metaphor. However, can the same be said of its value within the field of OD?

Brink (1993) sees three applications of metaphor in OD. First, metaphors are often more easily heard than rational explanations and as a consequence they encourage listening. Second, metaphors often provide opportunities for development. Third, they promote communication, because the symbolism employed is often creative and can attract other organisational members into discussion. Morgan also believes that metaphors can be of great use to managers and OD practitioners. Through their effective application the complexity of organisational life is illustrated and an awareness of the 'one-sided' nature of many of the established ways of viewing organisational phenomena is also provided (Morgan, 1986, 1989, 1993).

Beyer (1992), in her discussion of the role of science in organisational analysis, argues that managers and scientists are essentially playing different language games, and that for understanding to occur between them what is required are 'translators', without which 'none of the meanings scientists intend would be transferred from scientists to managers when managers adopt scientists' language' (1992: 469).

Perhaps one of the translators, or vehicles through which managers and scientists can begin to communicate, is metaphor. Beyer sees the use of 'conceptual and symbolic' language which both managers and scientists have access to as encouraging, and possibly an indication that 'empirical organisational science [can] contribute to managerial practice' (1992: 473).

In considering the usefulness of metaphor when analysing organisations it is important to include the processes involved in their application. A metaphor takes a term from one domain, the original domain, to another, the target domain, where the term does not usually apply. In short, metaphors treat things which are dissimilar in material ways as if they were not (see, for example, Ortony, 1975). Consequently, while metaphor may be viewed as an efficient way to understand a complex reality, it should not be viewed as an exact replica, or precise explanation, of the phenomenon under study. The metaphor does not itself explain the resemblance between two objects (Tsoukas, 1990; Pinder and Bourgeois, 1982); and, as Trice and Beyer observe, 'metaphors are not precise, something is usually lost and added in the translation process' (1993: 96).

Tinker (1986) sounds a further note of caution regarding the application of metaphors in organisational settings. He believes that particular types of metaphor can act to shape individuals' conceptions of the phenomenon they purport to represent, namely the danger of reification. Tinker focuses on a number of metaphors, including some of the human metaphors discussed in this chapter (i.e. those implied by social Darwinism, socio-biology and biology). The crux of his argument is that metaphors are never neutral representations when applied to social affairs:

> These metaphorical constructions achieve the same ends; they remove the social environment of corporations from the scrutiny of critical social analysis; they leave unarticulated the structural conflicts in which corporations are embedded. . . The implication is that the corporate environment is not merely unknowable and unanalyzeable, it is also immutable, unchangeable and uncontrollable in terms of its structural inequalities. Consequently organisational theory is purged of political and social content. (Tinker, 1986: 375)

Tinker's concern is that the representation of organisations in terms of biological, organismic or other systems, which by their very nature have to behave in a particular way (i.e. biological organisms have to pass through certain stages in their growth cycle, while living organisms can only exist through an exchange with their environment) means that organisations are also viewed as automatically adhering to the same behaviour. In such thinking, inequality, social position and power distribution within organisations are accepted as 'given' and are not seen for what they actually are – a functioning social system, in the hands of organisational members to shape as they see fit.

Thus, while understanding that metaphors can be useful in their ability to free us from the constraints of traditional ways of viewing an organisation and organisational activity, it is apparent that metaphorical constructs should be used with caution, ensuring that they do not further confuse the issue under study through imprecise or inappropriate explication. Bearing this in mind, we now move on to an analysis of whether the use of human metaphors can aid us in gaining a better understanding of the complex phenomenon of OD.

ANTHROPOMORPHISM AND THE INDIVIDUAL: THE ORGANISATIONAL RELATIONSHIP

The use of anthropomorphism can be seen in, for example, Weick's (1979) work, and the process has subsequently been discussed at some length by Doving (1994). Using anthropomorphism to construct human-oriented metaphors in organisational theory can lead to some confusion. This occurs due to the fact that organisations only exist through individuals who are their members, while at the same time we use an individual human being as a metaphor for the organisation as a whole (Doving, 1994). The problem is related to the 'level' of analysis. Is the metaphor attempting to draw a perfect identity between the development of an individual and that of an organisation, or are the two in fact so dissimilar in their developmental processes that the metaphors used in this context are inappropriate?

If we were to consider the relationship between the organisational phenomenon and the human phenomenon (metaphor) to be identical or very close, then we would expect the constructs and relationships to be replicated in the original and the target domain of the metaphor (Rousseau, 1985). In short, such a close relationship would entail organisations and humans sharing the main features or concrete properties inferred from the metaphor (Tsoukas, 1990). On this basis, a metaphor used to describe individuals within an organisation could correctly be used to describe the total organisation.

In reality, of course, the relationship between organisational phenomenon and human phenomenon is far less simplistic. We tend to assume only a partial analogy between the original and target domains, and therefore the use of human metaphors in the development of organisational theory should proceed cautiously (Bourgeois and Pinder, 1983; Pinder and Bourgeois, 1982). As previously mentioned, the metaphors themselves do not indicate where organisations and humans resemble one another in relation to particular phenomena under investigation. The task is to identify 'what' it is that is similar between the two and where the differences lie. If this is not achieved then the metaphor's value is significantly undermined. In effect, then, we must not assume that human properties are automatically replicated in the organisational arena. Nevertheless, this is exactly what happens – metaphors which are literary devices aiding an alternative way of thinking of the phenomenon to which they pertain are confused with reality (Weber, 1971; Weick, 1979).

By their very nature, anthropomorphisms used to describe organisations may be construed as providing a real or literal description of the organisation. This often arises from the fact that, while organisations are inhabited by individuals for whom the constructs can be applied literally, at the organisational level the same constructs are more likely to be figures of speech. Doving (1994) uses the example of organisational knowledge to illustrate this point, arguing that we cannot conclude that 'organisational knowledge' exists from a recognition that individuals have knowledge, and that organisations are comprised of individuals. The claim of the existence of 'organisational knowledge' cannot be based solely on the fact that knowledge exists at the individual level.

Perhaps the most problematic issue in relation to the use of the human metaphor to explain organisational phenomena stems from the argument that ideally organisational phenomena should be measured at the organisational level (Rousseau, 1985). However, the organisation is an 'ambiguous' object, which 'cannot be weighed and measured. It cannot answer questions about feelings, preferences or beliefs. Neither can the organisation as such be observed. Only persons can be observed and questioned, but never the total organisation'. (Doving, 1994: 10)

We are thus only able to infer organisation-level data from data obtained at other levels of analysis, such as the individual level. To do this adequately requires that we have a solution to the problem of 'aggregation', and that this solution (and thus the theory emanating from it) is reliable, enabling the extrapolation of valid organisation-level data. In the absence of such a solution (theory) the data aggregation will be uninformative and in some extreme cases utterly misleading (Cook and Campbell, 1979). Data about individuals in the organisation may be extracted, but less about the organisation itself (Rousseau, 1985).

It seems, then, that personification of organisations via human metaphors can be extremely valuable for students and organisational members. They must, however, be used cautiously and the relationships between the original and target domains adequately tested, so that, once found, the extent of the relationship is not lost in the translation. The next section considers three of the most influential human metaphors which have been advanced as an aid to understanding the phenomenon of OD.

THE ORGANISMIC METAPHOR

Spencer (1873, 1876) represents one of the first examples of an approach to management theory which is built on an analogy of the organisation with biological organisms (Clegg and Dunkerley, 1980). Spencer regarded an organism as a system of 'mutually connected and dependent parts constituted to share a common life... An organism is typically seen as a combination of elements, differentiated yet integrated, attempting to survive within the context of a wider environment' (Morgan, 1980: 614).

Morgan's *Images of Organization* (1986) provides us with some valuable insights into the nature of the organismic metaphor. He notes that it is based on the recognition that an organisation, like an organic system, exists through a continuous exchange with its environment. This exchange is essential for the survival of the life and form of the system, since interaction with the environment is the basis of 'self-maintenance' (Morgan, 1986: 46). Through the recognition that organisations cannot act independently of the environment in which they operate comes the metaphor of the organisation as an 'open system' or living organism. In its simplest form, an open system consists of a continuous cycle of input, internal transformation (throughput), output and feedback; organisations, like biological organisms and societies, are fully open systems.

The open systems approach recognises the interactive relationship between an organisation and its environment, emphasising that the relationship is of such critical importance that the organisation depends for its very survival on its ability to develop appropriate responses to these demands. The external environment is viewed as an input to the organisation, through social, legal, technical, economic and political factors; and it is the organisation's ability to respond appropriately to these inputs, through its internal transformation processes (converting the inputs to outputs), which will determine its continued survival. From the notion of 'appropriate' response to external stimuli determining continued existence, theoreticians began to recognise that not all organisations are suited to all environments, and that certain organisational types showed markedly greater survival rates in certain types of environment than others (Morgan, 1986).

Burns and Stalker (1961) studied organisations operating in a number of industries, e.g. man-made fibres, engineering and electronics. They concluded that when an organisation's environmental conditions are turbulent, such as at times of high product market uncertainty, 'open and flexible' styles of management are necessary. However, they also acknowledge that bureaucratic (or metaphorically mechanistic) organisational forms remain appropriate in environments which are stable in nature, or artificially protected from the vagaries of their natural environment, for example through government regulation. Burns and Stalker propose the notion of a 'continuum' of organisational forms, ranging from the mechanistic to the organic, correlating increasingly flexible forms of organisation with more dynamic organisational environments.

The organismic metaphor also recognises that organisations cannot simply react to environmental stimuli without due regard to their own internal needs and functions which must be satisfied in order to maintain an ongoing relationship between the organisation and its environment. It was thus recognised that individuals and groups within organisations, like living organisms, operate to best effect only when their internal needs are satisfied; leading theorists to attempt to 'identify essential life sustaining activities' (Morgan, 1980: 615). Integrating the needs of individuals and organisations was the aim of the human relations school. Through the modification of organisational factors such as structure, managerial style and the organisation of work, authors such as Argyris (1964), Herzberg (1959) and McGregor (1960) believed that they could create jobs which were intrinsically motivating, would foster personal growth and would increase commitment and motivation. It was believed that applying these processes at the individual level would enable the organisation as a whole to achieve its aims and objectives (Morgan, 1986).

Burns and Stalker (1961) found that successful adaptation to the organisational environment depended on top management's ability to adopt and implement appropriate courses of action in response to the environmental conditions facing the firm. These findings supported those of Woodward (1965), who suggested that the technology employed within the organisation gave rise to a number of options in relation to organisational structure. Successful organisations were those which achieved the best 'fit' between technology and structure, although ultimately the choice was of a strategic nature.

The work of Lawrence and Lorsch (1967) was important because it highlighted the need for organisations operating in turbulent, dynamic environments to achieve a greater degree of internal differentiation (i.e. between an organisation's departments) than was necessary for an organisation operating in a more stable environment. Unlike in nature, where species are differentiated by discrete, observable characteristics, organisational characteristics can be distributed in a more continuous way. One form may often intermingle with another, producing organisations with 'hybrid' characteristics (Morgan, 1986). However, as Mintzberg (1975) and more recently Peters and Waterman (1982) have shown, successful organisations seem to display distinctive characteristics, enabling them to deal successfully with their environment.

Emphasising the satisfaction of the needs of the organisation for its continued survival ensures that survival is seen as the key aim or primary task facing the organisation. This is in contrast with the classical focus on achieving particular operational goals. The process of survival takes precedence over the rigidity often imposed in the pursuit of set targets or goals. Thus action can be focused where it is necessary, and not rigidly in one direction. Strategy, structure and technology, and the human and managerial dimensions of organisation, are seen as organisational sub-systems with 'living' needs, which require satisfaction in such a way that the needs of both are met – otherwise the 'health and openness' of the entire system may be affected (Morgan, 1986).

In viewing the organisation as a living organism, we tend to forget that organisations are formed through social interaction and social constructs, and rely for their shape and structure on the dominant visions, ideas, norms and beliefs. Unlike the material structure of an organism, their structure is thus dependent on a variety of factors and may develop in a number of ways, according to the organisational response to internal needs and the external environment. It can thus be said that to suggest that organisations need to 'adapt' to their environments, as do the contingency theorists, is misleading, as it tends to neglect the fact that organisations and their members are not simply reacting to forces operating in an external world, but rather they are active participants operating in concert with others to construct that world.

A further limitation of the metaphor rests in its assumption of 'functional unity'. Organisms in the natural world are usually characterised by a functional interdependence; every element of the system (when operating normally) is working for all the other elements. Morgan (1986) gives the example of the human body where the blood, heart, lungs, arms, legs etc. normally co-operate for the homeostatic functioning of the body as a whole.

Circumstances when one element works in a way which is against the interests of the whole, such as when illness occurs, arise when elements of the whole are not co-operating to sustain the system and could lead to its demise, i.e. death. Within organisations, however, times when they operate in harmony, as discussed above, are the exception rather than the rule. The elements within an organisation are capable of operating independently and usually do so. At times organisations may be highly unified, as people in different sections abandon their own self-interest, for a time, for the good of the organisation as a whole; at other times the same organisation may be characterised by the pursuit of diverse and often conflicting interests.

THE POPULATION ECOLOGY METAPHOR

Astley and Van de Ven (1983) provide a useful analysis of the population ecology model. As they see it, the population ecology model as formulated by Aldrich (1979) is based on the notion that environmental resources are structured in the form of 'niches', whose existence and distribution across society are only marginally influenced by the actions of a single organisation. This view rather deterministically states that there are definite boundaries to the extent to which strategic choice is available to individual organisations (Aldrich, 1979). The ability of organisations to alter their internal 'form' to meet the demands of different niches is also seen as constrained. Organisations are thus placed at the mercy of their environment as, should they not fortuitously 'fit' into a niche, they will be 'selected' out and fail (Hannan and Freeman, 1977). This view implies a population level of analysis, since whole species of organisation are seen to survive or fail, irrespective of the aggressive or defensive actions taken by single organisations within them.

The population ecology view defines a 'population' as an aggregate of organisations that are relatively homogenous (Hannan and Freeman, 1977). All organisations within the population share certain 'key elements' constituting their common form. As a consequence, they also share a mutual vulnerability to the environment. Such common vulnerability goes some way to explaining the occurrence and distribution of different species of organisation across differing environmental conditions.

Populations depend on distinct combinations of resources, called niches, to support them. Populations are formed as a result of processes which segregate one set of organisations from another, such as incompatible technologies and government regulations (Hannan and Freeman, 1986). Blending processes also occur which blur the boundaries between populations. These processes include the increasing use of shared technologies, common markets and institutional action such as deregulation (Aldrich, 1993).

The population ecology view has, on occasion, attracted considerable criticism. This is due to its challenging the assertion that changes in organisational form are explained by internal adaptation. Instead it argues that the process is characterised by environmental selection (Astley and Van de Ven, 1983). However, it is the internal adaptation view that has historically dominated organisational theory. Based on the work of systems theorists, who view organisations as 'complex adaptive systems' (Buckley, 1968), contingency theorists have emphasised that organisations respond to change by adapting their internal structures appropriately to maintain an isomorphic relationship with the environment. For example, environmental heterogeneity must be matched by internal differentiation and integration within the organisation's operating sub-units, if organisational performance is not to suffer (Lawrence and Lorsch, 1967).

Population ecologists believe that the adaptation perspective exaggerates the degree to which managers of organisations are able to adjust their structural forms to suit the demands of the environment (Aldrich and Pfeffer, 1976). They argue that sunk costs, historical precedent, political resistance to change and so on may contribute to 'structural inertia' (Hannan and Freeman, 1977). If we accept this view of 'structural inertia', it follows that once the niche that an organisation occupies ceases to attract sufficient resources to maintain its current organisational form, that form becomes obsolete and is selected out. Those holding the adaptation view would reject this position, arguing that organisations respond to change by tuning in to the necessities of their local and task environment, and adapting appropriately (McKelvey, 1979). The adaptation view analyses at the unit level, whereas in the selection view at this level any fine tuning within the localised confines of an organisation's niche is futile, since eventually the niche which makes it possible for a certain type of organisation to exist may disappear altogether. Thus the focus moves from the unit level to entire species or populations of organisations that come and go in 'waves', as whole industries or organisational forms are born and extinguished (Aldrich, 1979).

Population ecology focuses attention on the 'natural' environment, emphasising that this is comprised of forces beyond the control of the organisation. Organisations can vie for environmental resources with other organisations in a competitive bid for survival, but such action is futile as their fortunes are ultimately environmentally determined. This contrasting focus on 'natural' versus 'social' environments carries implications for the assessment of each perspective in relation to what it is that constitutes the essential determinant underlying organisational activity. Population ecologists believe that it is 'environmental pressures [which] make competition for resources the central force in organisational activities' (Aldrich, 1979: 27–8), and that the population ecology model is most effective in environments with dispersed resources, i.e. environments which closely approximate perfectly competitive markets.

To summarise, the natural selection or population ecology view sees the evolution of corporate society and its economic infrastructure as driven by environmental forces. Change occurs through the natural drift of resources through the economy, rather than in terms of internal managerial action. Primacy is ascribed to the environment as the determining force which inhibits organisational choice by channelling organisations into predetermined directions. The view thus sees the managerial role as inactive, or at best symbolic (Pfeffer and Salancik, 1978).

Morgan (1986) sees the major strength of this metaphor as lying in its focus on ecology and inter-organisational relations. By adopting ecological views, the idea is reinforced that a theory of inter-organisational relations is essential if we are to gain an understanding of how the world of organisation actually 'evolves'. Morgan adds that, if the population ecologists are right, we will also be able to look to new forms of inter-organisational relations to begin to deal with the complex environments faced by modern organisations.

Morgan's (1986) discussion of this metaphor also leads him to identify its limitations. He suggests that the population ecology view is far too deterministic to be capable of providing an acceptable explanation of the ways in which organisations evolve or develop. The population ecologists would have us believe that environments 'select' organisations for survival; that in the long run, what managers and decision makers do is irrelevant. Thus even efficient and successful firms which adopt appropriate courses of action in response to changes in their environment are doomed to failure as a result of environmental changes that influence the structure of their resource niche. The population ecology view has been heavily criticised for underestimating the influence and element of choice implied by an organisation's strategic direction; despite inertial pressures, there is evidence to suggest that organisations are able to transform themselves from one kind of organisation to another. Doving (1994) also sees this metaphor as inappropriate because organisations have the ability to migrate from one population to another, or from one niche to another, and because organisations are capable of 'purposive mutation', i.e. organisational redesign.

THE ORGANISATIONAL LIFE CYCLE OR STAGE MODEL METAPHOR

The main focus in stage models is an examination of the dual variables of organisational size and age of firm. The theme running through all stage models is that as an organisation grows, like a human being, it will pass through clear and marked stages of development; with reliance shifting from the owner–manager in the early stages, towards more formalised and bureaucratic structures as the organisation matures.

One of the first life cycle models was developed by McGuire (1963). He believed that organisations passed through five stages in their development process; these he termed 'traditional small company', 'planning for growth', 'take-off', 'drive for professional management' and 'mass production'. A number of stage models have been developed since; however, the work of Greiner (1972) is of particular interest.

Greiner believes that five key dimensions emerge as necessary for building a model of organisational development. These he gives as age of the organisation; size of the organisation; stages of evolution; stages of revolution and growth rate of the industry. Greiner contends that as an organisation progresses through each developmental phase, each evolutionary period (defined as 'prolonged periods of growth where no major upheaval occurs', 1972: 38) results in its own 'revolution' (defined as 'periods of substantial turmoil in organisational life', 1972: 38). Each evolutionary period is characterised by a particular management style, used to achieve growth, and each revolutionary period is identified by a management problem requiring resolution before growth can continue.

Stages of revolution occur in more turbulent times, and usually require a major upheaval in managerial practices. Traditional managerial practices are no longer applicable to the organisation at its present stage; organisations which fail to abandon the practices of the past and institute widespread organisational change face the possibility of a reduction in their rate of growth, or possibly total demise. In each revolutionary period, it is essential that management develop a new set of organisational practices, tailored to manage the next period of evolutionary growth. However, Greiner points out that it is these same new practices which will, in the future, lead to the next period of revolution.

The pace at which an organisation will progress through these phases of evolution and revolution is inextricably linked with the nature of its environment. Thus in fast-growing, dynamic environments, evolutionary periods tend to be rather short, while they will be much longer in a mature or slower-growing industry.

Greiner goes on to discuss the factors which lead to 'revolution' within the organisation. The first of these he terms the 'leadership crisis'. As an organisation grows, the informal managerial practices which were once sufficient are now incapable of dealing with current organisational problems. The issue as to who will lead the organisation has to be confronted. The organisation's founders are often not the best managers, and it is their willingness to step down in favour of a professional business manager which determines whether the organisation moves on to the next stage of evolutionary growth. Other revolutionary crises occur when the organisation's growth necessitates that its members are given more autonomy, and when delegation, co-ordination and collaboration become necessary in order that work is more effectively channelled and conducted. The key to weathering the periods of 'revolution' and embarking on the next phase of evolutionary growth is in Greiner's view an understanding, not only of the action necessary to get through the current revolution, but that the action taken will also ensure smooth progression through the next stage of growth. He also points out that managers must understand that the action they take at the current time will create future problems, i.e. a decision to delegate will lead to a problem of control in the future. Historical actions are largely responsible for what happens to organisations in the future; it is through an understanding of this, i.e. an appreciation of the organisation's past, that managers may actually improve the job they do in the future.

Greiner's model is certainly not the only stage or organisational life cycle model, but it is one of the most influential in the field (others include Churchill and Lewis, 1983; Kanzanjian, 1984; Flamholtz, 1986; Dodge and Robbins, 1992). Stage models are useful because, as Churchill and Lewis

(1983) point out in relation to small business, an understanding of the stages the business is going to pass through can aid in assessing current challenges, e.g. the necessity to buy new equipment or to groom individuals within the organisation to become future managers. (For a detailed discussion of the role of metaphor in understanding small businesses, see Perren in Chapter 14.) Such models can also be of use if managers understand, as pointed out by Greiner (1972), that actions taken at key periods in the organisation's past can be a clue to the best way to deal with current problems and crises.

The main disadvantage of such models is that, although biological systems pass through predictable and largely unavoidable stages in their development, from simple to more complex (Kimberley and Miles, 1980), there is no imperative for organisations to behave in the same way. As Moore (1993: 85–6) points out: 'Business communities, unlike biological and social systems are made up of real people who make decisions; the larger patterns are maintained by a complex network of choices, which depend, at least in part, on what participants are aware of.'

'COGNITIVE' METAPHORS: THE CASES OF ORGANISATIONAL LEARNING AND ORGANISATIONAL MEMORY

If through the application of human metaphors an organisation can assume human forms and behaviour, it therefore follows that it thinks and acts like a human; perhaps, as discussed by Oswick, Lowe and Jones in Chapter 7, it can even be said to develop a human personality. Not surprisingly, then, one of the most prominent metaphors to be applied to organisations endows them with 'cognition', i.e. knowing, perceiving or conceiving (*The Oxford English Dictionary of Current English*).

The idea of organisational cognition has been used in a number of ways. Probably the best known example is given by Morgan (1986), who discusses the organisation in terms of a brain metaphor. This draws attention to the distributed nature of many organisational functions and the networks through which they are connected. It also highlights the concept of a learning organisation. The application of a brain metaphor might also take account of the part played by meaning and imagination, and perhaps captures the idea of creating or adding value.

This section will focus on the concepts of organisational learning and organisational memory; concepts which are aligned to the brain metaphor, but which themselves are important contributions to the theoretical body of OD knowledge. The concepts are implicit in all of the literature models discussed above and are therefore key facilitative features of the human metaphors that the models incorporate. As evidence of this relationship take for example Greiner (1972), who points to the importance of organisations memorising historical events in order to determine appropriate future action. Similarly, look at contingency theory which highlights the importance of adopting appropriate courses of action in response to environmental pressures. These appropriate courses of action are often based on memory and previous learning experiences. In short, applying the lessons of history, and acting appropriately to the environment, are only possible if we believe that:

- the organisation is capable of 'learning' from the past; and
- it has some way of 'remembering' the lessons learnt.

Organisational learning

'All organizations learn whether they consciously choose to or not – it is a fundamental requirement for their sustained existence' (Kim, 1993: 37). Organisational learning can be viewed as a metaphor, building on the similarity with individual learning. Thus, theories of individual learning are necessary to aid an understanding of organisational learning. In line with such an approach, the learning process has been described in the following way:

> a person continually cycles through a process of having a concrete experience, making observations and reflections on that experience, forming abstract concepts and generalizations based on those reflections and testing those ideas in a new situation which leads to another experience. (Kim, 1993: 38)

Another element in a model of organisational learning is the organisation as a behavioural system. For learning to serve any purpose requires the ability to act on the experience, i.e. to alter behaviour in the light of experience. Thus organisations have to be viewed as behavioural systems. An example of such a view is given by Cyert and March, who see the organisation:

> as an adaptively rational system that basically learns from experience. A firm changes its behavior in response to short-term feedback from the environment according to some fairly well-defined rules and adapts to longer-term feedback on the basis of more general rules. At some level in this hierarchy, they suggest lie 'learning rules'. (Kim, 1993: 41)

Organisational learning can therefore be seen as having both a cognitive (interpretative) and behavioural element. Indeed, one of the defining characteristics of organisational learning is a change in behaviour. In order to act on the lessons of the past (i.e. alter behaviour), the organisation must be capable of interpreting the consequences of previous actions and experiences of individuals appropriately. Thus the organisation must also be viewed as an 'interpretation' system. Such a view is apparent in Daft and Weick's (1984) model of the organisation's learning process. The key stages to their model are scanning, interpretation and learning.

Organisational memory

Walsh and Ungson (1991: 61) define organisational memory as:

> Stored information from an organization's history that can be brought to bear on present decisions. This information is stored as a consequence of implementing decisions to which they refer, by individual recollections and through shared interpretations.

These authors analyse the constituents of organisational memory, which they see as being acquisition, retention, individuals, culture, transformations, structure and ecology.

Acquisition occurs through interpretations about organisational decisions, and their subsequent consequences. Information which is useful is retained, and that which has served little purpose is discarded. Individuals store their organisational memory in their ability to recall and take action on experience in respect of the cognitive processes required to effect organisational decisions. To aid memory, individuals and organisations keep records and files, which as many authors have observed constitute the physical, tangible aspects of an organisation's memory (Huber, 1991; March and Olsen, 1975; Simon, 1976). The role of culture in organisational memory is that it embodies past experience, which can be of use in the future. Culture is thus one of the retention facilities of organisational memory. Transformations include practices such as work design (Taylor, 1911), selection (Arvey, 1979) and socialisation (Van Maanen and Schein, 1979). All of these transformations are built on past experience and are housed in the organisation's memory.

The concept of organisational memory has been the focus of some debate. Commentators seem to disagree on the specific form of organisational memory and at what level it might reside in the organisation. The result has been a wide divergence of views. On the one hand, for example, Sandelands and Stablein (1987: 136) have suggested that 'organisations are mental entities capable of thought'. On the other hand, Argyris and Schon (1978: 11) have posited that organisational memory is only a metaphor, 'organizations do not literally remember'.

CONCLUSIONS

This chapter has focused on the application of human metaphors within OD. In doing so, it has examined three of the most prominent of these metaphors, highlighting their associated strengths and weaknesses. An explanation has also been advanced of two cognitive metaphors – organisational learning and organisational memory – and their role in facilitating OD where human metaphors are in use.

The chapter has not sought to preach the use of human metaphors in the analysis of organisations, nor has it sought to undermine their value. Instead, it has sought to show that we cannot deny the prevalence of human metaphors in OD. The use of anthropomorphisms in organisational theory will not simply stop – we will continue to think of organisations as human entities. For this reason, human metaphors will continue to play a major role in shaping our understanding of organisational change.

What is necessary, however, is to use human metaphors in the most effective way. It is imperative that we learn how and when it is best to apply them and that we acknowledge their limitations. In respect of OD, an inappropriate metaphor serves no purpose other than to add confusion to the situation in which an organisation finds itself. Students studying organisations, as well as those managers and OD practitioners who work within them, should therefore see this chapter as having provided a framework within which key metaphors in OD can be applied and scrutinised.

REFERENCES

Aldrich, H. (1979) *Organizations and Environments*. Englewood Cliffs, NJ: Prentice-Hall.

Aldrich, H. and Pfeffer, J. (1976) 'Environments of organizations', in Inkeles, A. (ed) *Annual Review of Sociology*. Vol. 11, Palo Alto, CA: Annual Reviews.

Aldrich, H. (1993) 'Incommensurable paradigms? Vital signs from three perspectives', in Reed, M. and Hughes, M. (eds) *Rethinking Organisation: New Directions in Organisation Theory*. London: Sage.

Argyris, C. (1964) *Integrating the Individual and the Organization*. New York: Wiley.

Argyris, C. and Schon, D.A. (1978) *Organizational Learning: A Theory of Action Perspective*. Reading, Mass.: Addison-Wesley.

Arvey, R.D. (1979) *Fairness in Selecting Employees*. Reading, Mass.: Addison-Wesley.

Astley, W.G. (1984) 'Toward an appreciation of collective strategy', *Academy of Management Review*, Vol. 9, No. 3.

Astley, W.G. and Van de Ven, A.H. (1983) 'Central perspectives and debates in organization theory', *Administrative Science Quarterly*, Vol. 28.

Beyer, J.M. (1992) 'Metaphors, misunderstandings and mischief: a commentary', *Organisation Science*, Vol. 3, No. 2.

Bourgeois, V.W. and Pinder, C.C. (1983) 'Contrasting philosophical perspectives in administrative science: a reply to Morgan', *Administrative Science Quarterly*, Vol. 28.

Brink, T.L. (1993) 'Metaphor as data in the study of organizations', *Journal of Management Inquiry*, Vol. 2, No. 4.

Buckley, W. (ed) (1968) *Modern Systems Research for the Behavioral Scientist*. Chicago: Aldine.

Burns, T. and Stalker, G.M. (1961) *The Management of Innovation*. London: Tavistock.

Churchill, N.C. and Lewis, V.L. (1983) 'Growing concerns: the five stages of small business growth', *Harvard Business Review*, Vol. 62, May–June.

Clegg, S. and Dunkerley, D. (1980) *Organization, Class and Control*. London: Routledge and Kegan Paul.

Cook, T.D. and Campbell, D.T. (1979) *Quasi-Experimentation: Design and Analysis Issues for Field Settings*. Boston: Houghton Mifflin.

Daft, R.L. and Weick, K.E. (1984) 'Toward a model of organizations as interpretation systems', *Academy of Management Review*, Vol. 9.

Dodge, R.H. and Robbins, J.E. (1992) 'An empirical investigation of the organisational life cycle model for small business development and survival', *Journal of Small Business*, January.

Doving, E. (1994) 'Using anthropomorphistic metaphors: organizational action, knowledge and learning'. Paper presented at the conference on *Metaphors in Organisational Theory and Behaviour* at King's College London, 28–30 July.

Flamholtz, E.G. (1986) *How to Make the Transition from Entrepreneurship to a Professionally Managed Firm*. San Francisco: Jossey-Bass.

Greiner, L.E. (1972) 'Evolution and revolution as organizations grow', *Harvard Business Review*, Vol. 51, July–August.

Hannan, M.T. and Freeman, J.H. (1977) 'The population ecology of organizations', *American Journal of Sociology*, Vol. 82.

Hannan, M.T. and Freeman, J.H. (1986) 'Where do organizational forms come from?', *Sociological Forum*, Vol. 1, No. 1.

Herzberg, F.B. (1959) *The Motivation to Work*. New York: Wiley.

Huber, G.P. (1991) 'Organizational learning: the contributing processes and the literature', *Organization Science*, Vol. 2, No. 1.

Kanzanjian, R.K. (1984) 'Operationalizing stage of growth: an empirical assessment of dominant problems', in Hornday, J., Tarpley, F., Timmons, J.A. and Vesper, K. (eds) *Frontiers of Entrepreneurial Research*. Wellesley, Mass: Babson College, Centre for Entrepreneurial Studies.

Kim, D.H. (1993) 'The link between individual and organizational learning', *Sloan Management Review*, Fall.

Kimberley, J.R. and Miles, R.H. (1980) *The Organizational Life Cycle*. New York: Jossey-Bass.

Lakoff, G. and Johnson, M. (1980) *Metaphors We Live By*. Chicago: University of Chicago Press.

Lawrence, P.R. and Lorsch, J.W. (1967) 'Differentiation and integration in complex organizations', *Administrative Science Quarterly*, Vol. 12.

Manning, P.K. (1979) 'Metaphors of the field: varieties of organizational discourse', *Administrative Science Quarterly*, Vol. 24.

March, J.G. and Olsen, J.P. (1975) *Ambiguity and Choice in Organizations*. Berger: Universitetsforlaget.

McGregor, D. (1960) *The Human Side of Enterprise*. New York: McGraw-Hill.

McGuire, J.W. (1963) *Factors Affecting the Growth of Manufacturing Firms*. Bureau of Business Research: University of Washington.

McKelvey, W. (1979) 'Comment on the biological analogy in organizational science, on the occasion of Van de Ven's review of Aldrich', *Administrative Science Quarterly*, Vol. 24.

Mintzberg, H. (1975) *The Structuring of Organizations*. Englewood Cliffs, NJ: Prentice-Hall.

Moore, J.F. (1993) 'Predators and prey: a new ecology of competition', *Harvard Business Review*, Vol. 72, May–June.

Morgan, G. (1980) 'Paradigms, metaphors, and puzzle solving in organization theory', *Administrative Science Quarterly*, Vol. 25.

Morgan, G. (1983) 'More on metaphor: why we cannot control tropes in administrative science', *Administrative Science Quarterly*, Vol. 28.

Morgan, G. (1986) *Images of Organization*. Newbury Park, CA: Sage.

Morgan, G. (1989) *Creative Organization Theory: A Resource Book*. Newbury Park, CA: Sage.

Morgan, G. (1993) *Imaginization: The Art of Creative Management*. Newbury Park, CA: Sage.

Ortony, A. (1975) 'Why metaphors are necessary and not just nice', *Educational Theory*, Vol. 25, No. 1.

Peters, T.J. and Waterman, R.H. (1982) *In Search of Excellence*. New York: Harper and Row.

Pfeffer, J. and Salancik, G.R. (1978) *The External Control of Organizations: A Resource Dependence Perspective*, New York: Harper and Row.

Pinder, C.C. and Bourgeois, V.W. (1982) 'Controlling tropes in administrative science', *Administrative Science Quarterly*, Vol. 27.

Pullinger, D. (1992) 'Slimming down and wasting away: case for the process doctor', *Management Education and Development*, Vol. 23, No. 4.

Rousseau, D.M. (1985) 'Issues of level in organizational research: multi-level and cross-level perspectives', *Research in Organizational Behaviour*, Vol. 7, No 1.

Sandelands, L.E. and Stablein, R.E. (1987) 'The concept of organization mind', in Bachrach, S. and DiTomaso, N. (eds) *Research in the Sociology of Organizations*. Greenwich, CT: JAI Press.

Simon, H.A. (1976) *Administrative Behavior*. New York: Free Press.

Spencer, H. (1873) *The Study of Sociology*. London: Kegan Paul and Trench.

Spencer, H. (1876) *Principles of Sociology*. London: Williams and Norgate.

Taylor, F.W. (1911) *Principles of Scientific Management*. New York: Harper and Row.

Tinker, A. (1986) 'Metaphor or reification: are radical humanists really libertarian anarchists?', *Journal of Management Studies*, Vol. 23, No. 4.

Trice, H.M. and Beyer, J. (1993) *The Cultures of Work Organizations*. Englewood Cliffs, NJ: Prentice-Hall.

Tsoukas, H. (1990) *The Role of Metaphors in Organizational Theory Development: A Review and a Suggestion*. Working Paper No. 188, Manchester Business School.

Tsoukas, H. (1991) 'The missing link: a transformational view of metaphors in organizational science', *Academy of Management Review*, Vol. 16, No. 3.

Van Maanen, J. and Schein, E.H. (1979) 'Toward a theory of organizational socialization', in Staw, B. (ed) *Research in Organizational Behaviour*. Greenwich, CT: JAI Press.

Walsh, J.P. and Ungson, G.R. (1991) 'Organizational memory', *Academy of Management Review*, Vol. 16, No. 1.

Weber, M. (1971) *Power and Bureaucracy: Politics and Class, Social Research and Values*. Oslo: Gyldendal.

Weick, K.E. (1979) *The Social Psychology of Organizing*. Reading, Mass.: Addison-Wesley.

Woodward, J. (1965) *Industrial Organization: Theory and Practice*. London: Oxford University Press.

PART II

Organisational culture and change

INTRODUCTION

The chapters in this part of the book concern two fundamental aspects of OD, i.e. planned change and the corporate culture. Both of these areas have clear overtones of a journey. At one level there appears to be an ongoing search, perhaps even a quest, among management theorists and consultants for the illusive 'corporate culture recipe' . More discrete forms of a journey are to be found in change programmes. Although OD is increasingly being portrayed as an exploratory journey, planned change is still frequently treated as a linear process – a clear and direct, albeit on occasions slow, movement from the current state to a desired one. In this way change is often presented, either explicitly or implicitly, as a journey towards a specified destination.

Chapters 5 and 7 offer critical insights into the nature and complexity of organisational culture. In particular, they serve to illustrate the limitations of the standardised quick-fix solutions to cultural problems presented in the popular management literature. Chapters 4, 6 and 8 present differing perspectives of organisational change. Of these, Chapters 4 and 6 explore the benefits of using metaphors as a means of instigating and facilitating major change interventions. By contrast, the limitations of change initiatives are graphically illustrated in Chapter 8 using a football metaphor.

Chapter 4, by Broussine and Vince, presents the findings of an applied research project. As part of a structured programme, they encouraged managers to express their feelings and emotions about change through drawings. This was followed by a period of reflection and then discussion of the drawings. Two sources of metaphor emerged: first, from the drawings themselves; second, further metaphors were created as a result of the subsequent interaction between managers. It is argued that these metaphors provide insights into managers' emotions in relation to change and that the metaphors also combine to generate new possibilities with regard to the perceptions, and management, of change.

In Chapter 5, Hocking and Carr argue that the study of organisations has been dominated by the culture metaphor. It is suggested that the holistic view of organisational culture, which arises out of the structural-functionalist tradition, is overly simplistic. An approach which views organisations as multiple realities is advocated. A forceful case is made for treating organisations as sub-cultures as this acknowledges the existence of conflicting interests and facilitates a better understanding of the role which diversity plays in organisational life.

Chapter 6 examines the benefits of developing a metaphoric gap as a basis for attempting to change an organisation. Keizer and Post assert that OD can be seen as a process of bridging a gap. They advocate an approach similar to gap analysis but which relies on metaphor to indicate both the 'is' and the 'should be' situations. It is posited that effective organisational change is dependent on the generation of a pair of metaphors (present and desired) that symbolise and emotionalise the key characteristics of the situation and which identify in a meaningful way the nature of the gap to be bridged. The authors go on to offer a typology of gaps and outline a six-step approach for applying the technique. In addition, the limitations and constraints of the approach are also discussed.

The study of personality and organisational culture are juxtaposed in Chapter 7. Oswick, Lowe and Jones argue that lessons can be learnt from the more mature, and concrete, domain of personality. In particular, ideographic and nomothetic methodologies are used to classify research into organisational culture. The chapter highlights the highly polarised nature of cultural research. It is suggested that far greater collaboration is required between the ideographic-phenomenological position of anthropologists and ethnographers, and the nomothetic-positivist stance of management theorists.

The final chapter in this part, by Currie and Kerrin, uses English football as a metaphorical vehicle for a macro-level analysis of organisational change issues. Football is enlisted as a form of generative metaphor. It encourages managers to be creative and develop new perspectives and insights into change that can be translated into, and utilised within, the workplace. The possibilities for change are illustrated by applying the metaphor to two case study organisations: a manufacturing company and a district health authority.

CHAPTER 4

Working with metaphor towards organisational change

Mike Broussine and Russ Vince

INTRODUCTION

This chapter describes how the metaphors expressed by managers within their teams can be utilised to create possibilities for organisational change. We describe an applied research project which encouraged managers to address both perceptions of change and resistance to change through analysing individual and organisational metaphors. Metaphors at different levels of the organisation provided insights into the emotions present in relation to change. These metaphors also combined to create or 'generate' new possibilities in the team's awareness of the changes they are managing.

Change in organisations is often constrained by the rationalisation that change = problem (Garratt, 1987). When approaching change, managers usually consider a range of 'problems to be solved' allowing them to 'move forward' in policy, strategy or implementation. This tendency can suppress the emotional, relational and political complexities and paradoxes present in the change process. Through a focus on metaphor, such complexities can be retained and worked with as key factors in the management of change.

Our concern, both as management developers and as researchers, is to learn more about change in organisations. We are particularly concerned with highlighting ways of thinking about and working with the emotional complexities of teams and with inter-hierarchical dynamics between teams at different levels. Consequently, the aim of this research has been to bring managers' emotions to the surface and to encourage managers to work with and through these emotions in a contained way. We have experimented with the notion of metaphor as a container for the expression of emotion and developed methods that try to be creative as well as challenging.

In this chapter we:

- review and discuss the importance of metaphor in understanding change in organisations;
- outline our research approach and methods;
- present and discuss the emotional states that key metaphors within the study described;

- suggest ways in which metaphors that express different emotional states between different levels of an organisation combine in order to 'generate' different possibilities for working with change in organisations.

THE IMPORTANCE OF METAPHOR IN THE MANAGEMENT OF CHANGE

The aim of this section of the chapter is to highlight and discuss three functions of the use of metaphor in the management of change. These are:

- metaphor as a method of diagnosis and planned change;
- metaphor as an invitation to interact;
- metaphor as a container for emotional and unconscious forces at work.

These three functions reflect different perspectives in the writing on metaphor. We feel these are related rather than distinct, and combine into a useful framework for working with metaphors in the management of change.

Metaphor as a method for diagnosis and planned change

'Changing the organization involves changing the metaphors' (Smith, 1982). The notion that metaphor can be used as a method for diagnosis and planned change in organisations is perhaps the most common conceptualisation of the function of metaphor in organisational change. Marshak (1993) outlines the use of metaphor for highlighting underlying, unarticulated understanding about what is happening in an organisation. For Marshak metaphors can provide opportunities to prepare for change, to align in relation to it, or to confuse and mislead managerial and organisational understanding of change.

Barrett and Cooperrider (1990) describe four 'principles' of metaphor related to organisational change. They argue that metaphors can be: transformative, facilitative, provide a steering function for action, and that they invite active experimentation. Brink (1993) sees three particular 'applications' of metaphor in organisations. First, metaphors are often more easily heard than rational explanations, they thereby encourage listening. Second, since metaphors often promote the possibility for formulation, they provide opportunities for development. Third, they attract other organisational members into communication because the symbolism seems creative. All of these perspectives position metaphor as an essential route towards the discovery of something different. Metaphor is also an element in the *process* of change, it stimulates both reflection and action, and hence the praxis that emerges from the interface between reflection and action. Therefore, metaphor can be instrumental in bringing about some form of organisational transformation (Sackmann, 1989).

Metaphor as an invitation to interact

When something is defined metaphorically this is not just an invitation to *think* about it in a certain way, it is also an invitation to *interact* in terms of certain implied assumptions (Schon, 1979). Metaphors express particular concerns and interests in ways that make claims on the nature of the target of those concerns and interests (Danziger, 1990). This is one definition of the 'generative' properties of metaphor – that they promote engagement and, through such engagement, change.

The notion of metaphor as an invitation to interact is based on a definition which acknowledges not just a similarity between two apparently distinct subjects. Metaphors also make possible both the identification of links between sub-systems and the creation of new connections. Thus, two different hierarchical levels of an organisation with distinct metaphors describing the same thing may generate new connections or new ways of seeing an issue or direction. Such connections are particularly powerful in facilitating an organisation's capacity to change (Barrett and Cooperrider, 1990). This process is also visible in research on conflict in organisations (Kolb and Bartunek, 1992), whereby 'second-order change' (shifts in the frameworks informing action) is generated through the 'dialectical interaction' of different views. Metaphors are powerful tools for second-order change because they lend themselves to dialectical interaction. In other words, metaphors arising from separate and/or conflicting organisational groups are often perceived to be simultaneously different *and* valid. This can promote the generation of new perspectives.

Metaphor as a container for emotional and unconscious forces at work

The power of metaphors is that they 'provide vivid, memorable and emotion-arousing representations of preconceived experience' (Ortony, 1979). Averill (1990) asserts that emotional aspects of experience which are difficult to contain often become the subject of metaphor. She highlights six different areas in which this particularly occurs, identifying six 'major metaphors of emotion' (1990: 112). Another perspective is that emotions are the 'target' of metaphor (Sarbin, 1986) in the sense in which such metaphors are seeking to explain emotion. This emotion is not solely related to the individual but to the organisation as well. This is why Burke (1992) asserts that metaphors are 'windows into the soul of the social system'.

In organisations, where direct emotions are often suppressed and avoided, individual and organisational defences against emotion become very powerful. Metaphors often provide an opportunity for managers to look indirectly at emotional and unconscious forces at work. Unconscious defences are very immediate and powerful. It is rather like looking directly into the eyes of Medusa: the fear of emotion can turn managers to stone.

Metaphors serve a reflecting function, allowing managers to look indirectly (through their shields) at powerful emotions without being turned to stone.

This therefore provides a second definition of the generative properties of metaphor in the ability of metaphor to assist both individuals and organisational groupings to align their emotional states with their task needs (Krantz, 1990). Indeed, this allows organisational members to undertake their work roles more 'deeply and passionately', and offers access to the organisational or systemic sub-strata of experience (known to Tavistock theorists as 'relatedness') that are evoked by interaction within an organisation. This relatedness leads to the illumination of 'the structure of inter-subjectivity and results in the uncovering of organisational identity' (Diamond, 1990). 'The compelling aspect of metaphor is not therefore the mental image itself but the way in which the image reaches into the subjective terrain of unconscious experience' (Krantz, 1990).

RESEARCH APPROACH AND METHODS

The research discussed here has been undertaken in public sector organisations at a time when the public services are experiencing a high degree of turbulence and change. The issues they face include privatisation, compulsory competitive tendering, the contract culture, the creation of health care trusts and the prospect of wholesale structural reorganisation of local government. This has created a challenge to public service managers' ability to manage change. We have found that managers have particular difficulties in this context in working with their feelings and emotions about the change process. The study particularly sought to enable managers to work with conscious and unconscious emotions about change and to work through the contradictions and paradoxes within the change process.

The method used in order to capture both emotional and unconscious data, and metaphors reflecting organisational experience or relatedness, was based on drawing (Vince, 1993). This approach was seen to be particularly effective in this context for two reasons: first, because metaphors were captured very powerfully and directly within managers' imagery; second, because 'informants often possess more copious and meaningful information than they can communicate verbally' (Meyer, 1991). This is especially true when the researcher is seeking emotionally based data (Vince, 1993).

Drawing as a process for encouraging learning and change has an established place in various fields, including psychology, education, organisation behaviour and management development. Yet, with a few exceptions (e.g. Randall and Southgate, 1981; Zuboff, 1988; Meyer, 1991), drawing has rarely surfaced as an applied method in management and organisational research. The reliability of drawings in research depends on the acceptance of underlying or unconscious process; on capturing a variety of contextually specific dialogues (intra/inter-personal and intra/inter-group); and on various patterns that seem to emerge regularly in drawings, providing a flexible, guiding analytical framework (see Vince, 1993).

We invited senior managers (e.g. the management team) and a sample of middle managers in each of six public service organisations (local government and health care) to express their feelings and emotions about change through drawing in (initially) separate workshops. This was the beginning of an experiential process which generated five types of inter-connected data:

1 *Emotional/subjective data* (obtained by individual drawings) – managers were asked: 'Draw a picture using the resources provided which expresses your feelings about change at work in your organisation.'
2 *Individual construing of the drawing* (the individual was invited to set down notes on the reverse of his/her drawing).
3 *Group reflections on the data generated through drawings and individual construings* (a written-up group discussion, the accuracy of which was checked with each group).
4 *Inter-group sharing of emotional data, individual construings and group reflections* (joint middle and senior management enquiry groups, tape-recorded).
5 *Joint synthesis: middle and senior managers collaborate in convergence of the data and sense making* (tape-recorded).

The first three types of data were obtained in separate middle management and senior management groups, the fourth and fifth in joint meetings of previously separate groups six to eight months later. A total of 86 managers produced drawings and associated sets of data as outlined above.

In this chapter we will concentrate on discussing two categories of metaphor that emerged from the research process. These are:

● *those that emerged through individuals' drawings* and were subsequently made available to the joint middle and senior management enquiry groups;
● *those that emerged as a result of the interaction of middle and senior managers* in the same organisation.

METAPHORS GENERATED THROUGH DRAWINGS

The spontaneous drawings produced by the 86 public sector managers gave rise to a rich and diverse set of symbols representing a range of emotions about organisational change. We discuss some examples of these drawings in this chapter as a means of communicating the types of metaphors generated. Nine categories of emotion relating to change were identified. The first interpretation of the drawings was carried out by the managers themselves, who wrote on the reverse side of each picture their own reflections on their drawing. The drawings and the written reflections were used to generate the categories described below, and the consistency of these reflections was checked against the transcripts of what the managers said about their drawings later in their group. Managers were able, through the drawings, to make available to colleagues data on this range of emotion in a novel way, to express what was underlying their emotional state at the time, and therefore to share experience about concerns, fears and assumptions about change.

Anxiety, fear and dread about the effects of change on organisations

The 'organisational ship' swamped by an enormous tidal wave, and the hospital being systematically demolished, are examples of drawings which communicated anxiety about the continued existence of the organisation, its values and ability in the future to provide services to the public. The research process enabled managers to share their feelings of being threatened by a sustained attack by central government on the very notion of public service. Phrases in the first workshops like 'They're neutering local government', and 'It's about political imperatives, cutting waiting lists and finance' convey a sense of feeling besieged, and managers' sense of public service ('what I came into the job for') being no longer valued: 'The feeling used to be that I was doing good, but it doesn't feel like that any more', was how one senior NHS manager put it.

Fear of personal catastrophe potentially resulting from change

Collapse, redundancy etc. were portrayed by the drawings of, for example, a person receiving his P45 (UK unemployment card), gravestones, clearly unhappy faces and menacing clouds on the horizon. While in our first category the anxiety was more about the threat to the organisation and the values which it stood for and which they believed in, here the fear was focused more on the potential personal threat anticipated as a result of change. Thus managers often used the word 'casualties' either on the reverse of their drawings or in the subsequent conversation. Sometimes the sense of personal vulnerability and the anticipated loss of current colleagues was conveyed by 'before and after' drawings, most powerfully by the senior manager who drew a full football crowd observing a team of eleven players in the top half of her picture, and a sparsely populated football ground in the lower half with eight team members remaining standing, and the three others lying 'dead' on the pitch.

Anger, vengefulness, violent feelings directed towards perpetrators of change

Many managers reported that our research process enabled them to unleash a hitherto repressed anger, the intensity of which they had not consciously realised. These managers sometimes drew pictures of intense violence – the local authority portrayed as a 'maiden' being decapitated by a sinister force (in this case representing central government), or the organisation being drawn as a castle being blown apart by cannon. The use of such metaphors communicated vengeful attitudes towards the 'perpetrators' of change, sometimes coupled with a pessimistic foreboding about their own and their organisations' futures. The senior local government officer who drew the castle under attack wrote on the back of his drawing the words 'hostility, unenlightened, chaos, spite, double standards', capturing, for him, the characteristics of those who had caused destructive pressures.

Change as an opportunity for personal and organisational development and empowerment

An ugly duckling transformed into a swan, a smiling face on a stronger body, and a very verdant and firmly rooted tree – these are examples of optimistic imagery which the process sometimes produced. Out of the 86 drawings, however, only three managers produced wholly optimistic drawings, many more conveying more complex, paradoxical and dual feelings such as those described in our fifth and sixth categories below.

Denial and rationalisation about change

Some managers who used other optimistic images admitted in the group discussions that their images could also be interpreted as communicating rationalisation and denial, e.g. by drawing an unrealisable idyll (oases, holiday and leisure scenes) of stability and personal growth, such managers were unable to begin with to countenance, consciously or unconsciously, the grim realities which were actually anticipated. These managers therefore unconsciously or consciously began by communicating the opposite of their true feelings. One senior local government manager found it difficult to produce a drawing at all, preferring instead to write in big letters the words 'Challenge', 'Excitement', 'Fun', 'Humour', 'Communication' and 'Enthusiasm'. As an 'afterthought' he added in very small writing the words 'Anxiety!' and 'Doubt!' at the foot of the sheet. The manager subsequently felt he had denied difficult feelings that he had not been able to explore.

Paradoxical feelings about change.

Mixed feelings – optimism *and* pessimism about change – were conveyed in many of the drawings. These public service managers employed a combination of imagery to reveal their feeling of change as risk, that change could 'go either way'. Therefore one senior manager drew a highly distorted and angry image of a politician associated with seeing change as pushing a boulder up a steep hill. But in the bottom half of his picture was a 'First Prize' gold cup, and a peaceful image of a dinghy sailing towards a benign sunset. Both the 'hatred' (as the manager put it) and the 'hope' which was felt about change were thus combined in the one drawing. As we shall see, metaphors concerning this duality of emotion about change resurfaced in the subsequent joint middle and senior management enquiry groups, e.g. frequent mention was made of 'double-edged swords' when referring to organisational change, and one manager was not sure whether she was a 'kamikaze pilot' or an 'astronaut' when it came to managing change.

Change resulting in powerlessness and debilitation

This was either as a result of having to handle increases in workload, 'hassle' and barriers to effectiveness, or because they felt unable to control either the substance or pace of events involved in change, or both. Often this was expressed in terms of having more to do with fewer resources, leaving little or no time for self (enjoyment, development). In some of the drawings which come into this category, two levels of metaphor are discernible within the one drawing. To take an example, a health service middle manager drew six cartoon images on her sheet, e.g. piles of paperwork on her desk, lots of people knocking at her door requiring attention, a computer spewing out 'info', etc. (On the reverse of the drawing she wrote 'Constantly asking more... do they know we're here?') At the obvious level, each of the cartoons she included give interesting insights into her role and her attitudes to it in a period of change. At another level, however, the sheet is crowded. Consciously or unconsciously she conveyed a sense of the cumulative effects of all six situations portrayed by the 'busyness' of her drawing. In contrast, another NHS middle manager drew a small, pathetic tree with a single acorn lying on the floor. The tree was placed very much at the centre of the sheet, leaving a large amount of blank space surrounding the image. The metaphor as a container for emotion is therefore not only conveyed by the *content* of the drawing (or sub-sets of the drawing) but also by the *spatial context* of the image or images. Indeed, Furth (1988) confirms the potential significance of both centrality and size of items drawn in pictures in the person's feelings or thinking. The placement of oneself in a picture can have unconscious significance for the author, e.g. has she placed herself at the centre of a drawing or on the edge somewhere? Similarly, the size of items may indicate the emphasis or the devaluing of the person or thing which has been included.

Change as creating a diversion from self-concept of desired role

Others experienced organisational change as a destabilising, alien process which detached them from their self-concept about what they should be doing. For these managers change stopped them from getting on with their 'real job' and all that is attached to this. One middle manager drew himself on a treadmill by which was a notice saying, 'Business as usual during alterations'; a colleague wrote on the back of his picture (frowning, unhappy faces), 'Confusion, not getting the job done properly, trying hard to please everyone, *moving away from real engineering*, living in the hope it will work out in the end...'

Change as a journey to endure in order to reach a new stability

Change was seen by some to be an 'additional burden' to endure, a journey to get through, to work around, with the hope of emerging to idyllic stability. The arrival at this ideal state would not, they felt, be without casualties, as some would not survive the change (as we saw in our second category of emotional states). Ethereal castles in the air, oases, beach scenes with bucket and spades were among the drawn metaphors used to express this hope. Journeys were drawn as horse and carts travelling through ominous valleys, people vaulting over barriers, or boats being tossed around on shark-infested seas as they try to reach the tropical island.

The nine categories provided by our qualitative analysis have given us a powerful, even poignant, insight into the paradoxical, sometimes contradictory and generally messy emotional reality that managers experience in a period of tremendous change. The process of enquiry with the separate middle and senior management groups led to considerable learning about 'the management of change'. The potency, range, complexity and subtlety of the drawings, e.g. enabling analysis of different levels of metaphor in the one drawing, all required a revision of a view that change could be managed by a reliance solely on rational strategic processes.

METAPHORS GENERATED THROUGH INTERACTION

Managers who participated in the first groups agreed to continue the process by bringing the groups together to enable interaction between the sample of middle managers and their management team. This interaction could now take place with the benefit of the emotionally based data generated in the earlier, separate group sessions at which the drawings were produced. While there were naturally some misgivings and risks concerning this, all the groups agreed that the developmental impetus provided by the research process so far, together with the novelty of the approach, made the risks, if perceived as such, worth taking. As it turned out, the process of interaction between top managers and a group of their subordinates resulted in further learning and organisation development benefits (in two of the participating organisations, the processes described have been repeated). The joint sessions at which each group made available to the other their drawings, construings and group reflections from the first enquiry groups took place some six to eight months later. These sessions were tape-recorded to assist subsequent analysis.

We were particularly interested to discover whether the metaphors used respectively by senior managers and by middle managers (perhaps with the drawings from the earlier sessions acting as a catalyst) would in turn generate shared metaphors, signifying possible emotional relatedness about change, its meaning and its management.

In this section we present examples of dialogue in which metaphors were produced as a result of the interaction between middle managers and top managers. We were thereby able to listen to the use of metaphor by colleagues from different hierarchical levels of the same organisation who needed to communicate to each other in relation to their feelings about change. Our analysis of the data suggests that metaphor was consciously or unconsciously used for four primary purposes in these interactions:

- to make the giving of feedback to each other, especially by middle managers to their senior managers, more safe and acceptable;
- to explain and enable others to learn about how change is or was experienced by the individual: thus the use of metaphor facilitated joint reflection on episodes of change, providing deeper understanding of each other's perspectives on change;
- to enable managers unconsciously to conspire to avoid dealing with change;
- to enable exploration of the possibility of securing shared diagnoses about change, how it should be managed, and about the difficulties and dilemmas anticipated.

The use of metaphor to make the giving of feedback more safe and acceptable

Example 1

MIDDLE MANAGER A No, no. You'd expect the Management Team to be the initiators and the **drivers** of the change programme...and everybody else to be on the receiving end.

MIDDLE MANAGER B But on the other hand maybe it would be more efficient... uh rather than to be **pushing** – I think one drawing had, was it the **sheep, pushing the sheep out of the flock** into the... – and the other thing was [the Chief Officer]'s **Woah, pull them up, pull them up hill**. Wouldn't it be better to get people actually **walking up hill** on their own – rather than either **pushing them or driving them or pulling them,** that you actually say 'This is where we're going – let's all go up together'?

DEPARTMENTAL MANAGEMENT TEAM MEMBER If you'd like to tell us how to do that! [*laughter*]

MIDDLE MANAGER B No. Is that 'following the leaders', as opposed to 'facing the same direction'? You see the **pulling** one is an antagonistic point of view because they're facing each other, not going in the same direction. Whereas if you've got people pulling and leading, you're going in the same direction as you're trying to take people, and you're going in the same direction. Is there any thought given as to the direction you're facing when you're **pulling**?.

MIDDLE MANAGER C – That's an interesting metaphor. I think what it is, is that the leaders feel they start off **running and leading** and they **look over their shoulder** and find they're on their own. [*laughter*]

This group of middle managers are discussing their perceptions of the style of leadership displayed by their senior managers in a department which had experienced a high degree of reorganisation ('pushing' v. 'pulling'), with little interruption by any representative of top management. The shared assumption is that change involves going uphill – the question is whether staff ('flock', 'sheep') are pushed or pulled up this hill. The example demonstrates how metaphors can be used by more junior staff to achieve something – revealing your feelings about how your boss manages – which is normally difficult to achieve more directly and easier to avoid.

The use of metaphor to explain and reflect on how change is or was experienced

Example 2

MIDDLE MANAGER Nothing ever turns out what you think it's going to be in terms of change. And, although it's a threat there's a lot of excitement and a lot of opportunity built into it as long as you keep the team going. But it's this communication bit that's important because if you're taking extra strain and extra load, and then feel that something else is happening around you, **the ground's shifting**, that's a really **frightening situation** to be in.

This example paints a picture of an insecure manager finding it difficult to control or cope with the turbulence.

Example 3

SENIOR MANAGER A I felt that we were... I drew the **rocket ship**, and I felt that we were moving extremely fast **out into space** but we didn't quite know where, um... we were just **hurtling into it at a rate of knots**. I wasn't sure um whether... it was **a rocket** or whether it was actually **a missile** that was going to **bomb something**... whether I was **an astronaut** or a **kamikaze pilot**.

SENIOR MANAGER B Have you been taking the tablets? [*laughter*]

Senior Manager A conveys, in a relatively short piece of conversation, a set of contrasting metaphors which demonstrates well the duality and paradoxical nature of emotion about change as she experienced it.

The use of metaphor to avoid development and dealing with change

Example 4

MIDDLE MANAGER And I think the problem is trying... in no false way, trying to... get people sort of to look at **the horizon** and hope there is something actually over there even though... there doesn't appear to be anything there, anything new there... I mean the only way you can come to terms with that is that you've got to do something about that, adapting yourself to that environment... I mean I would have gone long ago if one felt... it was just all **demolition, a derelict landscape, nuclear holocaust**. It isn't just trying to pretend... it is something other than it is, but somehow you adapt – I suppose you adapt yourself to your environment.

MEMBER OF MANAGEMENT TEAM I think that's right... change was unsettling for myself – the actual amount of change. I mean you can even adjust to living in the **nuclear aftermath** if there isn't the fear that things are going to change...

MIDDLE MANAGER That's right, that's right... **there isn't a bigger bang** coming up.

The use of some very powerful shared metaphors in this interaction has unlocked a joint reflection between middle and senior managers, facilitating their display to each other of their considerable fear surrounding change. In this alone the process has a high degree of utility. However, the relatedness between the middle and the senior manager in this dialogue, assisted by the use of apocalyptic metaphors, could be described as 'Yes, isn't it awful'. The risk may be that both managers remain with the same set of metaphors ('It's awful isn't it?', 'Yes, isn't it!'). They become stuck in a mutual comfort without developing the means together to get out of their 'awful' situation to which, paradoxically, they are attached. The metaphor has not changed.

The use of metaphor to explore the possibility of securing shared diagnoses about change

Example 5

CHIEF OFFICER I tell you what I... I find it very frustrating when I think we – I mean we may not have done – but I think we've done a good job in the particular area, and we've tried desperately to introduce... to get something across, um... and we get **a blank wall** from... managers let's say, we get **a blank wall**. Now it may be the way we've presented it... I'd rather somebody said to me you know, 'Why the hell did you present it that way: this is how you should get it across' – we get **a blank wall** and we don't get the support that I think we should be getting. It's the old sort of, 'They have told me to do this, I don't agree with it, but they have told me to do it.'

MIDDLE MANAGER Just... just to make a comparison, just to go over what you said, **it's a bit like a car manufacturer** who makes a **brilliant car** and then is surprised because no one comes and buys it – **best car in the world**, super innovation, super **car**, but nobody comes to buy it: the reason they don't come to buy it is that there's no onus on **the purchasers** to find out how good it is. The onus is on **the manufacturer** to tell people how good it is and why they should buy it. Now reflecting on that analogy with what you said – [initiating a change] – and then we're surprised that people don't buy into it. The reason **they don't buy into it** is that **we don't sell it** enough by stressing the benefits, or maybe the consequences of not buying in which is the other side of, but I mean it's really – we shouldn't be surprised if people don't find out the good points themselves!

CHIEF OFFICER I don't... I mean I partly agree with you except we're not talking to pure **customers**, we're actually talking to people who...

MIDDLE MANAGER Who want **cars**.

CHIEF OFFICER Yes, who want **cars**.

The Chief Officer expresses his frustration with some resistant middle managers ('blank wall') who not only may not support any change initiatives, but will, as he sees the situation, comply reluctantly without being open about their misgivings about the change. The middle manager confronts his senior manager with his diagnosis of the cause of some resistance within the Chief Officer's department. The fact is the middle manager is in effect saying that the change initiatives coming from the management team are good ('brilliant car', 'best car in the world') but they are not 'sold' effectively, and the onus is on top management ('manufacturer') to 'tell people how good it is'. Therefore, by implication, senior management is not communicating sufficiently with middle managers about proposed changes.

In this example the senior manager, by joining the metaphor and participating in its change (**blank walls** to **cars**), signalled his willingness to participate in a joint diagnosis about the management of change with the middle managers. This is a good example of metaphors enabling middle and senior managers to relate their previously unstated experiences to reach a conclusion about managing change. The example also shows the middle managers' concern that senior management should communicate the reasons for change more effectively. We think that it demonstrates a 'generative' metaphor (blank wall → people who want cars) in that the emotional relatedness between the Chief Officer and the middle manager has led them to new ways of thinking and working with the management of change.

These five examples illustrate the potential of metaphor to move a group on to different ways of seeing and working with change, by enabling managers to give feedback, share with each other how change was for them, and by giving the opportunity for joint diagnosis of the need to manage change in potentially different ways – sometimes all three at the same time. The use of metaphor may also show the possibility of enabling managers to avoid development and remain stuck by not changing the metaphor, allowing them comfortably to continue to avoid and deny their responsibilities for handling change differently.

CONCLUSIONS

It is usually difficult to give feedback to your boss about the sense of fear or powerlessness which change can bring. It is rare for organisations to build in the opportunity for organisational members to learn how change affects each other emotionally. Moreover, it is difficult usually for top and more junior managers to learn about the consequences for each other of the ways in which they manage and implement change. However, in their various ways these examples of spoken and visual metaphors convey in a vivid way managers' emotional feelings about change arising out of the reflective process which the research process stimulated. The fact that this reflective process was *between* and *within* hierarchical levels gave them the opportunity to transcend together the more usual defence and inhibition to the expression of emotion in their organisations.

We have sought in this chapter to explore the utility of metaphor in adding to our and managers' understanding about organisational change. Our research process enabled groups of managers to learn about, and struggle with, the emotional reality and complexity of change. We think that accessing this emotional reality provides the possibility for the development of different ways of managing change based on organisational members' feelings and perceptions. However, this does not mean that this possibility is always taken up. For example, a middle and senior manager may avoid making connections between different emotional sub-systems within the organisation, and thereby deny the relatedness between these sub-systems, by consciously or unconsciously not associating, playing with or changing the metaphor.

These episodes are useful in so far as they add to the possibility of thinking about and making sense of the struggles and challenges which a high degree of change brings. Participating managers emphasised the developmental advantages to them and their organisation of going through a process which worked with vivid emotional data rather than just at the rational and strategic level (this was expressed, for example, in a local authority as how much had been achieved from a series of meetings 'with no agenda'). In this chapter we have attempted to engage with the emotional forces that drive and complicate decision making in teams. We would suggest that attempts to understand and work with emotion in teams are essential, and that this is often best achieved by an analysis of the metaphors which managers have used to express their struggles over change.

REFERENCES

Averill, J.R. (1990) 'Inner feelings, works of the flesh, the beast within, diseases of the mind, driving force, and putting on a show: six metaphors of emotion and their theoretical extensions', in Leary, D.E. (ed) *Metaphors in the History of Psychology*. Cambridge: Cambridge University Press.

Barrett, F.J. and Cooperrider, D.L. (1990) 'Generative metaphor intervention: a new approach for working with systems divided by conflict and caught in defensive perception', *Journal of Applied Behavioral Science*, Vol. 26, No. 2.

Brink, T.L. (1993) 'Metaphor as data in the study of organizations', *Journal of Management Inquiry*, Vol. 2, No. 4.

Burke, W.W. (1992) 'Metaphors to consult by', *Group and Organization Management*, Vol.17, No. 3.

Danziger, K. (1990) 'Generative metaphor and the history of psychological discourse', in Leary, D.E. (ed) *Metaphors in the History of Psychology*. Cambridge: Cambridge University Press.

Diamond, M.A. (1990) 'Psychoanalytic phenomenology and organisational analysis', *Public Administration Quarterly*, Vol. 14, No. 1.

Furth, G.M. (1988) *The Secret World of Drawings*. Boston, Mass.: Sigo Press.

Garratt, B. (1987) *The Learning Organisation*. London: Fontana/Collins.

Kolb, D.M. and Bartunek, J. (eds) (1992) *Hidden Conflict in Organisations*. London: Sage.

Krantz, J. (1990) 'Comments on the Barrett and Cooperrider article', *Journal of Applied Behavioral Science*, Vol. 26, No. 2.

Marshak, R.J. (1993) 'Managing the metaphors of change', *Organizational Dynamics*, Vol. 22, No. 1.

Meyer, A. (1991) 'Visual data in organizational research', *Organization Science*, Vol. 2, No. 2.

Ortony, A. (ed) (1979) *Metaphor and Thought*. Cambridge: Cambridge University Press.

Randall, R. and Southgate, J. (1981) 'Doing diological research', in Reason, P. and Rowan, J. (eds) *Human Inquiry: A Sourcebook of New Paradigm Research*. Chichester: Wiley.

Sackmann, S. (1989) 'The role of metaphors in organisation transformation', *Human Relations*, Vol. 42, No. 6.

Sarbin, T.R. (1986) 'Emotion and act: roles and rhetoric', in Harre, R. (ed) *The Social Construction of Emotions*. Oxford: Blackwell.

Schon, D.A. (1979) 'Generative metaphor: a perspective on problem-setting in social policy', in Ortony, A. (ed) *Metaphor and Thought*. Cambridge: Cambridge University Press.

Smith, K.K. (1982) 'Philosophical problems in thinking about organizational change', in Goodman, P.S. et al (eds) *Change in Organizations*. San Francisco: Jossey-Bass.

Vince, R. (1993) 'Every picture tells a story: inquiry into learning and change using drawings'. Paper presented at the *European Foundation for Management Development Research Conference*, Paris, December.

Zuboff, S. (1988) *In the Age of the Smart Machine*. New York: Basic Books.

CHAPTER 5

Culture: the search for a better organisational metaphor

Joy Hocking and Adrian Carr

INTRODUCTION

The study of organisations which utilise culture as a metaphor has tended to focus on culture's holistic nature. The argument put forward in this chapter not only addresses the domination of the holistic view of culture, but also its influence on the way the culture metaphor has been utilised as a substitution for organisation theory.

An exploration of the many layers of culture is undertaken, recognising that none of these layers is sufficient in themselves to explain both the formal and informal attributes of organisations. The dominant metaphor advocating a holistic view of culture (single layer) arises out of the structural-functionalist approach to organisations. It views culture (corporate culture) as an intervening variable, which is considered fundamental to an understanding of organisational life. Here the structural-functionalist view of culture is challenged in two ways. First, by exploring the conscious/unconscious negotiation of meaning, arguing that the meaning of a situation, culture and object can be different for each individual. And second, by a critical examination of the relationship between culture and collectivity, suggesting that the integration of individuals, groups and sub-units is problematic and hence a holistic approach to culture oversimplifies a complex process.

This chapter views organisations as multiple realities and thus argues that organisations are better understood as sub-cultures. It examines how sub-cultures emerge, their contribution to organisational diversity, and how they negotiate their needs within the formal and informal structures of the organisation. The use of sub-cultures as a metaphor for organisational analysis presents significant problems to the study of organisations, as the current dominant metaphor guides and reinforces the conceptual view that culture is a unitary concept. Nevertheless, the benefit of viewing organisations as sub-cultures is that it facilitates a better understanding of the role which diversity plays in organisational life. An interpretative approach suggests that organisations are multiple realities and as such the organisation's structure is continuously being constructed and reconstructed through the interactive nature of human agency. In the following sections the issues outlined here are explored in greater depth.

ORGANISATIONAL CULTURE AS A 'SOCIALISED OUTCOME'

It has been argued that structural-functionalism has served as the dominant 'ideological prism' or metaphor for the development of literature concerning organisational theory and organisation behaviour (Carr, 1986, 1989). The conception of culture in that same literature implies and largely continues to bear the hallmarks of the broader framework within which it was conceived (Linstead and Grafton-Small, 1992: 332). It is argued later in this chapter that inadequate understanding of the origins and development of sub-cultures is largely the result of the myopia that the structural-functionalist conceptual prism tends to encourage.

Talcott Parsons (1959), a key figure in the development of structural-functionalism, argued that there are certain patterns of social activity and interaction that settle into a relationship of 'equilibrium'. For Parsons the individual is functionally required to be integrated into the 'system' through 'socialisation' and 'social control' if the theoretical state of equilibrium is to be attained. Placed in this context culture is defined as the 'transmitted and created content and patterns of values, ideas and other symbolic-meaningful systems as factors in the shaping of human behaviour' (Kreober and Parsons, 1958: 86). The individual is to 'learn' (be socialised into) the expectations contained in certain social situations. The 'system of expectations', it can be argued, makes culture a term that is shorthand for the acquisition of social 'facts' – facts that are the bearers of an ideological message.

The view of culture that emerges from a structural-functionalist conceptual lens is one that leads to a myopia in which integration, harmony and the acquisition of 'social facts' becomes *the* focus. The development of sub-cultures, the phenomenon of work groups and their dissent from 'the' culture goes unexplained (Reichers, 1987; Wanous, Reichers and Malik, 1984; Schein, 1971). What has happened is that there has been an abstraction of the individual and a translation from person into 'action' (Carr, 1989; Leivesley, Carr and Kouzmin, 1993). Intention, interaction and meaning have been reified as social facts – a state of being – which enable structural-functionalists like Parsons to ascribe conformity and predictability to the individual as an integrated component or 'unit' of a social system. This orientation has also been noted by Silverman (1970) who argues:

> Parsons may, therefore, be criticised for having adopted an 'over-socialised
> conception of man' which overlooks the fact that role expectations are not
> just given by society but arise from and depend upon on-going human
> interaction. Social order is, therefore, problematic. (Silverman, 1970: 137)

Parsons, other structural-functionalists and systems theorists offer a
view *about* human agency but not *of* human agency. Effectively, they turn
into an *object* something which is really a *process*. Adorno (1967, 1968)
explains that one must draw insights from both psychology and sociology
in order to understand and explain the dynamics of the society–individual
connection. He singles out Parsons' understanding (or lack of understanding) of psychoanalysis as an example of a 'primitive notion of a single
universal science' . He argues that:

> While Parsons discerns the inadequacy of many of the usual psychological
> explanations of societal phenomena, he does not suspect behind this incom-
> patibility any real clash between the universal and the particular, any
> incommensurability between the objective life-process, the 'in itself' and
> the individual that is really 'for himself'. (Adorno, 1967: 69)

Much of the organisation theory/behaviour literature has been caught in
the structural-functionalist preoccupation with the need for harmony and
integration. This view has influenced the application and interpretation of
culture not as a metaphor but as a variable. Indeed, many of the models of
socialisation in this literature take the positivistic assumptions that 'integration' will occur, and overlook the dynamics of human agency that lead to
an individual associating with or disassociating from 'the' dominant culture (Schein, 1971; Wanous, Reichers and Malik, 1984). Thus what we are
implying is that the theoretical conception of how an organisation culture
arises, is 'transmitted' and sustained needs to be capable of explaining how
and why individuals and groups might not 'associate' with the 'dominant'
or intended culture. The foundation for such a theoretical conception, we
would argue, is to be had from an understanding of human agency and the
recognition of the psychodynamics that are involved. It is to this endeavour
that we now turn our attention.

CULTURE AND THE NEGOTIATION OF MEANING: THE PSYCHOLOGICAL CONNECTIONS

Meryl Reis Louis (1987), in a 'classic' paper in organisation theory on the
matter of organisation culture, commences her discussion of the 'psychological context' by arguing the following:

> At the individual level, 'human beings act toward things on the basis of the meanings that the things have for them...' (Blumer, 1969: 2). And those meanings, or significances, are the products of an in situ interpretative process. Meaning is essentially and endlessly negotiated by social system members. In one sense of negotiated, meaning production represents navigation of an experiential landscape by which one controls one's course or position. In the other sense of negotiated, it represents bargaining among alternative meanings differentially preferred by the various parties to an interaction. (Louis, 1987: 512)

Louis is embracing a symbolic interactionist perspective and using the term 'negotiation' in the metaphorical sense as originally intended by Anselm Strauss (1959, 1978). The meaning that a 'thing' has for an individual is a complex interplay of their 'experiential landscape' and the intra-psychodynamics of the provinces of the mind (i.e. id, ego and superego). Thus the meaning of a situation, culture and object, can be different for each individual and in fact can arise from motivations of which the individual is not consciously aware. In relation to organisation culture the individual encounters the various forms, e.g. myths, stories, rituals, symbols, language etc., which serve to convey the substance or ideology that seek to produce the 'relatively implicit sets of taken-for-granted beliefs, values and norms' (Trice and Beyer, 1993: 2). It is in the interaction with the cultural forms that the cultural substance is negotiated or navigated for its meaning.

While recognising that this dynamic may, and often does, occur at an unconscious level and that a culture may itself not be rational and may contain contradictions, a dominant theme nonetheless emerges to which the individual will respond. But what is it that is at the core of the negotiation/navigation for the individual in relation to the dominant ideology? Symbolic interactionists would argue that 'the central object to be negotiated in interaction is personal identity, or the self-meaning of the person' (Denzin, 1992: 26). This argument is also supported by the literature of psychoanalytic theory. It is in the latter context that elsewhere it has been argued by Carr (1993a) that the notions of identification and narcissism are pivotal.

Freud (1985) originally used the term 'identification' to describe a psychological process in which the ego makes an identity between an aspect of itself and some other object. The dynamics involved in this earliest of life experiences is captured in the following argument:

> Finally, the ego was faced with demands originating in the *superego*, a specialised subdivision of itself which was based on identification and internalisation of the more competent, dominant egos which the child found around itself. In the main, the superego took on its definitive form with the resolution of the Oedipus complex, involving an identification of

the child with the values and ideals of the parents. Consequently, the superego provided a sense of moral and aesthetic self-judgement (conscience and values, in other words), both in a positive sense as acting as an *ego-ideal* and in the negative one in performing the role of censor of the ego's wishes. . . Failure to meet the demands of the superego created a feeling of *moral anxiety*. (Badcock, 1988: 122)

The capacity for self-love (healthy narcissism) is enhanced if not largely dependent on significant other(s) approving of one's behaviour. The organisation and indeed its leaders (Freud, 1985; Diamond, 1991) may assume a status similar to that experience of the ego ideal and the individual can thus 'feel loved and protected by a powerful entity' (Baum, 1989: 194) and, as Benjamin similarly notes, 'the wish to restore early omnipotence, or to realise the fantasy of control, never ceases to motivate the individual' (Benjamin, 1988: 54). A psychological bonding between the individual and the organisation, its culture and/or leaders may result (Carr, 1993a). That is progressive and in a sense a revival of an earlier dependency. The impetus in this dynamic is clear, but at the same time the individual may find an alternative to an association with the dominant culture in their quest for 'a social identity' rather than a personal identity.

ORGANISATIONAL CULTURES: SOCIAL CONTEXT AND BELONGING

The structural-functionalist view of culture suggests that the integration of individuals, groups and sub-units is a realistic and achievable goal (Schein, 1971; Wanous, Reichers and Malik, 1984). Earlier in this chapter it has been argued that the integration of the individual into the organisation and the group is problematic. The structural-functionalist view of culture fails to appreciate the metaphorical nature of culture by attributing to it concrete properties, whereas an interpretivist approach views culture as a system of meanings (Gregory, 1983: 363).

In developing her cultural dynamics perspective, Hatch (1993) has argued that, while Schein's model continues to have relevance, it must be combined with symbolic-interpretive perspectives and she disputes that a founder's beliefs and values are taught to new organisational members. Further, in exploring the dynamics of organisations she argues:

that culture is constituted by local processes involving both change and process and that these processes need to be explained in the mundane terms of everyday organisational life. (Hatch, 1993: 658)

Therefore to substitute the use of metaphor as an explanatory tool for theory is to ignore the complexity of both the context and substance of culture. Psychological theories emphasising personal identity have given organisational researchers an insight into the complexity of human behaviour, although these theories have overlooked the sociological setting in which behaviour occurs.

Louis (1983) notes that the notion of culture does not rest with the objects studied but rather their interpretation. Where Louis differs from culture theorists such as Schein is that she does not view the study of culture as either individual or collective. She suggests that the study of culture should be examined from both sociological and psychological perspectives and hence her use of the term 'culture-bearing milieux'. This approach argues that interpretation occurs at different levels within an organisation: the individual subjective (within the individual), the cultural intersubjective (between persons) and finally the universal objective (within the social system), with the latter being the sociological context.

Diamond (1991: 192) has also noted the oversight of context when he discusses the stresses associated with group membership:

> The central dilemma for the individual in the work group rests on his or her ability to maintain a balance of relative independence (personal identity and self esteem) and group membership (a sense of belonging and affiliation) without becoming overly distressed. Establishing a separate identity in a group is essential to ego integrity and emotional well being. That requirement of independence and autonomy is what distinguishes us from each other. However, group affiliation draws on narcissism – both healthy and pathological. Individual requirements for self esteem and assurance differ. Some require finding others that make them feel more powerful and safe. Regardless, all of us need others and therefore require some degree of affiliation.

Diamond suggests that an understanding of the individual without reference to their social context is in a sense only half the picture. For example, while independence may be important to individuals in work groups, membership and affiliation are predominant drives for many, as being part of a group gives individuals a sense of being larger, greater and better than they really are. A consequence of this is that people often go to great lengths to maintain their affiliation to the group, frequently doing things that they would not consider outside the group.

The collective notion of cultural organisation has been drawn from anthropology where researchers have concentrated their study on small, remote and self-contained societies. Holistic cultural metaphors have resulted in a view of culture as an integrated system. Therefore the prototype for holistic cultural research is extended ethnography within an isolated social group (Gregory, 1983: 361). However, Van Maanen and Barley (1985: 32) argue that the conclusions arising out of this research must be re-examined when they are generalised to fragmented, mobile and highly industrialised societies. They suggest the term culture implies that human behaviour is partially prescribed by a collectively created and sustained way of life that cannot be totally personality based because it is shared by diverse individuals. Their view supports an interactionist perspective of culture, proposing that while organisations harbour sub-cultures, this does not preclude the possibility of a homogeneous culture.

That few scholars doubt the presence of sub-cultures in organisations and that sub-cultures undoubtedly develop more readily than do organisation-wide cultures have been noted by Trice and Beyer (1993: 13). Nonetheless, the issue of the emergence of sub-cultures as sub-units of an organisation or ones which span laterally across organisations has been largely unexplored. Management's attachment to the notion of managerial prerogative based on a unitary world view also blinds it to the existence of multiple cultures within organisations.

ORGANISATIONAL CULTURES: THE IDENTIFICATION OF SUB-CULTURES

The most highly organised, distinctive and pervasive sources of sub-cultures in work organisations are people's occupations (Van Maanen and Barley, 1985; Trice and Beyer, 1993). Occupations provide a starting point for the examination of sub-cultures in organisations and they facilitate the growth of sub-cultures at two levels. First, they provide the basis for diffuse sub-cultures in the general society; and second, their members often form face-to-face sub-cultures in the organisation that employs them. Some examples are doctors, lawyers, accountants and engineers, who are employed by organisations while at the same time having strong links to their professional associations outside the organisation. Members of many occupations derive favourable images and social identities from their work and this is projected onto others as a presentation of themselves.

Organisations also intentionally differentiate their members by assigning them relatively insulated roles and positions creating specific niches. When these niches are occupied by people facing the same problems, who have both opportunities and motives for interaction, organisational sub-cultures are born (Van Maanen and Barley, 1985: 38). They suggest that the importation of new organisational members via acquisition and merger can also result in the creation of sub-cultures. In addition, technological innovation can segment an existing cohesive group.

A study of Silicon Valley cultures found that the terms 'culture' and 'organisation' can be described in two ways:

> (1) culture coterminous with the focal organization's boundaries (i.e., organizational culture) and/or (2) noncoterminous culture, including cultural context (e.g., national, geographic, or industrial cultures); culture that cross-cuts the organization (e.g., occupational or ethnic cultures); or subcultures of the focal organization such as departmental or project cultures. (Gregory, 1983: 374)

Gregory (1983: 364) also illustrates how the value and interpretation placed on similar issues by different professional groups within the same organisation suggests one cannot assume that organisational integration is enough to guarantee shared priorities. Values are often expressed differently when they intersect with cross-cutting occupational cultures and hence it may be more accurate to separate the notion of organisational integration from cultural integration. Gregory notes that the positive value placed on 'innovation' is expressed in different ways by engineers and scientists. Engineers concentrate on developing new products, whereas scientists emphasise developing new technology. Rentsch (1990), on the other hand, has observed that organisations consist of different social interaction groups who interpret the same organisational events differently.

Some researchers have attempted to explain the existence of sub-cultures by focusing on cognitive components such as assumptions, beliefs and values as being the essence of culture. Others have explained it in terms of cultural diversity suggesting that ideologies should form the central concept of culture (Trice and Beyer, 1993). The research has demonstrated that our knowledge of culture is dependent on how the culture metaphor is interpreted, and that the concept of culture as multiple realities has not received the same attention as the holistic view favoured by the majority of researchers and practitioners (Barley et al, 1988: 24).

CULTURES AND MESOLAYERS: THE EMERGENCE OF MULTIPLE CULTURES

While research has observed that differences occur between groups, the question arises of how these groups become sub-cultures, what distinguishes a sub-culture from other work groups, and what the implications are for an unfettered holistic interpretation of the culture metaphor. Sub-cultures have been defined as:

> representing distinct *symbolic domains*, with some members frequently and routinely switching domains between domains, while others stay in one domain and thus in one subculture. (Trice and Beyer, 1993: 175)

Ashforth and Mael (1989) propose that an organisation displaying a common set of values and beliefs is a rarity, thus the notion of a single blended organisational identification is problematic. An individual's identity may be derived notably from their organisation but also their work group, lunch group, age group and others. The 'corporate culture' approach views organisational members as 'emotional, symbol-loving, and needing to belong to a superior entity or collectivity' (Ray, 1986). However, this perspective has, according to Yoon et al (1994), emanated out of studies of groups displaying high levels of interpersonal attachment who display more cohesion, greater goal attainment, greater compliance to group norms and many other positive organisational outcomes. The cohesion approach has been questioned by the classic studies of Mayo and Homans, who have observed that sub-groups formed by local inter-personal attachments can be barriers for members' commitment to that larger organisation (Yoon et al, 1994).

The subsequent discussion undertaken in this chapter will examine a number of theoretical approaches which not only serve to explain group attachment, but also the reason for such an attachment creating difficulties for cohesion occurring at the organisational level. This issue and the complexity of the term 'culture' requires an in-depth examination of ideologies, social identification and ethnocentrism.

Ideologies

It can be argued that sub-cultures have the same elements that cultures have: distinct patterns of shared ideologies and distinctive sets of cultural forms. Although some sub-cultural elements resemble the culture in which they are embedded, others can vary significantly. Trice and Beyer (1993: 175) have stated:

> **The more unique the elements of a subculture, the more it encourages members to loosen their commitment to the overall culture and generate shared rationalisations that allow them to violate significant aspects of it.** (Trice and Beyer, 1993: 175)

The focus on ideology, according to Trice and Beyer, is necessary because they consider ideology to be the substance of organisational culture. Their interpretation of ideology is to view it as a rather general set of ideas which are powerful in specific situations because they link actions and fundamental beliefs. They also suggest that ideologies are emotionally charged: fundamental belief systems that impel people to act in certain ways. It is suggested that ideologies can best be defined:

> **as shared, relatively coherent interrelated sets of emotionally charged beliefs, values, and norms that bind some people together and help them to make sense of their worlds.** (Trice and Beyer, 1993: 33)

Solidarity is realised when ideologies knit a group together, as they lend dignity to everyday activities and elicit members' commitment.

A more negative aspect of ideology is put forward by Alvesson (1991) who defines it as a 'consciousness-restricting' of ideas and beliefs, having primarily negative consequences. The negative aspect of ideological elements of groups can have such an impact that it is impossible to change beliefs without first changing behaviours. According to Starbuck (1982), people in closely knit groups can reinforce each other so strongly that groups have to be dismantled before the people are able to internalise new ideas. Sinclair (1991) has noted that professional values are often characterised as having intransigent, resource-ignorant perspectives which undermine the organisational good and make managers' jobs difficult. Professionals, on the other hand, do not want to be managed. Professional values devalue management skills and management's mandate to curtail professional autonomy. Sinclair identifies the professional and manager interface which supports theories outlining the emergence of sub-cultures in organisations.

Ideologies that can enter an organisation from the outside come, according to Trice and Beyer (1993: 46), from at least six external layers of its environment: (1) large-scale cultural systems or national cultures; (2) national cultures; (3) regional and community cultures; (4) industry cultures, (5) occupational cultures; (6) other organisations' cultures. Occupational ideologies are formed through the training and indoctrination received prior to entering the organisation, suggesting that groups which contain the self are likely to be regarded positively.

Social identification

Ashforth and Mael (1989) have stated that, despite the longevity of the social/group identification construct, little or no research has been conducted on identification of individual/groups with organisations. They suggest that:

> Social Identity Theory (SIT) conception of organizational identification as a shared identity is new to the organizational behavior literature. To date, the perception of identification has been confused with internalisation of organisational goals and values. (Ashforth and Mael, 1989: 23)

SIT can be considered to be much more closely linked to sociological perspectives. Hogg and Abrams (1988: 17) suggest that SIT 'turns the traditional social psychological approach on its head, to use a familiar phrase, and examines the group in the individual'.

In keeping with symbolic interactionists rather than the structural-functionalist view of Parsons, SIT considers identity and self-definition to mediate between social categories. However, Hogg and Abrams (1988) indicate that SIT goes further than a social psychological approach, as it explores the psychological processes by translating social categories into human groups. These processes, which include acknowledgement of the psychoanalytic notions of identification and narcissism discussed earlier in this chapter, create identity and generate behaviours which have a characteristic and distinctive form, that of group behaviour.

In complex organisations the pervasiveness of the categorisation of individuals, group distinctiveness and prestige, out-group salience and group formation factors suggests that group identification is likely to be prevalent. Thus an organisation is more likely to be comprised of disparate and loosely coupled identities. Social classification cognitively segments and orders the social environment, providing the individual with a systematic means of defining others. SIT consists of those aspects of an individual's self-image that derive from social categories to which he or she perceives as 'belonging'. Three theoretical principles arise out of this view:

- individuals strive to achieve and maintain a positive identity;
- a positive identity is based to a large degree on favourable comparisons that can be made between the in-group and relevant out-groups: the in-group must be perceived as positively differentiated or distinct from the relevant out-groups;
- when social identity is unsatisfactory, individuals will strive either to leave their existing group and join some more positively distinct group, or make their existing group more positively distinct. In doing so they continue to meet the need for a social identity and healthy narcissism.

Hogg and Abrams (1988: 18) stress that while 'psychological processes ensure groups are inevitable, they do not directly govern what groups they are, what characteristics they have, or how they relate to other groups. Functionalism of this sort is more in keeping with that specified in anthropology and seeks to legitimise the status quo.' The implications for organisations and in particular management's quest for a uniform culture are far reaching. First, SIT research suggests that identity is associated with the immediate group culture rather than the organisation as a whole. Second, the organisation needs to be certain that it is not considered to be the out-group by sub-units. Individuals belong to many different social categories and potentially have many different identities on which to draw. The group is thus in the individual, and the psychological processes responsible for this also determine the form that the group takes.

Ethnocentrism

Ethnocentrism concerns the relationship between inter-group behaviour at the societal level and attitudes and perceptions at the individual level. The concept provides a link between sociological theories of group conflict and psychological theories of inter-personal attraction (Brewer 1986: 90). Ethnocentrism also provides some insight into the reasons that sub-culture boundaries may be difficult to transact using the normal processes of communication; hence the need for a negotiated order.

Ethnocentrism, according to Trice and Beyer (1993), contributes to the formation of sub-cultures. Among the sub-cultures that frequently occur in organisations those forming around occupations seem prone to ethnocentrism. Brewer (1986) outlines Sumner's theory of inter-group relations which states that ethnocentrism is a technical term for the view in which one's own group is the centre of everything, and all others are scaled and rated with reference to it. Ethnocentrism is a 'syndrome'. It involves mutually reinforcing interactions among attitudinal, ideological and behavioural mechanisms that promote in-group integration and out-group hostility. In addition, this 'syndrome' is a universal concomitant of the formation and differentiation of social groups; and it is also related to inter-group conflict and competition.

Brewer (1986) argues that Sumner's statement concerning the origin of inter-group hostility postulates a direct relationship between proximity and intensity of conflict between two social groups. This prediction reflects the 'realistic group conflict' perspective, in which inter-group hostility is viewed as a rational response to the presence of incompatible goals and competition over scarce resources. This is in keeping with resource dependency theory. Brewer suggests that the relationship between distance and hostility arises out of the psychoanalytic-based theory of frustration and displaced aggression. The theory rests on the assumption that the requirements of intra-group co-operation are inevitably associated with some frustration of individual gratification, which produces a tendency to aggress against the source of the frustration.

Finally, an examination of ideologies, SIT and ethnocentrism provides some understanding of the complexity associated with the formation of groups. However, while these theories give some insight into the reasons for these groups forming several key questions still remain: Why do groups negotiate their way across and within the formal and informal organisational structures to achieve their objectives? How does this happen? And, why might only some groups persist as sub-cultures?

NEGOTIATING THE BOUNDARIES: FROM WORK GROUP TO SUB-CULTURE

Pfeffer and Salancik (1978) argue that in social systems and in social inter-actions, inter-dependence exists whenever one actor does not entirely control all of the conditions necessary for the achievement of an action or the desired goal of that action. They characterise organisations as multiple coalitions engaged in a contest for the acquisition and control of resources.

Similarly, Lawler's (1992) theory of sub-group attachment explains why individuals develop stronger ties to sub-groups than to the larger group. Positive outcomes are attributed to the sub-group, while negative outcomes are attributed to the larger group. Therefore the constraining and enabling effects of social structure are two sides to the same coin. Actors interpret social structure primarily in terms of either the constraints it imposes or what it enables them to do. This interpretation can be characterised as the actor's 'sense of control'. This control can assist the actor to determine whether they can or cannot manipulate their environment, implies that the need for self-determination and efficacy produces positive emotions when the choice process realises this need, and produces negative emotions when the choice process blocks it (Lawler, 1992). Furthermore, Lawler argues that interacting actors are likely to develop commonsense rules that indicate implicitly which collectivities are the primary sources of human freedom and choice. The sub-group is then perceived to be the most empowering, enjoying the strongest affective attachments; while those responsible for constraining choice (the organisation in some instances) receive the blame and affective attachments to a group or collectivity are either strengthened or weakened in proportion to the credit or blame, and hence reinforce the need to form coalitions to achieve goals.

In addition, resource dependency theory (RDT) suggests that it is the competition for scarce resources which may transform a normally co-operative organisational group into one which pursues its own self-interest to the exclusion of others.

SIT explains social competition in terms of two complementary processes: social categorisation and social comparison. Hogg and Abrams (1988) describe the social comparison as a situation where the self is favoured through the medium of in-group favouritism using selected dimensions where the in-group is more favourably placed than the out-group.

Kramer (1991) links resource dependency theory with social identity theory, suggesting that inter-group relations are related to the level of salient social categorisation. He proposes that an individual's decision to behave co-operatively or competitively with other individuals with whom they are inter-dependent is directly linked to how they perceive that inter-dependence. These perceptions are influenced by:

> **(1) the actual interdependence which exists between them and (2) the transformed psychological representation of that interdependence.** (Kramer, 1991: 211)

In addition, social comparison flows across organisational boundaries and Kramer (1991) cites as an example the salary expectations of workers in rival airlines (performing the same duties), who compare notes on their conditions of work. Actual resource inter-dependence depends on the actual availability of resources to the groups. While internal organisation factors and political processes affect the distribution of resources, Kramer argues that it is the relative power and status of groups which become important considerations in determining how much is received. Groups may employ co-optational strategies by forming coalitions to neutralise competitors. Kramer (1991) also addresses the perceptions, motives and expectations of individuals as being affected by the social categorisation process which is grounded in SIT. All these factors affect the decision by groups whether to co-operate or compete.

However Kramer, unlike Lawler, fails to recognise that the origin of the competition arises out of the organisation's need to control both work and resources (Clegg, 1981); or that sub-cultures may be formed to counteract some of that control (Trice and Beyer, 1993). Another point dealt with only in passing by Kramer was the power–dependence relationship and the impact on the strategies used by groups to reduce inter-dependence.

Strauss's concept of a negotiated order also has implications for understanding and explaining how the social competition between groups (as identified by Social Identity Theory and Lawler's Choice-Process Theory) is negotiated. Maines (1982) provides a brief account of the development of the negotiated order perspective in order to grapple with the fundamental questions of structure and process. He proposes:

> that the term 'negotiated order' was introduced into the literature by Strauss (1959) as a way of conceptualising the ordered flux they found in their study of two psychiatric hospitals. Their conceptualisation outlined the stable features of an organisation, while features such as rules, policies, work groups, hierarchies and divisions of labour, ideologies, career lines and organisations' goals, were regarded as the organisational background through which and within which people interact on a daily basis in an attempt to get their work done. Ambiguities inherent in an organisation require negotiation, either implicit or explicit, in order for organisational work to take place. (Maines, 1982: 269)

Maines (1982) believes that Strauss's central contention is that all social orders are negotiated orders and is therefore essential to our understanding of social organisation. Furthermore, he suggests that Strauss is asserting that understanding negotiation processes and their bearing on social orders might well provide important insights into how social orders are maintained, how they change, and how structural limitations interact with the capacity of humans to reconstruct their world creatively. Therefore Strauss's concept of social orders as negotiated orders provides a strong challenge to the metaphor of culture, which is more indicative of the static perception of organisations promoted by the structural-functionalist perspective.

CONCLUSIONS

The rather static interpretation of culture as a metaphor and its application to the study of organisational life have stifled the discourse which views organisations and the individuals within as dynamic processes. An interpretive approach to culture suggests that organisational processes are socially constructed and that these reconstructions are in a continual state of change.

The study of informal processes within organisations, such as sub-cultures, and the investigation of theories associated with group formation and identification emphasise the complexity of inter-group relations. If a holistic approach to the culture metaphor continues to be taken by management, expecting employees to have a uniform view of the organisation's goals, then management's objectives become increasingly more difficult to realise.

The unitary influence can be evidenced by the current normative search for excellence and the emphasis on quality. The often quoted successful outcomes are, at best, problematic. These and other panaceas for organisational ills may be interpreted in the future as only another passing fad which has failed to produce the expected efficiencies initially promised to managers.

Management's pursuit of culture as a unifying agent neglects or fails to adequately appreciate the issue of human agency. If uniformity is largely dependent on human endeavour then, it is argued, a more rigorous understanding of human agency is essential. The view of organisations using the metaphor of sub-cultures creates an understanding that appreciates the interactive nature of identity, the psycho/social significance of which underpins the formation of groups, sub-cultures and the multiple layers of 'negotiations'. It is the occurrence of these interactions which gives meaning to the individual 'as a group'. Such an understanding recognises an organisation's structure and process as continuously being constructed and reconstructed. Finally, it is important to emphasise that if organisation theory is reduced to a discourse in metaphors without a substantial theoretical debate, then the field could be reduced to focusing on language games. Therefore the culture metaphor requires the label *caveat emptor*, let the buyer beware.

REFERENCES

Adorno, T. (1967) 'Sociology and psychology: Part 1', *New Left Review*, No. 46.

Adorno, T. (1968) 'Sociology and psychology: Part 2', *New Left Review*, No. 47.

Alvesson, M. (1991) 'Organisational symbolism and ideology', *Journal of Management Studies*, Vol. 28, No. 3.

Ashforth, B.E. and Mael, F. (1989) 'Social identity theory and the organization', *Academy of Management Review*, Vol. 14, No. 1.

Badcock, C. (1988) *Essential Freud*. Oxford: Blackwell.

Barley, S.R., Meyer, G.W. and Gash, D.C. (1988) Cultures of culture: academics, practioners and the pragmatics of control', *Administrative Science Quarterly*, Vol. 33.

Baum, H. (1989) 'Organisational politics against organisational culture: a psychodynamic perspective', *Human Resource Management*, Vol. 28.

Benjamin, J. (1988) *The Bonds of Love*. New York: Pantheon.

Blumer, H. (1969) *Symbolic Interactionism: Perspective and Method*. Englewood Cliffs, NJ: Prentice-Hall.

Brewer, M.B. (1986) 'The role of ethnocentrism in intergroup conflict', in Worchel, S. and Austin, W.G. (eds) *Psychology of Intergroup Relations*. Chicago: Nelson Hall.

Carr, A. (1986) 'The political economy of technological change', in Watkins, P., Rizvi, F. and Bates, R. (eds) *Theory and Practice of Educational Administration*. Sydney: Deakin University Press.

Carr, A. (1989) *Organisational Psychology: Its Origins, Assumptions and Implications for Educational Administration*. Sydney: Deakin University Press.

Carr, A. (1993a) 'The psychostructure of work...', *Journal of Managerial Psychology*, Vol. 8, No. 3.

Carr, A. (1993b) 'From psychological contracts to psychological audits: some ethical and conceptual issues'. Paper presented at the ANZAM Conference, December.

Clegg, S. (1991) *Organisation Democracy, Power and Participation*. Brisbane: Griffith University Press.

Denzin, N. (1992) *Symbolic Interactionism and Cultural Studies: The Politics of Interpretation*. Cambridge, Mass.: Blackwell.

Diamond, M. (1991) 'Stresses of group membership...' in Kets de Vries, M. (ed) *Organizations on the Couch*. San Francisco: Jossey-Bass.

Freud, S. (1985) 'Group psychology and the analysis of ego', in *Civilisation, Society and Religion (Vol. 12)*. London: Pelican Freud Library (first published 1921).

Gregory, K.L. (1983) 'Native-view paradigms: multiple cultures and culture conflicts, *Administrative Science Quarterly*, Vol. 28.

Hatch, M.J. (1993) 'The dynamics of organizational culture', *Academy of Management Review*, Vol. 18, No. 4.

Hogg, M.A. and Abrams, D. (1988) *Social Identifications*. London and New York: Routledge.

Kramer, R.M. (1991) 'Intergroup relations and organisational dilemmas: the role of categorisation processes', *Research in Organisational Behaviour*, Vol. 13.

Kroeber, A. and Parsons, T. (1958/1970) 'The concepts of culture and of social systems', in Hammel, E. and Simons, W. (eds) *Man Makes Sense: A Reader in Modern Cultural Anthropology*. Boston: Little, Brown.

Lawler, E. (1992) 'Affective attachments to nested groups: a choice-process theory', *American Sociological Review*, Vol. 57.

Leivesley, R., Carr, A. and Kouzmin, A. (1993) 'Max Weber: victim of ethnocentric mishandling or how Weber became a management consultant', in Farazmand, A. (ed) *Handbook of Bureaucracy*. New York: Marcel Deker.

Linstead, S. and Grafton-Small, R. (1992) 'On reading organisational culture', *Organisation Studies*, Vol. 13, No. 3.

Louis, M.R. (1983) 'Organisations as culture-bearing milieux', in Pondy, L.R., Frost, P.J., Morgan, G. and Dandridge, T. (eds) *Organizational Symbolism*. Greenwich: JAI Press.

Louis, M.R. (1987) 'Organizations as culture-bearing milieux', in Shafritz, J.M. and Ott, S.J. (eds) *Classics of Organization Theory*. 2nd Edition, California: Brooks/Cole Publishers.

Maines, D.R. (1982) 'In search of mesostructure: studies in the negotiated order', *Urban Life*, Vol. 11, No. 3.

Parsons, T. (1959) 'The social class as a social system', *Harvard Educational Review*, Vol. 19, No. 4.

Pfeffer, J. and Salancik, G.R. (1978) *The External Control of Organizations: A Resource Dependence Perspective*. New York: Harper and Row.

Ray, C.A. (1986) 'Corporate culture: the last frontier of control', *Journal of Management Studies*, Vol. 23, No. 3.

Reichers, A. (1987) 'An interactionist perspective on newcomer socialization rates', *Academy of Management Review*, Vol. 12, No. 2.

Rentsch, J. (1990) 'Climate and culture: interaction and qualitative differences in organisational meanings', *Journal of Applied Psychology*, Vol. 75, No. 6.

Schein, E. (1971) 'Organizational socialization and the profession of management', in Kolb, D., Rubin, I. and McIntyre, J. (eds) *Organizational Psychology: A Book of Readings*. Englewood Cliffs, NJ: Prentice-Hall.

Silverman, D. (1970) *The Theory of Organisations*. London: Heinemann.

Sinclair, A. (1991) 'After excellence: models of organisational culture for the public sector', *Australian Journal of Administration*, Vol. 50, No. 3.

Starbuck, W.H. (1982) 'Congealing oil: inventing ideologies to justify acting ideologies out', *Journal of Management Studies*, Vol. 19, No. 1.

Strauss, A. (1959) *Mirrors and Masks*. New York: Free Press.

Strauss, A. (1978) *Negotiations*. San Francisco: Jossey-Bass.

Trice, H. and Beyer, J. (1993) *The Cultures of Work*. Englewood Cliffs, NJ: Prentice-Hall.

Van Maanen, J. and Barley, S.R. (1985) 'Cultural organisation fragments of a theory', in Frost, P.J., Moore, L.F., Louis, M.R., Lundberg, C.C. and Martin, J. (eds) *Organisation Culture*. London: Sage.

Wanous, J., Reichers, A. and Malik, S. (1984) 'Organizational socialization and group development: towards an integrative perspective', *Academy of Management Review*, Vol. 9, No. 4.

Yoon, J., Baker, M. and Ko, J.-W.(1994) 'Interpersonal and organisational commitment: subgroup hypothesis revisited', *Human Relations*, Vol. 47, No. 3.

CHAPTER 6

The metaphoric gap as a catalyst of change

Jimme A. Keizer and Ger J.J. Post

METAPHOR AS A MISSING LINK TO ACCEPTANCE

The interplay between client system representatives and OD consultants, in terms of role definition, tends to differ from situation to situation. In some instances the services of a consultant are enlisted to provide a diagnosis which isolates the major underlying problems. On occasions the relationship extends beyond the diagnostic phase and into the realms of implementing a remedy or solution. Although the relative involvement of interested parties may vary, the overriding objective of an OD intervention is to instigate some form of behavioural change within the organisation.

The effectiveness (E) of a consultancy process can be expressed as a formula: $E = Q \times A$, the success of a consulting process depending both on the quality (Q) of the given advice or recommended solution and the readiness to accept (A) that advice or solution within the organisation. From the outset of the process the OD practitioner attempts to establish and enhance the client system's readiness and ability to change. They work on morale and motivation within the organisation, try to make the most of the momentum, and take precautions to make sure that the organisation does not fall back on its existing reflexes and routines in the wake of the implemented solutions.

'Acceptance' is often very difficult to achieve and maintain and many change efforts fail to produce bottom-line performance improvements. Schaffer and Thomson (1992) report that a 1991 survey of over 300 electronics companies found that 63 per cent had failed to improve quality defects by 10 per cent. They contrasted activity-centred programmes with results-driven programmes and suggest that results-driven programmes have a much greater chance of success. They argue that measurable short-term performance indicators are needed and that management should take steps aimed directly toward improvement. They also highlight the need for 'acceptance', referring to the formation of a common conviction that action is necessary. They make clear that 'acceptance' is not soft. The most usual and direct way to realise 'acceptance' includes defining goals that are seen as attractive and leading to desired results. Such an approach is effective if direct activity is required and feasible. In cases in which direct action is not obvious, or desirable goals are difficult to define, this approach is likely to have only limited applicability.

In this chapter an alternative route to 'acceptance' is described, an approach which can be utilised in circumstances where the alternatives regarding action and goals are unclear, hazy or ambiguous. The approach is based on the notion of a 'gap'. It requires the deliberate generation of metaphors. Metaphors are created on the one hand to indicate the *current situation*, and on the other hand to indicate the *desired state* of the organisation.

METAPHOR AS CATALYST

Schaffer and Thomson may attribute the failure of many change programmes to their reliance on activity-driven aspects; however, the benefits accruing from a total switch towards a result orientation in change programmes is questionable. Clearly in a case of acute crisis an orientation to results may be necessary and effective. Nevertheless, results-driven change programmes suffer from the same inherent deficiency as activity-driven ones. Both orientations fail to acknowledge that the internal commitment of those who are involved is needed to achieve fundamental change. In change processes a gap between 'is' and 'should' must be bridged, thus preparing the way for fundamental change. An action- or results-driven programme will lead to changes in procedures and systems. Changes in principles and beliefs can only be achieved if people develop commitment to change.

The methodological foundations of action- and results-driven change programmes stem from the quantitative research paradigm. Actions are 'logically' derived from facts and analysis and then implemented. The choices about the direction of the change and the steps that have to be taken are made without the active participation of those involved. If the primary aim is to achieve change not only in people's behaviour but also in their attitudes and motives, the application of qualitative research techniques is far more appropriate. The qualitative design serves as a foundation for the understanding of the participants' worlds and the meaning of shared experience between the researcher or consultant and participants in a given social context (Janesick, 1994: 210).

In the qualitative orientation metaphors can be seen as filling the missing link between the more or less objective diagnosis (the 'is') and the design and implementation of action (the 'should'). Janesick (1994: 209) suggests:

'Metaphor in general creeps up on you and surprises. It defies the boiler-plate approach to a topic.' A common misconception about metaphors is that they are imprecise. This can be challenged, for example:

> **What is ironic is that. . .the use of metaphor is regarded as a sign of impreci-sion; yet, for making public the ineffable, nothing is more precise than the artistic use of language. Metaphoric precision is the central vehicle for revealing the qualitative aspects of life.** (Eisner, 1991: 227)

As suggested by Broussine and Vince in Chapter 4, metaphors also have emotional value. They provide a value-based representation of the way people experience the organisation and its environment. These qualities of the metaphor make it a catalyst *par excellence* if a meaningful and compre-hensive programme of change is required.

Metaphors are very powerful expressions of how people experience their situation. They include a 'normative perspective'. If people in a process of organisational reorientation or reorganising are invited to think in metaphors about their current versus their desirable situation and to create a metaphoric gap, a solid foundation for action is established. The emo-tional background of metaphors describing the situation in which people find themselves has a catalysing effect on the readiness to change. This quality of metaphors can be deployed for communication purposes and in change programmes.

CHARACTERISTICS OF METAPHORS IN THE CONTEXT OF ORGANISATIONAL CHANGE

In this chapter an approach is presented to using metaphors as catalysts in a process of organisational change. The starting point is that an organisa-tional change process, in which an OD consultant is involved, can be seen as a process of bridging a gap. The specific nature of this gap in a given sit-uation can be affected by designing a metaphoric gap, a pair of metaphors indicating the 'is' and 'should' situation.

The idea of a metaphoric gap shows resemblance to the technique of gap analysis widely used in the field of strategic management (see, for example, Hodge and Anthony, 1991; Bates and Dillard, 1992; Clark, 1992; Khan and Al-Buarki, 1992). The operating procedure for this technique consists of a comparison of the current situation and predicted develop-ments (current forecast) with an organisation's desired situation. The latter can only be established when management has a vision of the future organisation. In most situations the current and desired situation do not match and a strategic gap can be observed. Strategic management is aimed at bridging this gap.

Gap analysis serves both as a diagnostic tool and as an instrument for establishing organisational change, not only in the field of strategic management but in other fields as well. The gap analysis approach contains three major steps: gap identification, gap analysis and bridging the gap (Raynaud and Teasdale, 1992). Many scholars stick to the first two steps and use gap analysis purely as a diagnostic tool. Gap analysis as a diagnostic tool is used in various fields of research, such as marketing (Kontzalis, 1992; Cespedes, 1992; Chudy and Sant, 1993; Laczniak, 1993; Idasi et al, 1994), financial management (Meulemans, 1991; Grunewald, 1992; Galvin, 1994), quality management (Murphy, 1991; Headley and Choi, 1992; Boyett et al, 1992; Marash, 1993; Hampton, 1993; Remenyi and Money, 1994), manufacturing (Kochhar and Suri, 1992), facility management (Kincaid, 1994) and cultural management (Raynaud and Teasdale, 1992). Gap analysis encompasses a broad repertoire of techniques. Some are strongly quantitative (containing statistical procedures, modelling, and financial data), while others rely on qualitative methods, e.g. SWOT (strengths, weaknesses, opportunities and threats) analysis and the writing of *best case* and *worst case* scenarios.

In addition to its analytical or diagnostic use, gap analysis can also be used as an instrument for effecting organisational change. In these circumstances the third stage (bridging the gap) is emphasised, and the effect of the perceived gap on the willingness and ability to change is studied. Thach and Woodman (1994) provide an example of gap analysis as a change method for information technology in organisations. The concept of gap analysis can be applied in a broad range of situations where change is desired or required. Schein (1987), for example, underlines that establishing a gap facilitates the *unfreezing stage* of organisational change via the induction of guilt and anxiety.

OD consultants often make use of this technique. Many of the reports, and much of the general feedback, provided to clients contain either the implicit or explicit use of a gap in one way or another. In the gaps used by consultants one can even find a trend, maybe a fashion. It has become common practice to advise organisations to move from a 'classic paradigm' to a 'modern paradigm'. Characteristic of the classic paradigm is explicit reference to efficiency, division of labour, hierarchy and stability. The modern paradigm is presented in such concepts as the learning organisation, the lean organisation, network organisations and organisations with loosely coupled units. The references made to these paradigms are often tacit. They often use terms that are more common in practice, yet related to these paradigms. Some examples of these concepts found in consultants' presentations and reports are:

Classic	*Modern*
follower	initiator
low profile	high profile
easy going	quick and flexible
local	global
low tech	high tech
large, inflexible	small, flexible
risk avoiding	risk taking
product centred	client centred
introvert	extrovert
conservative	innovative
competitive	co-operative

Other interesting dichotomies can be found in Kanter et al (1992), Burke (1992) and Coulson-Thomas (1992).

Every pair of concepts is presented as a gap to be bridged. This is the heart of the metaphoric gap: a pair of metaphors is sought that symbolises and emotionalises the key characteristics of the situation and identifies the gap to be bridged. Thus the metaphoric gap combines two preconditions for effective organisational change: emotion and a challenging tension.

The metaphoric gap can be described as having two dimensions: a specification of the point of reference and a specification of the content.

Point of reference for the metaphoric gap

A metaphoric gap is constructed to make a powerful distinction between the situation as it is and as it should be or should become. There is a starting point and a reference point. The point of reference can be a within an organisation or it can be based on a comparison with another organisation. If the reference point is within the organisation, the focus is on the differences between departments, sections, units belonging to the same organisation, or even members of a work group. A frequently encountered in-company gap is the contrast between the marketing department and the research and development (R&D) department concerning customer orientation. In many companies the technology-dominated field of product development has certain limitations resulting from an inability to listen to the customer. R&D managers are perhaps likely to focus on the marketing department as a point of reference for an internal change of attitudes.

The reference point can also be outside the organisation. Here the organisation is compared with the situation found in a different organisation. Benchmarking has become an established technique for finding such differences. A well-known example is the competition between Apple and IBM/Microsoft engineers and software specialists, a rivalry that had its effect on the relationship between Mac consumers and MS Dos users.

The point of reference of the developed metaphoric gap is an important characteristic owing to psychological and social motives. Choosing a point of reference and comparing its qualities with certain characteristics of the own unit or organisation involves a normative element and may cause feelings of failure, guilt and inferiority. Although the comparison takes place on specific characteristics (the content of the gap, which will be discussed later) those involved may implicate other characteristics in the comparison. In fact, the phenomenon as a whole is taken as a normative point of reference, including all the unintended and detrimental attributes. For example, the customer orientation of the marketing department may function as a role model for the R&D department; the comparison, however, may be experienced as erroneous due to the commercial image and conflict in the past.

Content of the metaphoric gap

The impact of a metaphoric gap also depends on the content of the metaphors. The content of a metaphoric gap can be distinguished in at least three categories. First, metaphors can be chosen to indicate different types or classes, e.g. Donald Duck versus Gladstone Gander. The focus is on quite different qualities and properties. Second, metaphors can be chosen as different positions on one dimension, and the point is to indicate the distance on this dimension. The speed with which the organisation is moving or developing can be such a dimension. An example of such a couple of metaphors is tortoise versus hare. Third, a metaphoric gap can be formulated with respect to the mental framework of those who are concerned, e.g. focusing on the difference between espoused theory and theory in use, the difference between thinking and doing.

It is not easy to find a metaphoric gap that really satisfies. 'Imaginization' (Morgan, 1993) requires creativity and the ability to abstract. Every image chosen will correspond to the current and/or desired situation: at first sight the resemblance is striking. When we take a closer look the image shows some dissimilarities as well. It may be helpful to think of some sources from which one can borrow:

- *technology*: especially useful to indicate a difference between old fashioned and futuristic (e.g. horse and carriage versus jet aeroplane);
- *history*: useful to indicate a gap which focuses on the need to be contingent (e.g. World War I versus the war in the Gulf);
- *fairy tales, mythology, fables*: good source of 'types' (e.g. Snow White's Grumpy versus Doodle, Zeus versus Hades);
- *attributes of animals*: useful to point to the contrast between properties like weakness and strength (e.g. mouse versus elephant) or slowness and speed (snail versus cheetah);
- *cultures and rites*: useful to contrast values and traditions (e.g. Christian versus Islamic habits, Cockney versus Mersey);

- *sports*: especially useful to indicate a difference between success and failure (e.g. Manchester United versus Leicester City).

SIX-STEP APPROACH TO ORGANISATIONAL CHANGE

The change process is described from the perspective of the qualitative paradigm. The focus is to acquire from the start to the end of the change process as much internal commitment from those involved as possible. This implies a 'normative perspective' (Argyris et al, 1985) which leads to behavioural strategies that actively seek information and increased participation from others, and thus to greater effectiveness (Reason, 1994). Selecting the metaphoric gap is the crucial part in this process.

In most cases the instigation of, and impetus to, change rests with the management of an organisation. The management, in its responsibility for the quality and continuity of the organisation's performance, observes that a change will be necessary. If the situation is diagnosed as urgent and requiring direct drastic action, a quantitative, result-oriented strategy will be chosen. But even when changing behaviour is the first concern, often a flanking policy is required to ensure that not only behaviour but also attitudes and motives change. A structural change undertaken in isolation is rarely effective; cultural elements have to follow to make sure that things really become and remain different.

Various forms of change processes under different circumstances can be observed in practice. The decentralisation process of the UK's National Health Service to a large extent differs from the co-operation and collaboration between two universities. The first process is aimed at disentanglement, while the second concentrates on interweaving. These two change programmes bring forth different targets, different problems, different approaches and different psychological experiences. Similarly, the corporate turnaround processes of industrial 'giants' like Philips and IBM strongly differ from comparable transformation processes in thousands of anonymous small manufacturing enterprises (SMEs) all over the world.

Notwithstanding the differences, to a certain extent these processes and programmes show some similarities as well. The problems that these companies and public organisations face illustrate the difficulties involved in gaining personnel commitment and the managerial control of organisational change programmes. Often it is not the direction and the content of the intended change that obstruct and delay corporate transformation; the real problems are frequently connected to the dissemination of the change objectives to those involved.

In practice a change process needs to be steered, but participation needs to be elicited to create personnel commitment. To combine these two conditions, a team consisting of people from different levels and units in the organisation, line as well as staff, can function as a steering committee, regularly reporting to the management. Sometimes it is wise to have a consultant assist the team. The consultant's role can be particularly useful in helping the team handle the process carefully.

Figure 6.1 illustrates an approach to organisational change which uses the notion of a *metaphoric gap*. In the subsequent sections the step-by-step approach is discussed in greater depth.

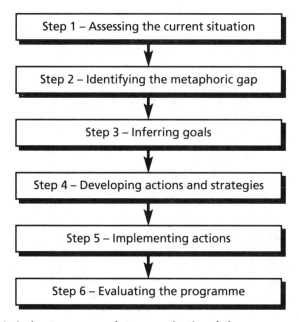

Figure 6.1 A six-step approach to organisational change

Step 1: Assessing the current situation

The change process starts with an assessment of the organisation's current situation by carrying out a critical evaluation of recent developments. There are many techniques available to carry out such an assessment, e.g. a SWOT analysis, benchmarking or scenario writing. The application and interpretation of these techniques results in a problemistic chart (a diagrammatic representation of problems) of the organisation's current situation. It is important that the results of the assessment are shared by those who are involved and that they understand the need to change. Therefore it is helpful to have the assessment made by a team, sometimes assisted by a management consultant. To share the results of the assessment with a wider group of involved employees the use of metaphors seems to be appropriate.

Step 2: Identifying the metaphoric gap

Conclusions must be drawn from the assessment and communicated and translated into action terms. The metaphoric gap plays a central role in the interpretation and communication of the assessment outcomes.

Two different approaches are possible in the identification of the metaphoric gap. The first approach is top down. The management interprets and discusses the problemistic charts and develops an in-depth managerial diagnosis of these problems. Often experts from several fields within or from outside the company are asked to contribute to this diagnosis. Once the diagnosis is made, management chooses the metaphoric gap that captures the change which needs to be made. These metaphors are used to communicate the outline of the change programme and to create commitment as a start for an MBO-like (management by objectives) development of change objectives.

A second, more generative and participative approach brings management and employees together in various settings to discuss the outcomes of the assessment. The assessment team and the management can prepare these conclusions in close co-operation with anyone who is involved. Ideally all departments or units involved are required to indicate what the assessment means for them: which pair of metaphors characterises the situation that they face versus the situation that they must attain as an organisation, as units within the organisation and as individuals within those units?

The process of formulating metaphors can be stimulated by delivering some instructions and examples. To increase the comparability of the developed metaphors, the process facilitator can ask participants to borrow images from a specific range of sources as described earlier in this chapter. On the other hand, a *carte blanche* assignment may be more challenging and may lead to more creative images and greater commitment from the personnel involved. Alternatively, the metaphoric gaps formulated within the separate groups may be shared and a form of aggregated gap may be identified. The latter is important to create a corporate identity for the overall change programme.

The result of this step is either a commonly understood metaphoric gap for the change programme as a whole or a series of metaphoric gaps for specific units or groups or sub-programmes. These metaphoric gaps serve as 'emotional' frameworks for the development of change objectives and action programmes.

Step 3: Inferring goals

Once the metaphors have been chosen, strategic and operational goals must be inferred. The members of the organisation can be asked to think of behavioural consequences of the metaphors: What targets fit with the metaphorical images of the organisation, the units and the individual members? To establish a company-wide change of attitudes and behaviour, every single unit and employee must be stimulated to discuss candidly these perceived consequences and to translate the commonly shared metaphoric gap into specific policies and objectives. In this process management has a facilitating role. Often it is necessary to slow down subordinates and to bring in a more realistic point of view. Managers are frequently required to play a contract-setting role. In some instances it might be helpful to enlist the services of an external consultant to act as a non-directive facilitator. It is important to think of appropriate goal formulations in terms of the extent to which they are meaningful, challenging yet attainable, measurable and manageable. Management literature offers a vast array of methods and techniques to develop sound policies, solid objectives and proper performance indicators.

Step 4: Developing actions and strategies

When the goals or targets have been formulated, a specified action programme must be established for the organisation as a whole (responsibility of the general management), for the different units (responsibility of the unit management) and for individual employees (responsibility of the individuals). As described earlier in this chapter, it is important that these action programmes are results oriented. In order to close the gap between aspiration and achievement, output responsibility needs to be established. As described by Coulson-Thomas (1992), it is important to match transformation capability with change strategy. In all organisations this capability is limited, therefore it is important to balance means and ends and to set the right priorities. To maintain the momentum for planned change short-term results as well as flanking policies must be considered.

Step 5: Implementing actions

Within certain parameters the implementation phase can be programmed. The hope must be that individuals within the organisation are increasingly willing to behave in a way which contributes to the set goals. The implementation can be segmentalised by management to ensure that short-term results become visible. Proving that the change programme does work by pointing to some appealing results works as a necessary and powerful accelerator of the change process. At the same time, change agents must remind those involved of the partial impact of such short-term success. In addition to short-term results, long-term improvements need to be achieved. The real test lies in the future: the continuous attention of all employees is necessary to pass this test. As stated by Coulson-Thomas

(1992) and Kanter et al (1992), attention must be given to empowerment and skill building, as well as to reinforcement via the adaptation of appropriate reward and remuneration systems.

Step 6: Evaluating the programme

The implementation route should contain milestones, points at which the results must be evaluated. Close evaluation is important to ensure that the process holds the attention of the members of the organisation. Obviously the results of such evaluation can give rise to new change activities or readjustment of the current process. It is important to evaluate the personnel and managerial commitment to the change objectives. Part of this evaluation is concerned with ascertaining whether the chosen metaphoric gap is still working. If there is reason to believe that the 'magic' has faded away, new images or better action schemes must be developed.

USING METAPHORS IN CHANGE PROGRAMMES: SOME ILLUSTRATIONS

Many large companies, because of macro-economic developments, have sought to reorganise or restructure their organisation and management systems. The inspiration for these changes has, in many cases, been provided by management gurus such as Peters and Waterman (1982). *In Search of Excellence* and other similar books advocate a change of values and beliefs. Changing an organisation culture is one of the most challenging, but at the same time one of the most difficult assignments for the company's change masters and management consultants. This section examines two case examples of large-scale, ambitious change programmes which rely on the use of metaphor.

In the case of Philips a metaphor is used in naming the change operations: Centurion. Centurion has an association with 'century', Philips celebrating its hundredth birthday, on its way to the twenty-first century. Centurion also relates to the famous tank that does not stop for obstructions along the way. The corporate change programme is built on a dramatic need for a change of values and profit improvement. There is no other way. The term centurion is also associated with the officer in the Roman army. Like this officer, Philips' managers have to get used to handling personal assignments which are laid down in a formal description or are implicitly covered in the psychological contract.

The example of Philips illustrates the possibilities of metaphor in facilitating change programmes within organisations. However, the origin of the centurion metaphor is located at corporate headquarters. Centurion as an image is a useful concept in bringing forward the *need* for change. However, the metaphor used does not give *direction* to the change programme. The programme therefore should be (and is) given further direction, via participative activities (e.g. Philips' Customer Days). At a business unit or operational level, some discretion is needed for creating 'local' metaphors that guide the change programme within the constraints of operation Centurion. The concept of metaphoric gap can facilitate change processes at these levels.

A second illustration stems from management consulting practice and refers to the ongoing reorganisation of the Dutch government. Like many industrial companies government organisations are confronted with the need to change. The challenges which these organisations face are changing role in society, downsizing the organisation, improving productivity, creating a customer orientation and introducing the concept of management contract. One of the building blocks of the government change programme is a concentration on core competencies; issues outside this domain, such as developing applied solutions to non-core competencies, are decentralised or subcontracted. In a specific consulting assignment the management and personnel from a government agency took part in a workshop. They were asked to describe both the current situation and the desired situation from the human relationship perspective (i.e. as a marriage, a divorce, a close friendship, etc.).

One of the metaphors created by the participating groups was that of the solid and caring family (describing the current situation). One of the older children has reached the age of 18 and leaving the family house becomes expedient. The child is offered accommodation downtown (describing the future situation). A *go* or *don't go* decision needs to be made. Leaving home typically creates an uncertain situation and sometimes even causes pain. But both the parents and the child must make the best of it and may support each other in getting used to the new situation.

This family metaphor made it possible to view organisational change as a process that is inevitable and not unique in its character and content. Just as in the family situation, it was made clear that a change in the organisation structure was possible without ending positively experienced relationships between current in-company partners. Other family scenarios also have strong metaphorical connotations for organisational change – for example, the notion of 'feuding relatives' might be helpful as a means of understanding and managing an intervention aimed at conflict resolution.

CONCLUSIONS

Although Morgan and others make out a case for the use of metaphors in diagnostic activities as well as in change programmes, the question of *how* to use these metaphors is left unanswered. In this chapter we advocate the use of a metaphoric gap in creating support for organisational change. However, there are some pitfalls. Those considering using the approach should bear in mind the considerations outlined below.

The use of metaphors requires some conceptual intelligence and social skills. Not every person will be able to contribute or participate in the process of 'imaginization' (Morgan, 1993). Notwithstanding this shortcoming, metaphors are generally easier to comprehend than most theoretical frameworks, especially when images are chosen that appeal to the everyday life of those involved. The concept of a gap to be bridged reduces the multiple-factor assessment to two single images and therefore results in a tremendous simplification of the intended change. The proposed participative approach will result in metaphors that are easy to comprehend for those involved. If necessary, management can support employees in developing metaphoric gaps by applying the suggestions and sources described earlier in this chapter.

Major change programmes in large companies require the development of company-wide metaphors. The result of this stage in organisational change must be a metaphoric gap understood and accepted by most members of the organisation. The participative approach implies divergence in metaphor creation. Special attention is needed to integrate from individual 'imaginization' to a collective metaphor. When an overall change metaphor is chosen it is essential that the metaphor is supported by extra information. Information is crucial in the case of metaphors that are not common. For example, Philips' Centurion metaphor needs further explanation to ensure that elements relating to the management contract and individual responsibility are made explicit. By contrast, the family metaphor, used by the Dutch government, needs far less information to be fully understood.

More than other ways of communicating and targeting change activities metaphors can be misunderstood. The simple fact that a metaphor as a symbolic message contains several, sometimes contradictory, aspects at the same time can lead to confusion and potentially is a source of conflicting views and ideas (see Chapter 1 for further insights into this problem). Special attention is required when communicating the metaphoric gap, the derived goals and action programme to avoid misunderstanding.

The concept of metaphoric gap closely relates to Lewin's (1951) unfreeze–change–refreeze model. The metaphors paint a picture of the current and undesired situation (which needs to be unfrozen) and the preferred situation to be attained and refrozen. In modern management literature Lewin's model of organisational change is regarded as outdated. Many scholars persistently emphasise that organisational change must be seen as a never-ending process. Change is the 'rule', stability is the 'exception'.

It seems reasonable to expect that within the context of organisational change a particular metaphor has a 'shelf life'. In a process of ongoing improvement change never ends. The gap will never be bridged completely: the longer the bridge gets, the wider the gap grows. In order to avoid discouragement, despondency and frustration the change process must be subdivided into feasible sub-programmes. To facilitate such ongoing improvement programmes metaphors must be refreshed from time to time. A striking illustration was offered to us by a TQM officer who compared the company-wide *kaizen* quality improvement programme to a rocket launch installation. Viewing the company as being like NASA enabled quality improvement to be compared to sending missiles into space – each time a bit further; a journey that never ends. The company went as far as naming the various sub-projects after famous space exploration missions like Explorer, Pioneer and Mariner (future sub-projects will be called Gemini, Voyager and Apollo). Despite the finite character of these sub-projects, like space exploration the main project of improving quality never ends. The NASA rocket launcher metaphor provided an effective vehicle for selling the idea within and outside the organisation.

In this chapter we have described and tried to sell the idea of the metaphoric gap as a catalyst of organisational change. The greatest scope for application is undoubtedly in situations where the intervention process requires attitudinal and motivational change. In recent years large companies such as Philips and IBM have embarked on extensive, radical change initiatives. They have downsized their firms considerably and taken pains to change the attitude within their companies. They have tried to get the employees at all levels to be more customer oriented. The first move – firing thousands of employees – can be carried out in a relatively short time. The second – building new attitudes – takes much more time, and possibly never stops. Applying metaphors and gap analysis could be helpful in the second stage of the process.

Today, we encounter an extraordinary level of interest by managers in the concept of metaphor. The work of Morgan and others has contributed to this. Yet managers have been using metaphors from time immemorial. The 'mouldability' of metaphors appeals to creative sentiments and the needs of managers in practice. The metaphoric gap approach may contribute to the readiness and the ability of managers, change agents and others to express their feelings about organisational change. As a result, it may help organisations in their struggle to accomplish significant and lasting change.

REFERENCES

Argyris, C., Putnam, R. and Smith, M.C. (1985) *Action Science: Concepts, Methods and Skills for Research and Intervention*. San Francisco: Jossey-Bass.

Bates, D.L. and Dillard, J.E. (1992) 'Wanted: a strategic planner for the 1990s', *Journal of General Management*, Vol. 18, No. 1.

Boyett, J.H., Kearney, A.T. and Konn, H.P. (1992) 'What's wrong with Total Quality Management?', *Tapping the Network Journal*, Vol. 3, No. 1, Spring.

Burke, W.W. (1992) *Organization Development: A Process of Learning and Changing*. Reading, Mass.: Addison-Wesley.

Cespedes, F.V. (1992) 'Sales coordination: an exploratory study', *Journal of Personal Selling and Sales Management*, Vol. 12, No. 3, Summer.

Chudy, B. and Sant, R. (1993) 'Customer-driven competitive positioning – an approach towards developing an effective customer service strategy', *Marketing and Research Today*, Vol. 21, No. 3, September.

Clark, D.N. (1992) 'A literature analysis of the use of management science tools in strategic planning', *Journal of the Operational Research Society*, Vol. 43, No. 9, September.

Coulson-Thomas, C. (1992) *Transforming the Company: Bridging the Gap between Management Myth and Corporate Reality*. London: Kogan Page.

Galvin, M. (1994) 'Credit union management', *Credit Union Management*, Vol. 17, No. 1, January.

Grunewald, A.E. (1992) 'Do risk measures exaggerate?', *Bank Management*, Vol. 68, No. 2, February.

Hampton, G.M. (1993) 'Gap analysis of college student satisfaction as a measure of professional service quality', *Journal of Professional Services Marketing*, Vol. 9, No. 1, Winter.

Headley, D.E. and Choi, B. (1992) 'Achieving service quality through gap analysis and a basic statistical approach', *Journal of Services Marketing*, Vol. 6, No. 1, Winter.

Hodge, B.J. and Anthony W.P. (1991) *Organization Theory: A Strategic Approach*. Boston: Allyn and Bacon.

Idasi, J.O., Young, T.M., Winistorfer, P.M., Ostermeier, D.M. and Woodruff, R.B. (1994) 'A customer-oriented marketing method for hardwood lumber companies', *Forest Products Journal*, Vol. 44, No. 7/8, July–August.

Janesick, V.J. (1994) 'The dance of qualitative research design', in Denzin, N.K. and Lincoln, Y.S. (eds) *Handbook of Qualitative Research*. London: Sage.

Kanter, R.M., Stein, B.A. and Jick, T.D. (1992) *The Challenge of Organizational Change: How Companies Experience it and Leaders Guide it*. New York: The Free Press.

Khan, G.M. and Al-Buarki, E.A. (1992) 'Strategic planning in Bahrain', *Management Decision*, Vol. 30, No. 5.

Kincaid, D. (1994) 'Measuring performance in facility management', *Facilities*, Vol. 12, No. 6, June.

Kochhar, A. and Suri, A. (1992) 'Gap analysis approach to the effective implementation of master production scheduling systems', *Integrated Manufacturing Systems*, Vol. 3, No. 2.

Kontzalis, P. (1992) 'Identification of key attributes, gap analysis and simulation techniques in forecasting market potential of ethical pharmaceutical products', *International Journal of Forecasting*, Vol. 8, No. 2, October.

Laczniak, G.R. (1993) 'Marketing ethics: onward toward greater expectations', *Journal of Public Policy Making*, Vol. 12, No. 1, Spring.

Lewin, K. (1951) *Field Theory in Social Science*. New York: Harper and Row.

Marash, S.A. (1993) 'The key to TQM and world-class competiveness', *Quality*, Vol. 32, No. 10, October.

Meulemans, D. (1991) 'Assessing the strategic gap: the first step in resource allocation', *Topics in Health Care Financing*, Vol. 17, No. 3, Spring.

Morgan, G. (1993) *Imaginization: The Art of Creative Management*. London: Sage.

Murphy, P.F. (1991) 'Six steps to quality improvement', *Journal for Quality and Participation*, Vol. 14, No. 6, December.

Peters, T.J. and Waterman, R.H. (1982) *In Search of Excellence*. New York: Harper and Row.

Raynaud, M. and Teasdale, M. (1992) 'Confusions and acquisitions: post-merger culture shock and some remedies', *Communication World*, Vol. 9, No. 6, May/June.

Reason, P. (1994) 'Three approaches to participatory inquiry', in Denzin, N.K. and Lincoln, Y.S., *Handbook of Qualitative Research*. London: Sage.

Remenyi, D.S.J. and Money, A.H. (1994) 'Service quality and correspondence analysis in determining problems with the effective use of computer services', *European Journal of Information Systems*, Vol. 3, No. 1, January.

Schaffer, R.H. and Thomson, H.A. (1992) 'Successful change programs begin with results', *Harvard Business Review*, Vol. 70, No. 1, Jan/Feb.

Schein, E.H. (1987) *Process Consultation, Vol II: Lessons for Managers and Consultants*. Reading, Mass.: Addison-Wesley.

Thach, L. and Woodman, R.W. (1994) 'Organizational change and information technology: managing on the edge of cyberspace', *Organizational Dynamics*, Vol. 23, No. 1, Summer.

CHAPTER 7

Organisational culture as personality: lessons from psychology?

Cliff Oswick, Sidney Lowe and Philip Jones

INTRODUCTION

The process of attributing human characteristics to organisations is firmly embedded within the management literature. Indeed, its usage is so commonplace that we are often unaware that we are talking in figurative, rather than literal, terms (Lakoff and Johnson, 1980). There are numerous examples of the personification of organisational activities and processes. For instance, when we refer to the learning organisation or the caring organisation we are effectively applying cognitive and emotional characteristics to an inanimate entity. Physiological properties – such as weak, strong, and healthy – are also frequently enlisted to describe organisations. So too are components of the body, e.g. the heart of the workforce, the backbone of the company, the lower limbs of the hierarchy, and the brains of the organisation. Even Organisational Behaviour, the terminology used to describe a mainstream academic discipline, relies on personification. Clearly, people within an organisation behave – they behave individually and collectively. But can an organisation, which is not in itself alive, exhibit behaviour? Arguably not.

The personification of the discourse on organisations rarely occurs in a random, haphazard way. It is driven by a particular way of thinking about events and actions. The language used is not merely an embellishment, it is often the product of a less obvious, but more deeply rooted, process of anthropomorphism. This kind of projection of the human condition is not restricted to organisations. It seems to pervade all walks of life. In his book aptly entitled *The Body in the Mind*, Johnson (1987: xv) explains this tendency more fully. He observes:

> Through metaphor, we make use of patterns that we obtain in our physical experience to organize our more abstract understanding. Understanding via

metaphorical projection from the concrete to the abstract makes use of physical experience in two ways. First, our bodily movements and interactions in various physical domains of experience are structured, and that structure can be projected by metaphor onto abstract domains. Second, metaphorical understanding is not merely a matter of arbitrary fanciful projection from anything to anything with no constraints. Concrete bodily experience not only constrains the 'input' to the metaphorical projections but also the nature of the projections themselves, that is, the kinds of mappings that can occur across domains.

The metaphorical projection undertaken in this chapter attempts to apply the above interpretation. Use is made of the patterns obtained through our experience and knowledge of personality (the concrete) to organise and structure our understanding of organisational culture (the abstract). Furthermore, the extent to which treating organisational culture and personality as synonymous shapes and constrains our understanding of the domain is also explored.

ORGANISATIONAL CULTURE AS PERSONALITY

In order to structure the subsequent discussion of organisational culture and personality, it is perhaps worthwhile briefly establishing how the terms are to be used. There are many definitions of culture; arguably the most comprehensive, and the most widely cited, has been provided by Edgar Schein (1985). He suggests that culture is:

1 A pattern of shared basic assumptions,
2 invented, discovered, or developed by a given group,
3 as it learns to cope with its problems of external adaptation and internal integration,
4 that has worked well enough to be considered valid, and, therefore,
5 is to be taught to new members of the group as the
6 correct way to perceive, think, and feel in relation to those problems.

For our purposes the definition of personality to be used here is 'the total pattern of characteristic ways of thinking, feeling and behaving that constitute the individual's distinctive method of relating to the environment' (Kagan and Havemann, 1976: 376).

If we consider the definitions of personality and culture provided above there appear to be a number of similarities. In fact, if we swopped the word 'group' for 'individual' in Schein's definition of culture, and replaced 'individual' with 'organisation' in Kagan and Havemann's definition of personality, the outcome would be fairly representative, interchangeable definitions. Further examination of the similarities, and the degree of overlap, between the two constructs is undertaken in later sections. However, given the common ground shared by the two areas it is somewhat surprising that there are very few examples of a direct metaphorical connection being made. One notable exception is provided by Bridges (1992) who describes organisations as having character – which seems to equate to culture. He comments:

> Character is the typical climate of the organizational country; it is the personality of the individual organization; or it is the DNA of the organisational life form. It is the organization's character that makes it feel and act like itself.

Other writers have drawn similar inferences regarding the personality metaphor. For example:

> The idea of viewing organizations as cultures – where there is a system of shared meaning among members – is a relatively recent phenomenon. Fifteen years ago, organizations were, for the most part, simply thought of as rational means by which to co-ordinate and control a group of people. They had vertical levels, departments, authority relationships, and so forth. But organizations are more. They have personalities too, just like individuals. They can be rigid or flexible, unfriendly or supportive, innovative or conservative. (Robbins, 1989: 466)

In the limited instances where the personality metaphor has been applied to organisational culture, it has operated at a surface level. That is to say that it has been mentioned as a passing observation, rather than being used as a vehicle for a more thorough investigation of culture. In this chapter the robustness and appropriateness of the metaphor are examined with a view to providing new insights into organisational culture. This deeper level of metaphorical projection requires a more detailed juxtapositioning of the two domains.

The similarities

Before attempting to compare personality and organisational culture, it is important first to acknowledge that they are inextricably linked. The dominant personality traits of employees have an impact on the culture of the organisation and vice versa, albeit that there is not a strong level of mutual determinism. Since an organisation is made up of a collection of people, all of whom have personalities, at least some impact on the prevailing culture is inevitable. Personality acts on culture in any one, or a combination, of three main ways:

1 Individually – via the dominant characteristics of key players.
2 Occupationally/departmentally – via the dominant traits found within sub-groups.
3 Collectively/organisationally – via the dominant attributes of the majority.

Implicit in the subordination of the goals of the individual to those of the organisation is the need to conform to a pattern of shared basic assumptions (or culture). This conformity is elicited via a process of socialisation for new members. In situations where there is a high degree of incongruence between individual values and the culture, coercive measures are frequently used. Although the impact of culture on personality is generally fairly limited, the demands of a strong corporate culture can lead to the suppression of particular personality characteristics, and nurture the expression of others. Thus, there is a dynamic interplay between the organisation's culture and the personality of employees. This relationship is summarised in Figure 7.1.

Personality and organisational culture are analogous in several ways. However, one of the most striking features is the extent to which both domains appear to be metonymous. Here the term metonymy is used in the following manner:

> **Metonymy is one of the basic characteristics of cognition. It is extremely common for people to take one well-understood or easy-to-perceive aspect of something and use it to stand either for the thing as a whole or for some other aspect or part of it.** (Lakoff, 1987: 77)

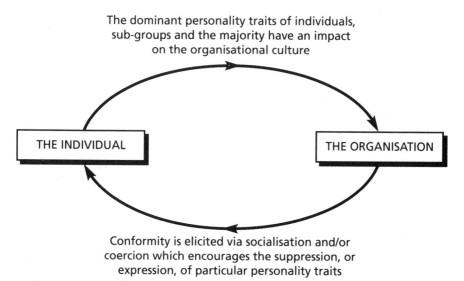

The dominant personality traits of individuals, sub-groups and the majority have an impact on the organisational culture

THE INDIVIDUAL

THE ORGANISATION

Conformity is elicited via socialisation and/or coercion which encourages the suppression, or expression, of particular personality traits

Figure 7.1 The interaction between organisational culture and employee personality

An example of this would be one air hostess saying to another, 'Seat 42 wants to move to a non-smoking area'.

Here 'seat 42' is standing for the person sitting in seat 42. Both organisational culture and personality are frequently used metonymically. Organisational culture is used to stand for the organisation as a whole and for a multitude of organisational problems. Similarly, personality is used to stand for the individual and the individual's actions. Some typical examples of this would be:

- He has no personality.
- There was a clash of personalities.
- It's a personality problem.
- The organisation's culture is all wrong.
- We need to change the culture.

In each of these cases, the domain is standing for something else. When we say, 'He has no personality', we do not mean it literally. Instead we are suggesting that the behaviour exhibited by the person is unacceptable or not consistent with our expectations. Equally, a clash of personalities translates into 'two parties having conflicting or opposing views'. Culture is also frequently used in an inappropriate, almost polysemic way. Organisational problems and issues which are framed in cultural terms are often more appropriately located in other domains, i.e. they can be classified as economic, structural or technical problems.

The metonymous usage of personality and organisational culture is perhaps strongly connected to their relationship with behaviour. Personality is an antecedent of behaviour; yet behaviour also influences personality. Therefore, behaviour is both an input and an output of personality. Hence it is often difficult to disentangle behaviour and personality, and to determine where one begins and the other ends. A parallel relationship also exists between behaviour and organisational culture. If we revisit the above examples of metonymy they appear to be using personality (or culture) to stand for some aspect, or aspects, of behaviour.

The tendency to attribute individual behaviour to personality, and organisational behaviour to the organisation's culture, is perhaps due to a form of cognitive myopia. The fundamental attribution error (Kelley, 1973) seems to have some bearing on this problem. Hellriegel et al (1992: 126) have described this form of perceptual error as 'the tendency to underestimate the impact of situational or external causes of behaviour and to overestimate the impact of personal and internal causes of behaviour when seeking to understand why people behave the way they do'. In overestimating the impact of personal and internal causes we are effectively attributing a person's behaviour to their personality. This is problematic. Behaviour is not simply a product of personality – situational variables often affect behaviour. For example, if someone behaves aggressively in a given situation it does not necessarily mean that it is typical of their behaviour or indeed an intrinsic part of their personality. The aggression displayed might simply be a reaction to an unpleasant event which occurred earlier in the same day.

If as suggested, the operationalisation of the fundamental attribution error leads us to believe that behaviour is primarily attributable to personality (internal causation), as opposed to situational factors (external causation), we have a plausible explanation for the metonymous usage of personality to represent behaviour. If we turn to organisational culture, the same process appears to apply. When organisations fail to achieve certain goals, or produce poor performances, they are inclined to attribute causation to the organisation's culture, rather than external factors. The existence of external factors (such as the environment, competition, consumers etc.) is normally acknowledged, but the culture is still held responsible. Even in situations where contrary evidence exists, the culture is nevertheless typically blamed on the basis of failing to anticipate or respond to external factors. Ironically, organisational culture is often seen as both the root cause and the solution of problems.

A further area of similarity between the two domains relates to definitional problems. Both seem to be easy to define in broad and vague terms; however, trying to place parameters on either domain or attempting to identify their constituent parts becomes extremely difficult. This appears to be due, at least in part, to the aforementioned issues (i.e. metonymy and their linkage with behaviour). The heterogeneous nature of both domains is perhaps another contributing factor. We know that an individual's personality is made up of a collection of traits and that an organisation's culture is a pattern of shared assumptions. However, the specific concoction of ingredients does not appear to be consistent, and hence there appear to be a number of dissimilar forms of personality and organisational culture. This is perhaps succinctly encapsulated in an adage provided by Kluckhohn and Murray (1948: 35) who said that, 'to some extent, a person's personality is like all other people's, like some other people's, and like no other person's'.

Finally, a further feature which personality and organisational culture seem to share is their stability. Many writers have highlighted the difficulties involved in trying to alter someone's personality. Personality has been described as being 'stable' and having 'continuity in time' (Maddi, 1980). Likewise, it is difficult to change an organisation's culture. Cummings and Huse (1985: 423) observe:

> **cultural change is an extremely difficult and long-term process. Some experts doubt whether large firms can even bring about fundamental changes in their cultures; those who have accomplished such feats estimate the process takes from six to fifteen years.**

The differences

There is a danger that when applying a metaphor to an object, or in this case a discipline, we focus on what Ortony (1975) refers to as the 'ground' (the aspects of similarity) and ignore the 'tension' (those which are dissimilar). One of the most significant areas of dissimilarity derives from the fundamental nature of human beings and organisations. An organisation is essentially a pluralistic phenomenon; a person is a unitaristic entity. For example, a person might have mixed or competing views about which direction to walk, but once this cognitive dilemma is resolved the body acts in unison, i.e. the left foot and the right foot go in the same direction. To a lesser or greater extent, an organisation is an amalgamation of collaborating, competing and conflicting parts. Therefore, even when a specific course of action is agreed on by an organisation, it is unlikely that the sub-units will have either the inclination or co-ordination required to pull together in the same direction. It is for this reason that sub-cultures are central to the study of organisational culture. No equivalent term exists in the study of personality. It is impractical to attempt to subdivide a personality into a series of sub-personalities.

The holistic nature of the personality metaphor limits its utility as a mechanism for studying culture. The projection onto organisational culture necessarily has to operate at a macro level – given that the metaphor does not provide sufficient common ground to facilitate a meaningful analysis of aspects of sub-culture. However, the tension between the two domains provides a cautionary insight into the inherent problems involved in attempting to explore organisational culture as a unitarist concept. A fuller discussion of this problem is provided in Chapter 5 by Hocking and Carr.

Another area of tension between the domains relates to their origins and formation. Organisational culture and personality have emanated from different disciplines and they have also developed over very different time frames. The notion of organisational culture has evolved from the broader study of culture found in the fields of anthropology and sociology (Adams and Ingersoll, 1990), while the study of personality can be firmly located within the realms of psychology.

In relative terms organisational culture is still in its infancy, having only emerged as a distinct area of organisational analysis during the past two decades. In fact, some commentators have suggested that focused research on organisational culture did not commence until the early 1980s (see, for example, Frost et al, 1991; Turner, 1990). By contrast, the study of personality has enjoyed a far longer research trajectory. One of the earliest contributions can be traced back to Hippocrates in 400 BC. He effectively developed the first 'type theory' of personality when he identified four basic temperaments, namely the sanguine, the melancholic, the choleric and the phlegmatic. Morea (1990: 1) has stated that, 'The science of personality began, conveniently, with the century when in 1890 Freud published *The Interpretation of Dreams.*' It is difficult to be precise about when the 'serious academic study' of personality first began. However, the major theoretical contributions seem to have been formulated more than 40 years ago (e.g. Allport, 1937; Eysenck, 1947; Jung, 1933; Kelly, 1955; Rogers, 1947).

It is possible to treat the two domains as if they were products. Using the notion of the product life cycle, we could describe personality as an established product while organisational culture is still in the early stages of development. Put another way, personality is a mature discipline compared to organisational culture which is currently in its adolescence. If organisational culture is at a pre-paradigmatic stage of development, then this source of dissimilarity may offer a means of increasing our understanding of the domain. In effect, it is feasible that lessons could be learnt from the more mature, and concrete, domain of personality which is further along a similar metaphorical path.

STUDYING ORGANISATIONAL CULTURE: ALTERNATIVE PARADIGMS

Allport (1937) identified two contrasting approaches to the study of human behaviour. First, the nomothetic approach which is concerned with law setting or giving, dealing with the abstract, the universal, or the general. Second, the ideographic which focuses on relating to, or dealing with, the concrete, the individual, or the unique. Luthans and Davis (1982) suggest that the defining characteristics of nomothetic perspectives are that they are group centred; employ standardised, controlled environmental contexts and quantitative methods; and seek to establish general laws. In contrast, ideographic perspectives are individual centred; use naturalistic environmental contexts and qualitative methods; and seek the exploration of the unique experiences of the individual. Even though the two appear to be based on fundamentally different and conflicting premises about the nature of the human condition, they can be seen as complementary in that both approaches have been used to increase our understanding of personality.

The characteristics of nomothetic and ideographic approaches as they are used in the study of personality have been highlighted by Huczynski and Buchanan (1991). The results of superimposing these approaches onto the cultural domain are presented in Table 7.1.

Most of the research into organisational culture can be described as being either ideographic or nomothetic. There appears to be a tacit understanding of these terms, although they are not explicitly used within the literature. Schein (1985) has referred to the need for 'clinical' and 'ethnographic' approaches which seem to be broadly comparable.

Table 7.1 Contrasting approaches to the study of organisational culture

The nomothetic approach	The ideographic approach
Tends to be quantitative in nature	Tends to be qualitative in nature
Is generalising: emphasises the discovery of laws of organisational action and decision making	Is individualising: emphasises the uniqueness of an organisation
Is based on the specific analysis of clusters of organisations/variables	Is based on the intensive study of a single organisation
Uses objective questionnaires and structured interviewing to collect data, which is limited in scope, from a large sample	Uses projective instruments and semi-structured interviews to collect data, which is not limited in scope, from a relatively small sample
Describes culture in terms of an organisation's possession of a prescribed set of common dimensions and/or core characteristics	Describes culture in terms of the organisational members' individual and collective understanding of their own organisation
Views culture as composed of discrete and identifiable elements	Believes that culture has to be understood and studied as an indivisible, intelligible whole

Figure 7.2 provides a classification of 40 of the most prominent studies into organisational culture using ideographic–nomothetic and theoretical–empirical scales. The research is drawn from both the academic and management literature.

All four quadrants in Figure 7.2 are relatively balanced in terms of the distribution of studies, which perhaps indicates a degree of healthy diversity and the potential for methodological richness. However, a reclassification of the same studies using a practitioner–academic orientation scale offers a very different impression (see Figure 7.3 on p.116). The greater proportion of nomothetic research is slanted towards a management audience, while the bulk of ideographic work has tended to have an academic focus. There are in fact numerous academically oriented studies which adopt a nomothetic approach, but instead of exploring organisational culture they merely use it as a variable in the study of other domains (see, for example, Brown and Starkey, 1994). There is a distinct dearth of research in this area which examines organisational culture in its own right. More rigorous quantitative research is necessary if we are to develop insights into the generalisable characteristics, and common constituent parts, of organisational culture. Also the generation of informed nomothetic findings should complement the work of ethnographers and anthropologists.

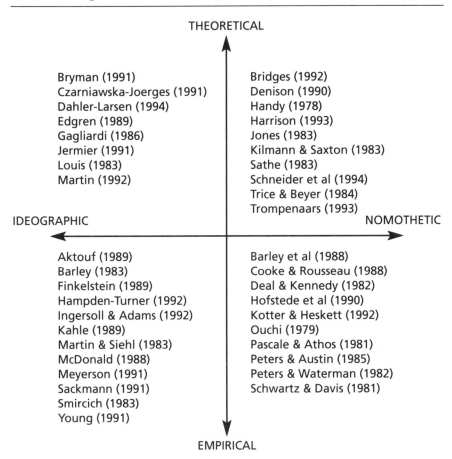

THEORETICAL

| IDEOGRAPHIC | | NOMOTHETIC |

Bryman (1991)
Czarniawska-Joerges (1991)
Dahler-Larsen (1994)
Edgren (1989)
Gagliardi (1986)
Jermier (1991)
Louis (1983)
Martin (1992)

Bridges (1992)
Denison (1990)
Handy (1978)
Harrison (1993)
Jones (1983)
Kilmann & Saxton (1983)
Sathe (1983)
Schneider et al (1994)
Trice & Beyer (1984)
Trompenaars (1993)

Aktouf (1989)
Barley (1983)
Finkelstein (1989)
Hampden-Turner (1992)
Ingersoll & Adams (1992)
Kahle (1989)
Martin & Siehl (1983)
McDonald (1988)
Meyerson (1991)
Sackmann (1991)
Smircich (1983)
Young (1991)

Barley et al (1988)
Cooke & Rousseau (1988)
Deal & Kennedy (1982)
Hofstede et al (1990)
Kotter & Heskett (1992)
Ouchi (1979)
Pascale & Athos (1981)
Peters & Austin (1985)
Peters & Waterman (1982)
Schwartz & Davis (1981)

EMPIRICAL

Figure 7.2 Methodological classification of research into organisational culture

Traditionally, ideographic and nomothetic approaches have served different aims in the study of personality. Ideographic methodologies have tended to be concerned with helping the individual within the workplace, e.g. employee counselling. Nomothetic instruments, such as psychometric tests, have been used as a means of comparing an individual to a set of criteria or to other individuals. The emphasis placed on comparisons ensures that a degree of breadth is achieved in the analysis, but this is often at the expense of depth.

The nomothetic work undertaken in the cultural domain suffers from similar limitations: there seems to an ongoing quest for the corporate culture recipe. The majority of studies in this area provide frameworks which are composed of a limited series of 'superficial pigeon holes' into which a given organisation can be slotted. The most common form is the four-box typology or what Hampden-Turner (1992) has termed 'the quadrants syndrome'. The appeal of these popular classifications for managers is their simplicity.

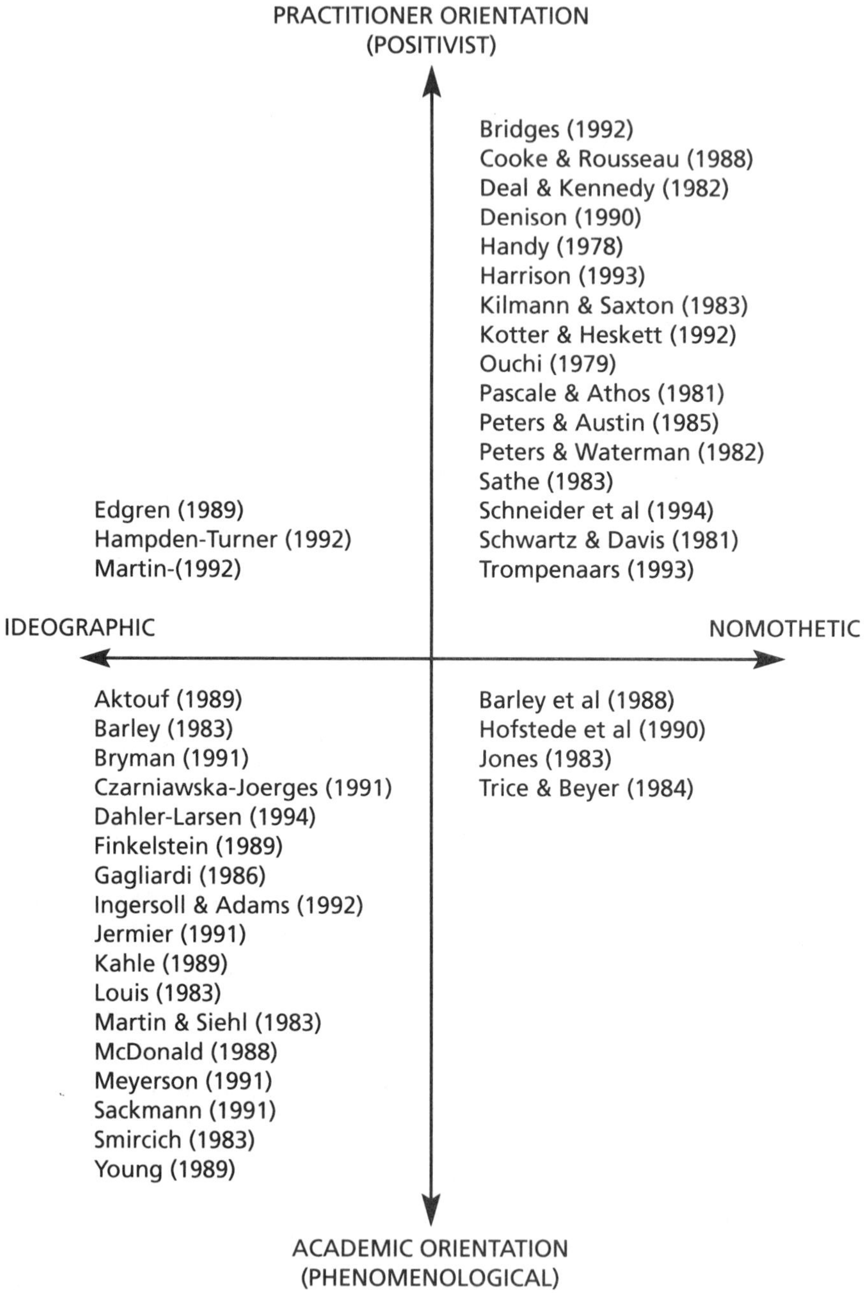

PRACTITIONER ORIENTATION
(POSITIVIST)

Bridges (1992)
Cooke & Rousseau (1988)
Deal & Kennedy (1982)
Denison (1990)
Handy (1978)
Harrison (1993)
Kilmann & Saxton (1983)
Kotter & Heskett (1992)
Ouchi (1979)
Pascale & Athos (1981)
Peters & Austin (1985)
Peters & Waterman (1982)
Sathe (1983)

Edgren (1989)   Schneider et al (1994)
Hampden-Turner (1992)   Schwartz & Davis (1981)
Martin-(1992)   Trompenaars (1993)

IDEOGRAPHIC   NOMOTHETIC

Aktouf (1989)   Barley et al (1988)
Barley (1983)   Hofstede et al (1990)
Bryman (1991)   Jones (1983)
Czarniawska-Joerges (1991)   Trice & Beyer (1984)
Dahler-Larsen (1994)
Finkelstein (1989)
Gagliardi (1986)
Ingersoll & Adams (1992)
Jermier (1991)
Kahle (1989)
Louis (1983)
Martin & Siehl (1983)
McDonald (1988)
Meyerson (1991)
Sackmann (1991)
Smircich (1983)
Young (1989)

ACADEMIC ORIENTATION
(PHENOMENOLOGICAL)

Figure 7.3 Epistemological classification of research into organisational culture

They are easily understood and they make the complex seem simple. Managers are also psychologically comfortable with being able to label their organisation. Unfortunately, the lack of depth inherent in nomothetic approaches means that the predictive value for a particular organisation in terms of organisational development and change is extremely low. In essence, the positivistic nomotheticism prevalent in the management discourse offers quick-fix, off-the-shelf solutions to cultural problems.

In order to gain the depth of understanding required to provide a meaningful platform for organisational change, ideographic methodologies are essential. Further management-oriented ideographic research would help to make managers more aware of the complexity, pervasiveness and embedded nature of organisational cultures. It may also nurture and encourage the development of unique tailor-made cultural interventions. The limited dissemination of ideographic research among practitioners perhaps goes some way to explaining why organisations have generally experienced low rates of success when attempting to implement cultural change programmes.

CONCLUSIONS

The highly polarised nature of academic–practitioner research into organisational culture is not so evident in the study of personality. There is a dialogue, overlap and productive tension between the fields of clinical psychology and occupational psychology which brings a form of synergy to the study of personality. By contrast, there appears to be very little similar interaction between the ideographic–phenomenological position of anthropologists and the nomothetic–positivist stance of management theorists with regard to the study of organisational culture. The implications of this form of academic stand-off have been pointed out by Frost et al (1991: 7):

> Organizational culture researchers do not agree about what culture is or why it should be studied. They do not study the same phenomena. They do not approach the phenomena they do study from the same theoretical, epistemological, or methodological points of view. These fundamental disagreements have impeded the exchange of ideas and the ability to build upon others' empirical work. It has therefore been difficult to clarify what has been learned or how cultural studies contribute to other traditions of enquiry. No wonder, then, that research on organizational culture has sometimes been dismissed as a 'dead end', as unrelated to mainstream theory, or as a fad that has failed to deliver on its promises.

If we are to move beyond a vague, partial understanding of organisational culture, further collaborative, interdisciplinary research is required – work which challenges and transcends the established dominant paradigms. This is perhaps one of the main lessons that can be learnt from psychology.

REFERENCES

Adams, G.B. and Ingersoll, V.H. (1990) 'Painting over old works: the culture of organization in an age of technical rationality', in Turner, B.A. (ed) *Organizational Symbolism*. Berlin: Walter de Gruyter.

Aktouf, O. (1989) 'Corporate culture, the catholic ethic, and the spirit of capitalism: a Quebec experience', in Turner, B.A. (ed) *Organizational Symbolism*. Berlin: Walter de Gruyter.

Allport, G.W. (1937) *Personality: A Psychological Interpretation*. New York: Holt.

Barley, S.R. (1983) 'Semiotics and the study of occupational and organizational cultures', *Administrative Science Quarterly*, Vol. 28.

Barley, S.R., Meyer, G.W. and Gash, D.C. (1988) 'Cultures of culture: academics, practitioners and the pragmatics of control', *Administrative Science Quarterly*, Vol. 33.

Bridges, W. (1992) *The Character of Organizations*. Palo Alto, CA: Consulting Psychologists Press.

Brown, A.D. and Starkey, K. (1994) 'The effect of organisational culture on communication and information', *Journal of Management Studies*, Vol. 31, No. 6.

Bryman, A. (1991) 'Street corner society as a model for research into organizational culture', in Frost, P.J., Moore, L.F., Louis, M.R., Lundberg, C.C. and Martin, J. (eds) *Reframing Organizational Culture*. California: Sage.

Cooke, R.A. and Rousseau, D.M. (1988) 'Behavioural norms and expectations: a quantitative approach to the assessment of organizational culture', *Group and Organization Studies*, Vol. 12.

Cummings, T.G. and Huse, E.F. (1985) *Organization Development and Change*. 3th Edition, St Paul: West Publishing.

Czarniawska-Joerges, B. (1991) 'Culture is the medium of life', in Frost, P.J., Moore, L.F., Louis, M.R., Lundberg, C.C. and Martin, J. (eds) *Reframing Organizational Culture*. California: Sage.

Dahler-Larsen, P. (1994) 'Corporate culture and morality: Durkheim-inspired reflections on the limits of corporate culture', *Journal of Management Studies*, Vol. 31, No. 1.

Deal, T. and Kennedy, A. (1982) *Corporate Cultures*. Reading, Mass.: Addison-Wesley.

Denison, D.R. (1990) *Corporate Culture and Organizational Effectiveness*. New York: Wiley.

Edgren, L.D. (1989), 'The commando model: a way to gather and interpret cultural data', in Turner, B.A. (ed) *Organizational Symbolism*. Berlin: Walter de Gruyter.

Eysenck, H.J. (1947) *Dimensions of Personality*. London: Routledge and Kegan Paul.

Finkelstein, E. (1989) 'Culture and crisis management in an English prison', in Turner, B.A. (ed) *Organizational Symbolism*. Berlin: Walter de Gruyter.

Frost, P.J., Moore, L.F., Louis, M.R., Lundberg, C.C. and Martin, J. (eds) (1991) *Reframing Organizational Culture*. California: Sage.

Gagliardi, P. (1986) 'The creation and change of organizational cultures: a conceptual framework', *Organization Studies*, Vol. 7, No. 2.

Hampden-Turner, C. (1992) *Creating Corporate Culture: From Discord to Harmony*. Reading, Mass.: Addison-Wesley.

Handy, C. (1978) *The Gods of Management*. London: Souvenir Press.

Harrison, R. (1993) *Diagnosing Organizational Culture*. San Diego: Pfieffer.

Hellriegel, D., Slocum, J.W. and Woodman, R.W. (1992) *Organizational Behavior*. 6th Edition, St Paul: West Publishing.

Hofstede, G., Neuijen, B., Ohayv, D.D. and Sanders, G. (1990) 'Measuring organizational culture: a qualitative and quantitative study across twenty cases', *Administrative Science Quarterly*, Vol. 35.

Huczynski, A.A. and Buchanan, D.A. (1991) *Organisational Behaviour: An Introductory Text*. 2nd Edition, Hemel Hempstead: Prentice-Hall.

Ingersoll, V.H. and Adams, G.B. (1992) *The Tacit Organization*. Greenwich, CT: JAI Press.

Jermier, J.M. (1991) 'Critical epistemology and the study of organizational culture: reflections on street corner society', in Frost, P.J., Moore, L.F., Louis, M.R., Lundberg, C.C. and Martin, J. (eds) *Reframing Organizational Culture*. California: Sage.

Johnson, M. (1987) *The Body in the Mind: The Bodily Basis of Meaning, Imagination, and Reason*. Chicago: University of Chicago Press.

Jones, G.R. (1983) 'Transaction costs, property rights, and organizational culture: an exchange perspective', *Administrative Science Quarterly*, Vol. 28.

Jung, C.G. (1933) *Psychological Types*. New York: Harcourt.

Kagan, J. and Havemann, E. (1976) *Psychology: An Introduction*. 3rd Edition, New York: Harcourt Brace Jovanovich.

Kahle, E. (1989) 'Interrelations between corporate culture and municipal culture', in Turner, B.A. (ed) *Organizational Symbolism*. Berlin: Walter de Gruyter.

Kelley, H.H. (1973) 'The process of causal attribution', *American Psychologist*, Vol. 28.

Kelly, G.A. (1955) *The Psychology of Personal Constructs: Vols 1 and 2*. New York: Norton.

Kilmann, R.H. and Saxton, M.J. (1983) *Kilmann–Saxton Culture Gap Survey*. Pittsburgh: Organizational Design Consultants.

Kluckhohn, C. and Murray, H.A. (1948) 'Personality formation: the determinants', in Kluckhohn, C. and Murray, H.A. (eds) *Personality*. New York: Knopf.

Kotter, J.P. and Heskett, J.L. (1992) *Corporate Culture and Performance*. New York: Free Press.

Lakoff, G. (1987) *Women, Fire, and Dangerous Things*. Chicago: University of Chicago Press.

Lakoff, G. and Johnson, M. (1980) *Metaphors We Live By*. Chicago: University of Chicago Press.

Louis, M.R. (1983) 'Organizations as culture-bearing milieux', in Pondy, L.R., Frost, P.J., Morgan, G. and Dandridge, T. (eds) *Organizational Symbolism*. Greenwich, CT: JAI Press.

Luthans, F. and Davis, T.R.V. (1982) 'An ideographic approach to organisational behavior research', *Academy of Management Review*, Vol. 7.

Maddi, S.R. (1980) *Personality Theories: A Comparative Analysis*. 4th Edition, Homewood: Dorsey.

Martin, J. (1992) *Culture in Organisations: Three Perspectives*. New York: Oxford University Press.

Martin, J. and Siehl, C. (1983) 'Organizational culture and counter-culture: an uneasy symbiosis', *Organization Dynamics*, Vol. 12.

McDonald, P. (1988) 'The Los Angeles Olympic organizing committee: developing organizational culture in the short run', in Jones, M.O., Moore, M.D. and Snyder, R.C. (eds) *Inside Organizations*. California: Sage.

Meyerson, D.E. (1991) 'Normal ambiguity? A glimpse of an occupational culture', in Frost, P.J., Moore, L.F., Louis, M.R., Lundberg, C.C. and Martin, J. (eds) *Reframing Organizational Culture*. California: Sage.

Morea, P. (1990) *Personality*. London: Penguin.

Ortony, A. (1975) 'Why metaphors are necessary and not just nice', *Educational Theory*, Vol. 25, No. 1.

Ouchi, W. (1979) *Theory Z: How American Business Can Meet the Japanese Challenge*. Reading, MA: Addison-Wesley.

Pascale, R. and Athos, A. (1981) *The Art of Japanese Management*. New York: Simon and Schuster.

Peters, T. and Austin, N. (1985) *A Passion for Excellence*. New York: Random House.

Peters, T. and Waterman, R. (1982) *In Search of Excellence*. New York: Harper and Row.

Robbins, S. (1989) *Organizational Behaviour: Concepts, Controversies, and Applications*. Englewood Cliffs, NJ: Prentice-Hall.

Rogers, C.R. (1947) 'Some observations on the organization of personality', *American Psychologist*, Vol. 2.

Sackmann, S.A. (1991) *Cultural Knowledge in Organizations: Exploring the Collective Mind*. California: Sage.

Sathe, V. (1983) 'Implications of corporate culture: a manager's guide to action', *Organization Dynamics*, Vol. 12.

Schein, E.H. (1985) *Organizational Culture and Leadership*. San Francisco: Jossey-Bass.

Schneider, B., Gunnarson, S.K. and Niles-Jolly, K. (1994) 'Creating the climate and culture of success', *Organization Dynamics*, Vol. 23.

Schwartz, H. and Davis, S. (1981) 'Matching corporate culture and business strategy', *Organization Dynamics*, Vol. 10.

Smircich, L. (1983) 'Studying organizations as cultures', in Morgan, G. (ed) *Beyond Method*. California: Sage.

Trice, H.M. and Beyer, J.M. (1984) 'Studying organizational cultures through rites and ceremonials', *Academy of Management Review*, Vol. 9, No. 4.

Trompenaars, F. (1993) *Riding the Waves of Culture*. London: Nicholas Brealey.

Turner, B.A. (ed) (1990) *Organizational Symbolism*. Berlin: Walter de Gruyter.

Young, E. (1991) 'On the naming of the rose: interests and multiple meanings as elements of organizational culture', in Frost, P.J., Moore, L.F., Louis, M.R., Lundberg, C.C. and Martin, J. (eds) *Reframing Organizational Culture*. California: Sage.

CHAPTER 8

English football as a metaphor for organisational change

Graeme Currie and Maire Kerrin

INTRODUCTION

In this chapter football is used as a metaphorical vehicle for exploring organisational change. It aims to engage the manager's and academic's imagination and creativity in an arena which removes them from the blinkered view they may take of the workplace. Paradoxically, some football managers may find that certain benefits can be gleaned from reversing the metaphor, i.e. does the process of organisational change offer fresh insights into the management and development of football teams?

The manner in which the football metaphor is enlisted here is in line with the argument that the major advantage of metaphors is often said to be their generative power, their ability to open up creativity and new insights (Czarniawska-Joerges, 1988; Morgan, 1980; Schon, 1979). The works of Morgan (1980, 1986) have provided a focus on the interest expressed in metaphors as a vehicle for organisational analysis. Morgan (1980: 607) states: 'Schools of thought in social science, those communities of theorists subscribing to relatively coherent perspectives, are based upon the acceptance and use of different kinds of metaphor as a foundation for inquiry.' In later work he states: 'Metaphor is often just regarded as a device for establishing discourse, but its significance is much greater than this. For the case of metaphor implies a way of thinking and a way of seeing which pervade how we understand our world generally.' (Morgan, 1986)

Alvesson (1993) suggested: 'A metaphor is created when a term is carried over from one system or level of meaning to another, thereby illuminating some central aspects of the latter (and shadowing other aspects). A metaphor allows an object to be perceived and understood from the viewpoint of another object.' Within the typologies developed by Alvesson, then the use of football as a metaphor is of the *second level*. It falls within the idea of viewing the organisation as a game (Crozier, 1985; Crozier and Friedberg, 1980), and is similar in its application and the way that it sees the explanation of the various work arrangements and social relations in the various units.

Metaphors will be used by the authors to show the possibility for change, utilising case studies, one manufacturing based and the other a district health authority. The notion that metaphor can be used as a method for diagnosis and planned change in organisations is perhaps the most common conceptualisation of the function of metaphor in organisational change, as outlined by Marshak (1993). For Marshak, metaphors can provide opportunities to prepare for change, to align in relation to it, or to confuse and mislead managerial and organisational understanding of change. Potentially, metaphor can be used to lead towards some form of organisational transformation (Sackmann, 1989).

For the authors, metaphor is used to illustrate organisational variables which come together under the headings of human resource management or Organisation Development as interventions in transforming organisations.

In the manufacturing case study, it was reported that Japanese managers working as internal consultants frequently used metaphors when illustrating problems in the organisation. For instance, they used the concept of a train to illustrate that all stress should not be placed on the engine but should be distributed along the carriages, and that this is a metaphor for organisational stresses. Aspects of 'Japanisation' are often taken as best practice, and hence notice should be taken of their use of metaphors as further reinforcing the value of metaphors in the management of change. Another example of a metaphor in the same case study was one whereby the manufacturing director likened the role of cell leaders to that of a player–manager in a football team, leading by example rather than being standoffish as some traditional football and manufacturing managers have been.

FOOTBALL: AN APPROPRIATE METAPHOR?

Some readers may not take to football as a metaphor because of their lack of interest in the game. However, the fact remains that around 20 million spectators attend Premier and Endsleigh league matches in England each season. Players invade the living rooms of those who don't even profess to be fans. You are likely to find games on two channels every Sunday, live European games midweek and two football highlights programmes every week. Twenty five million people in Great Britain, half of them women, saw Gascoigne weep as England lost that 1990 World Cup semi-final to West Germany. A report collated by the Sir Norman Chester Centre for Football Research at Leicester University (1994), as reported in *FourFourTwo* (1994) found that overall, one in ten Premier League fans earned over £30 000 per year and one in five over £20 000 per year. As James Walvin (1994) points out, the game has moved on from the terraces and its working class support. It can be argued that increasingly football spectators and television viewers are those who have an interest in the workplace as managers of change, and it is those at whom this chapter is aimed.

In using football as a metaphor, the authors hope to provide the right mix of similarity and difference between the 'source domain' and the focal one. As Alvesson (1993) suggested: 'Too much or too little similarity means that the point might not be understood and no successful metaphor will have been created.'

Football metaphors are often used in everyday life and language. We have sports celebrity endorsement of non-sporting products: Jack Charlton and Shredded Wheat, Kevin Keegan and Brut. Politicians have used football metaphors: Douglas Hurd is a safe pair of hands, Michael Heseltine isn't a team player, at Warrington the IRA scored an own goal. As Tom Shone (1994) suggests, the language the politicians and advertisers use, because they are both interested in pure persuasion, is the easiest rhetorical means to hand. Similarly, in analysing organisational change the authors use football as a metaphorical exploration of the subject.

Indeed, the recognition of football as a reflection of events in wider society is noted by Tom Shone who quotes Nick Hornby as stating: 'Anyone looking for a handy lazy symbol of our post-war decline can always rely on our international side to provide it. You need a weak and feeble football manager [Graham Taylor] to dramatise the plight of a weak and feeble Prime Minister? No problem.'

In taking a journey through English football, a metaphor will be provided for organisational change required in UK companies in the face of increasing international competition. For emergent African footballing nations read the tiger economies of the Pacific Rim countries.

CONTRASTING STYLES OF FOOTBALL AND CHANGE

In line with the increasing globalisation of business, it is appropriate to use metaphors of the international comparison of football styles across the globe. Of particular interest as a metaphor are the Dutch and English systems of football, as outlined by Kuper (1994). The Dutch system can be regarded as a 'benchmark' in the same way that the Japanese are regarded in manufacturing. Kuper reported that Ogechukwu, a Nigerian at a Dutch club, was surprised that the coach did not say much and that it was always the players who were talking. The Dutch players advise their managers on tactics and team selection. The AC Milan manager Arrigo Sacchi stated that the Dutch internationals Ruud Guillit, Frank Rijkaard and Marco Van Basten had given him 'new ideas and views', and he said that it was largely down to them that 'a new style was introduced that diverged from the traditional, Italian mode of thought and style of play' (Kuper, 1994: 94). If this is compared to Great Britain, and we make the assumption that Scottish football is of a similar nature to English, then Hans Gilhaus stated about British football: 'As a footballer there, you're just a number and you do what the boss says. That's what you call the manager: "Boss"' (Kuper, 1994: 94).

Kuper's interpretation of Dutch football was that it is successful because the Dutch footballer talks so much. The English method barely gives players a chance to argue: there is simply no debate. Whereas the 20-year-old Dutch footballer assumes that he is as likely to have the truth as his manager, the British view is that the manager is the manager.

Bobby Robson, when interviewed by *World Soccer* (Kuper, 1994: 96), provided an interesting comment when comparing the two styles: 'The players are all much more interested over there [the Netherlands] in tactics – how we play and how we change things.' PSV Eindhoven's full-back, whom Robson managed, told Nieuwe Revu, 'Robson's a nice man, really a very nice man. But the only thing he taught me in two years was English' (Kuper, 1994: 96). Helenio Herrera, the man who taught the world how to play defensive football in the 1960s, told Kuper (1994: 82) that 'when it came to modern football, the Britons missed the evolution'.

When we draw on the above as a metaphor, and embed it in the two case studies, then the following is suggested. If English football is to introduce organisational change in a similar fashion as the manufacturing industry, the multi-functional team/player approach which adapts to the formation of the opposing team and has been successfully developed in the Netherlands may be the way forward. The use of such a style of football permeates the language of Dutch coaches when discussing football tactics, to the extent that they describe the style as 'structured flexibility'. This is similar to manufacturing attempts to develop a multi-skilled labour force which can be deployed to any area of the factory when they are needed. An important part of Dutch football, which is taught at an early age, is the ability to understand what your nearest team-mates are thinking and how the game appears from their position. Exactly the same is true in the case study of the manufacturing company where management are teaching operatives through job rotation and multi-skilling how the 'game' appears to other workers. This enables workers to understand how their actions in one position affect another operator in another part of the factory and so reduce mistakes and cover-ups.

Within manufacturing the need to change to multi-functional teams was a reaction to international market pressures whereby companies needed to rationalise labour and create new ways of working to stay competitive. Much of this has emerged in the form of business process re-engineering and lean production. In terms of the Health Service change has come about through the Government White Paper *Working for Patients* (1988) and 'The Griffiths Report' (Griffiths, 1988) which call for a more efficient and effective service. The style of football known as 'total football' (demonstrated by the Dutch model) can be used to symbolise the need to reduce functional interfaces in the manufacturing case and the move towards multi-disciplinary and multi-agency teamwork in the health authority case.

INSULARITY IN UK FOOTBALL AND ORGANISATIONS

The extent to which English football is insular is revealed by a quote from Brian Clough to Kuper (1994: 108): 'If the African nations get their way, and only one British team plays in tournaments in future, I think I'll vote Conservative. Think about it, a bunch of spear-throwers who want to dictate our role in football. They still eat each other up.' Here, an extremely racist comment is expressed by an admired former domestic team manager and one which flies in the face of African teams' success in the 1990 World Cup (Cameroon) and 1994 World Cup (Nigeria). In a similar vein, the research carried out in the manufacturing organisation revealed that the skilled blue-collar element of the workforce were critical of Japanese managers who when visiting the plant gave constructive criticism about how processes and tasks were carried out. The UK skilled blue-collar workers regarded themselves in this case as a benchmark for the rest of the world and felt aggrieved that Japanese managers should be telling them how to do their jobs.

'There's still an idea here in Europe that Africans can't do anything better than the whites,' complained Alloy Ago, the keeper of Nigeria who plays for Club Liège in Belgium (Kuper, 1994: 102). In fact, as Professor Paul Nkwi explained to Kuper, Cameroonian football, reflecting African football in general, has combined the high balls of the British and the small passes of the French and Germans. This is paralleled by the development of a Japanese style in manufacturing utilising Western techniques such as those of Total Quality espoused by Deming, and outlined in, for example, Gabor (1990).

The insularity of British footballers and their unwillingness to learn is further revealed by the lack of success which British footballers have experienced as expensive imports in Italy. Kuper reported Ian Rush as having left Juventus after two sorry years saying: 'It was like playing in another country'; while Luther Blissett at AC Milan complained: 'No matter how much money you've got, you can't seem to get any Rice Crispies'. During his time at Lazio, Paul Gascoigne learnt little Italian and his public behaviour was often at odds with Italian expectations, such as the incident where he belched at Italian journalists.

As a metaphor for organisational change, the suggestions that English football needs to move towards a more European or Continental way of playing football (that is, short passes working the ball through midfield, as opposed to the long ball from defence to attack) is a reflection of the current change occurring within the two case study organisations. Indeed, the call for change in English football has intensified since England failed to qualify for the World Cup finals in America, and is thought to be due to the football industry being in desperate need of 'cultural cleansing' (*The Guardian*, January 1994). In *Newsnight* of the same week, the then CBI Director-General Howard Davis likened the condition of English football in the 1990s to that of British industry in the 1970s:

> **It is internationally uncompetitive, suffers from chronic over-capacity, is riven by demoralising disputes – and there is too much control by amateurs. Rather than address its real problems football's response is always to repackage itself without changing anything.**

Hence the absurd reorganisation of the English League, in which only the names are changed, reminiscent of the endless rebranding of the British car industry; hence the greater attention given to the remarketing of the England strip than to the style of football they play. Here, Davis uses football as a metaphor for the changes in British manufacturing in the past few decades. He suggests that manufacturing has begun to be proactive by changing the system of production and the way people work as a response to the international market and the growing competitive threat from Japan. This image of British manufacturing in the 1970s and English football in the 1990s is one of poor organisational self-image, a factor which may affect football's ability to understand and manage organisational change. The crisis in British manufacturing in the 1970s made the industry look at itself and initiate a reorganisation, something which English football needs to do in the 1990s if it is to compete within its own marketplace.

It may be the case that the arrival of Terry Venables as manager of England suggests that lessons from other countries will be taken on board. A football magazine, *FourFourTwo* (Blair, 1994), provides some substance for this in an interview with 'El Tel'. He is labelled as the 'thinking man's football manager', and was quoted as stating that he would like England to play like Brazil. This at least is a pleasant change for an England manager. His illustrious predecessor, Sir Alf Ramsey, remarked after the 1970 World Cup: 'We have nothing to learn from the Brazilians.' Against Norway, Venables persevered with the so-called 'Christmas tree' formation (one up front, two behind the striker, three in midfield and four in defence). However, in the interview with *FourFourTwo* he stated, 'I don't want to be rigid with one system. I'm looking forward to being able to change whenever necessary. We have the players to be able to do that, players who are adaptable, and who work hard to win.'

Given what has been presented earlier in this chapter, the adaptability of the players is questionable. Some months on, in the game against Nigeria, the selection of Wise – not regarded as an adaptable, creative player over Le Tissier who is – revealed the direction in which Venables' England is heading. *The Independent on Sunday* (Ridley, 1994) suggests that those who expected Venables to liberate the free spirits of the English game are likely to be left disappointed. Wise was a winner who could not easily be knocked off the ball, a player who robbed people in dangerous areas and kept possession. The pragmatism of Venables is illustrated by the fact that he was quoted as being impressed with the statistic that Wise had found another white (English) shirt with 39 out of the 45 passes he made.

SELECTION AND CONTINGENT STRATEGIES

The emphasis put on selection is evident in football, and provides a metaphor for the case studies. Graham Taylor, a former England manager, seemed to think that anyone over 30 was finished. Ron Atkinson, former manager at Aston Villa, during his time there seemed to prefer 'older' players. At Aston Villa, he transferred out many of the players he inherited and brought in new ones. Terry Venables, on taking over, picked older players such as Peter Beardsley who had been discarded under the old regime. Decisions such as these often revolved around the key area of midfield. In the case studies, key positions were seen as cell leaders in the manufacturing case and neighbourhood health team managers in the health authority case. As key positions, particularly in the manufacturing case study, sophisticated selection techniques were used. In place of the traditional interview an assessment centre was used, consisting of the interview supplemented by psychometric tests and group activities, using an external consultant who had formerly worked for Toyota. In the manufacturing and health authority cases, there were difficulties in recruiting a person with the right characteristics. Football and the England International football team have provided a metaphor for this in the difficulties of finding the right midfield player. The cell leaders and neighbourhood health team managers are the midfield of their respective organisations.

If we move on to another key actor in the English football game, Charles Hughes (FA coaching director), then we find another metaphor for issues of organisational change. Hughes is a proponent of the long ball game, a type of play which is associated with the English way and seen as unsuccessful at international level. However, in England's qualifying group for the 1994 World Cup Finals, Norway easily won the group utilising the diagonal 40-yard lofted pass into the penalty area as part of their winning formula. Contingency theory should be adopted in taking account of contextual variables in deciding on a solution. What doesn't work for English football might work for Norwegian football. In a similar vein, Aston Villa, supported by one of the authors, have resorted to the long ball game in the face of deteriorating results and confidence. Most of the time in the 1994/95 season this has resulted in the ball coming straight back at them, putting their defence under considerable pressure. Eventually, this leads to their conceding goals. This might suggest that the long ball game is unsuccessful and should not be used as a strategy to overcome opposition. However, against Tottenham Hotspur (November 1994), with the final whistle nearing and the score at 3–3, Parker hit a 35-yard crossfield ball to Houghton, who knocked it first time down the line 20 yards to Saunders who beat a Tottenham defender and scored the winner. Here, the long ball worked, even for Aston Villa, a struggling managerless team at the time. What we might draw from this as managers and academics concerned with organisational change is that there is no one sure-fire solution to a problem.

Regarding one of the research sites in which the authors have been involved, it was the case that competency-based management development had been adopted. One of the objectives of this, at least implicitly, was to contribute towards organisational change. After two years, in which not one person had obtained their NVQ Level 4 qualification through this programme, the organisation was reverting back to the 'old way of doing things'. Competency-based management development was being consigned to the bottom drawer; another 'flavour of the month', an initiative that was seen as 'not working'. When the reasons for its lack of success are analysed, it is found that it was adopted at an inappropriate time; that is, a period of restructuring and large-scale redundancies in the organisation. It was also implemented in an inappropriate way. It ignored overall business strategy and other human resource initiatives, as well as dismissing considerations of ownership by participants. In other organisations, competency-based management development initiatives have been implemented successfully (Greatrex and Phillips, 1989; McNichol, 1994). There is a direct parallel between discussions of the long ball game and the adoption of competency-based management development programmes, in that they should be implemented appropriately taking account of contextual variables.

TEAMWORK AND TEAM DEVELOPMENT

The interview with Charles Hughes in *FourFourTwo* (Lawrence, 1994) reveals other interesting statements about football which provide a metaphor for organisational change. He states:

Of primary importance in the basic tactics and coaching at international level is the developing of teamwork. Understanding between groups of players (the back four/midfield unit/attacking unit) is essential. They have to know how best to work together to co-ordinate into an effective unit. The more you chop and change, the more difficult it is to achieve that. It is imperative to stick to one method of playing. If you can't make up your mind about the method of play, compounded with you can't make up your mind about the choice of players, that is the worst case scenario for the development of the team. Therein lies the root of failure. (Lawrence, 1994: 77)

In terms of organisational change issues this touches on team structure, team development and team selection allied to strategic direction, reflecting general organisational behaviour concepts such as balance of team roles as espoused by Belbin (1981), and the stages of team development (Tuckman and Jensen, 1977).

In the case studies a metaphor can be drawn. In the health authority a decision was made, initiated by the Government White Paper (1988) and 'The Griffiths Report' (1988), to provide community health care in a neighbourhood basis using multi-disciplinary, multi-agency teams. Management development trainers, a role in which one of the researchers was employed, had to facilitate the implementation of the concept. This was done by the team identifying their objectives and their roles connected to this, utilising an in-tray exercise. This was aimed at moving the team towards balanced roles and through the initial stages of Tuckman and Jensen's model, focusing on clear objectives. Reversing the metaphor, then football in England could learn from gaining the commitment of the team members via this process. The above might happen in the Netherlands where the players are allowed their say, but in England decisions are imposed on team members.

In the manufacturing case study, 'understanding between groups of players and the working together to co-ordinate into an effective unit' provides a metaphor for the adoption of cell manufacturing. In both cases, as Charles Hughes suggests for football, you must make up your mind about the choice of players, which brings us back to the importance of selection. For Dennis Wise or Matt Le Tissier, read Joe or Josephine for cell leader, and Anne or Andy for neighbourhood community health team manager.

The process of culture change does not solely rely on selection but includes socialisation as an element. Thus, Hughes sees education as a priority. In the organisational context, training and development of the human resource are seen as priorities. This is reflected in government initiatives such as 'Investors in People', and academic debate around the concept of 'human resource management'. In football, Hughes sees the need to develop players with the right qualities to handle the pressures and adapt to international football temperamentally and psychologically. He suggests that there is a progression from under-15 to full international level, with young players gaining experience of different styles, temperaments and cultures.

However, in football as in the UK organisational arena, there is short-termism. Many managers of football teams do not pursue long-term strategies to develop youth teams, that is, home-grown players, but buy in players at extortionate fees. The role of the manager in this youth development depends on his job security and how success is measured at the club. For example, the emergence of Manchester United's young players in the 1994/95 European Cup campaign comes from the manager's input and work in this area. This stems from his security in his position at Old Trafford so that he can have long-term strategic plans which are now coming to fruition.

THE IMPLICATIONS FOR ORGANISATIONS

The notion of short-termism, as outlined above, has parallels in manufacturing in the UK where change is carried out by managers looking for short-term results which will enhance their career prospects. By the time the impact of their change has occurred they have left for a higher position either within the firm or outside. This is in contrast to the Japanese system where managers do not move around so much and are aware of the long-term effects of any change strategy. Again reversing the metaphor, perhaps there is a need for change within the management structure of football clubs so that long-term strategies can be developed and fulfilled.

In the case studies, management development in its content and mode of delivery, both explicitly and implicitly, is intended to have an impact on organisational culture as well as increasing competence. In the health authority, negotiating skills and financial budgeting skills modules are intended to emphasise business management rather than a professional management ethos; and problem-solving modules promote a participative decision-making model reflective of an organisational desire to move to multi- disciplinary teamworking compared to traditional hierarchical clinical ways of working.

In the manufacturing case, the content of competency-based management development around the NVQ framework includes a significant element of continuous problem solving. The self-managed learning which goes with this framework also encourages the continuing learning ethos. This supports the organisation's desire to obtain Investors In People (IIP) status and become what is termed a 'learning organisation'.

In broad terms, much of the preceding discussion about football provides a metaphor for the academic debate about organisational culture change (Ogbonna, 1992; Meek, 1992). Within the health service, research examining the constraints of culture on behaviour changes (Currie, 1994) suggested that only incremental behaviour changes were possible within a professional bureaucracy. Radical behaviour changes, such as participative decision-making styles, were not adopted. In the manufacturing case, tasks and roles were changed with little attention being paid to human resource management and culture change (Currie and Kerrin, 1994), yet success ensued, at least in the short term. However, there are doubts as to whether this strategy can be continued.

This research is mirrored by others, such as Brooks and Bate (1994) who, in examining culture in the British Civil Service, talked of a change *in* culture rather than a change *of* culture. What chance would radical change have in the English game where a new manager, Steve McMahon, on taking over his charges at Swindon Town, was quoted in *The Guardian* as saying that the team played pretty-pretty, namby-pamby football and it needed to change? Similarly in many manufacturing companies such machismo exists.

As an additional point in the discussion, what Hughes relies on for his views, as quoted in *FourFourTwo* (Lawrence, 1994), is hard data – and this is similar to Venables, who talks of passes to team-mates provided by Wise when playing for England. 'If you score first, you have a 90 per cent chance of not losing the game and an 80 per cent chance of winning', 'In USA 1994, 34 per cent of goals had an element of dribbling in them', and '45 per cent of all goals come from set plays' are figures Hughes comes out with off the top of his head. This provides a metaphor for the use of information in the case studies. In a tour of the plant at the manufacturing site, there are visual displays of data in each cell relating to Statistical Process Control (SPC), absenteeism, training records. In the health authority, information against government performance indicators is readily quoted, and neighbourhood profiles were drawn up by the newly formed multi-disciplinary community team as the basis for prioritising health care. Again reversing the metaphor, whereas in the organisations studied team members gathered and collected data, in football the 'manager' carried out the task and used the information to impose strategy on the team members.

CONCLUSIONS

What can we learn from football as a metaphor? Is it a metaphor for organisational change? Perhaps it is of interest to ask what can football learn from organisations. Organisational change in companies can provide lessons for football by taking on concepts used in management, such as continuous improvement, and applying them to football management. Within Rugby Union the new England manager uses management practices that are successful in his role as chief executive of a multi-million pound company and transfers this to the England training group. Rugby is an amateur sport, but here the connection between sport and business organisations has been sought. This type of move in rugby reflects the calls for a forward-looking business brain to take charge of English football to provide a product people want at a price they can afford.

A final comment on the wider scope of football as a metaphor lies within the political debate. As has been noted recently, our political debate and our footballing debate sound strangely similar. Both deal with the same identity crisis in terms of change. Should we be at the heart of Europe or not? In politics John Major argues that his policies are working. In football, however, failure tends to be starkly clear, and for now the Eurosceptics have lost (with the sacking of Graham Taylor). In contrast, Terry Venables, the newly appointed England manager, is described as a 'Europhile' while still retaining his 'Cockney Englishness'. Even his nickname, 'El Tel', provides evidence of his affiliation to Europe along with his experience of managing Barcelona. This political metaphor outlines the different sets of interests, conflicts and power plays that shape organisational activities and reflects the current struggle within English football as to how the national team should play.

To conclude and draw the discussion together, the debate about the way English football is played and organised provides a metaphor for what has happened, what is happening and what needs to happen in UK organisations. The themes explored have been international comparisons of styles, the amount of 'player' involvement, the insular nature of the English 'game' in football and organisations, the importance of selection and team development, the use of hard data, and finally the appropriateness of a contingency approach to problem solving. All of these themes are part of a wider debate about the manipulation of culture, the English football style and strategy providing a metaphor for traditional UK organisational styles and strategies.

It is hoped that what has been provided is a vehicle to engage the manager's and academic's imagination and creativity in handling organisational change issues. In addition what has come out in this discussion is a reversal of the metaphor. For those readers engaged in football team management, organisational change may provide a vehicle for consideration in assessing football styles and strategies.

REFERENCES

Alvesson, M. (1993) 'The play of metaphors', in Hassard, J. and Parker, M. (eds) *Postmodernism and Organizations*. Newbury Park, CA: Sage.
Belbin, E.M. (1981) *Management Teams: Why They Succeed or Fail*. London: Heinemann.

Blair, O. (1994) 'Kiss and tell: Terry Venables', *FourFourTwo*, September.

Brooks, I. and Bate, P. (1994) 'The problems of effecting change within the British civil service: a cultural perspective', *British Journal of Management*, Vol. 5.

Crozier, N. (1985) 'Comparing structures and comparing games', in Pugh, D.S. (ed) *Organisation Theory*. Harmondsworth: Penguin.

Crozier, N. and Friedberg, E. (1980) *Actors and Systems*. Chicago, IL: University of Chicago Press.

Currie, G. (1994) 'Teambuilding training in a clinical environment', *Journal of Managerial Psychology*, Vol. 9, No. 3.

Currie, G. and Kerrin, M. (1994) 'Implementation of JIT/TQ and associated human resource strategies: a case study.' Paper presented at the *Strategic Direction of Human Resource Management Conference*, Nottingham, December.

Czarniawska-Joerges, B. (1988) *To Coin a Phrase*. Stockholm: Study of Power and Democracy in Sweden.

FourFourTwo (1994) 'Old People are Terribly Fond of the Saints', *FourFourTwo*, October.

Gabor, A. (1990) *The Man Who Discovered Quality*. New York: Times Books.

Government White Paper (1988) *Working for Patients*. London: HMSO.

Greatrex, J. and Phillips, P. (1989) 'Oiling the wheels of competence', *Personnel Management*, August.

Griffiths, R. (1988) *Community Care – Agenda for Action*. London: HMSO.

Kuper, S. (1994) *Football Against the Enemy*. London: Orion.

Lawrence, A. (1994) 'That was route one', *FourFourTwo*, October.

Marshak, R.J. (1993) 'Managing the metaphors of change', *Organization Dynamics*, Vol. 22, No. 1.

McNichol, B. (1994) 'Right chemistry for developing NVQs', *Personnel Management*, May.

Meek, V.L. (1992) 'Organisation culture – origins and weaknesses', *Organisation Studies*, Vol. 9, No. 4.

Morgan, G. (1980) 'Paradigms, metaphors and puzzle-solving in organizational theory', *Administrative Science Quarterly*, Vol. 25.

Morgan, G. (1986) *Images of Organization*. Newbury Park, CA: Sage.

Ogbonna, E. (1992) 'Organisation culture and human resource management: dilemmas and contradictions', in Blyton, P. and Turnbull, P. (eds) *Reassessing Human Resource Management*. London: Sage.

Ridley, I. (1994) 'Wise man of substance', *The Independent on Sunday*, 20th November.

Sackmann, S. (1989) 'The role of metaphors in organisation transformation', *Human Relations*, Vol. 42, No. 6.

Schon, D.A. (1979) 'Generative metaphor: a perspective on problem-setting in social policy', in Ortony, A. (ed) *Metaphor and Thought*. Cambridge: Cambridge University Press.

Shone, T. (1994) 'It's a whole new ball game', *Sunday Times*, 29th May.

Tuckman, B. and Jensen, N. (1977) 'Stages of small group development revisited', *Group and Organisational Studies*, Vol. 2.

Walvin, J. (1994) *The People's Game: The History of Football Revisited*. London: Mainstream.

PART III

The intervention process

INTRODUCTION

The intervention process in OD can be seen as commencing with a diagnosis of problems, identifying changes required to address these problems and then putting the changes required into practice. Combined, the three chapters contained in this part of the book should give the reader an overall understanding of what the intervention process comprises and the role and impact of the actors involved in the process.

At a more specific level, each of the three chapters applies a metaphor to a particular facet of the intervention process. For example, Oswick in Chapter 9 examines the diagnostic phase of OD by comparing it to the visual process. To him, this metaphor operates at two levels. On the surface, likening the diagnostic phase to vision enables us to regard the consultant as the eyes, making sense of the situation they perceive at the client organisation. At a deeper, second level the metaphor is extended to take into account the possibility that vision can be distorted or obscured in a number of ways. Oswick's argument is that consultants as eyes are also subject to visual impediments and that these impediments can have a detrimental impact on the way they carry out their diagnosis. Moreover, if the diagnosis is flawed then one cannot be confident about the appropriateness and effectiveness of any changes suggested by the consultant in question.

Oswick's work suggests that we should pay special attention to the role of the OD consultant in the intervention process, and this is what Clark and Salaman do in Chapter 10. For them, existing OD literature is deficient in the way it examines the role of consultants and their relationship with their clients. It is deficient in that all too often it focuses either on the problems consultants are supposed to be able to resolve or on trying to describe the consultant as a professional expert. To Clark and Salaman, what is really needed in order to understand the true nature of consultancy work is a metaphor which explains how and why consultants are able to overcome what is probably their biggest problem – persuading clients of their value. The metaphor that is applied is of consultancy as a 'performance'. This provides us with a number of interesting insights, not least that the consultant has to involve the client in the performance in a way that arouses the client both emotionally and in terms of their actions and behaviour.

Consultants have been portrayed as agents of organisational change and it is the change process that Nic Beech analyses in Chapter 11. His application of the religious metaphor of change to the organisational setting allows us to make some valuable comparisons. To Beech, the process of organisational change can be equated to a process of religious conversion from one set of beliefs to another. For this to occur the discourse that dominates an organisation must alter and once accepted by the organisation's members it will go on to affect their actions and behaviour. A major strength of this metaphor is that it can be used to demonstrate the depth and extent of change that can occur within an organisation. By applying case study material to a fourfold typology of religious change, Beech shows that change can be confined to small numbers of, or even individual, organisational members, or that it can encompass all those involved in the organisation. Similarly, he shows that change can be revolutionary, i.e. that it can alter deeply rooted values and beliefs in a relatively short period of time, or that it can be incremental, slowly altering these values and beliefs over an extensive period. The problem for those managing the change, says Beech, is that different organisations and different organisational members fall into any of the four typologies at any one time. Thus a number of different change management styles are applicable to these different typologies. The challenge for management is to identify and apply the management style most appropriate for effecting the type of change for which they are striving.

CHAPTER 9

Insights into diagnosis: an exploration using visual metaphors

Cliff Oswick

INTRODUCTION

Many authors have discussed the way in which the diagnostic phase is a necessary stage of the OD process; however, most of the literature produced has tended to be of a prescriptive nature (see, for example, Cummings and Huse, 1989; French and Bell, 1990; Kotter, 1978; Lawrence and Lorsch, 1969). This perhaps reflects a perception of the make-up and needs of the target audience as primarily consisting of practising, or potential, consultants. In addition, the style of presentation is similar to that found in DIY (do-it-yourself) manuals for home improvements and car repairs – they tend to describe all of the components, to identify the tools required to carry out the task and to incorporate a sequential guide for action. Unfortunately, the overly optimistic stance which both DIY manuals and OD texts are inclined to adopt is heavily biased towards success. The underlying assumption is that everything will run smoothly and go exactly according to plan. This limits the inclusion of information on issues such as the dangers and pitfalls, spotting problems, why things might go wrong, and preventative and corrective action.

In the limited number of instances where the problems that can occur during diagnosis have been addressed, the emphasis has typically been on methodological issues pertaining to the appropriateness of different diagnostic frameworks and the relative merits of various data-gathering techniques such as interviews, questionnaires and secondary sources. Here, diagnostic problems are considered from a different viewpoint. The focus is a metaphorical examination of the diagnostic difficulties that arise owing to factors located within the client organisation, the abilities and approach of the consultant, and the interplay between the two parties. These issues have received far less literary attention; the work of Buchanan and Boddy (1992), Harvey and Brown (1992) and Pfeiffer and Jones (1976) are notable exceptions.

In this chapter the visual process is enlisted as a means of exploring the diagnostic phase of OD interventions. The use of metaphorical language, and more specifically visual terminology, has pervaded organisational discourse. In analysing organisational problems OD consultants and client representatives frequently resort to a repertoire of clichéd visual metaphors, such as 'seeing the wood for the trees', trying to hit 'a moving target', looking at 'the big picture', and the *post hoc* observation that 'hindsight is 20:20'. There are also examples of a more embedded, and less obvious, usage of the vision metaphor in diagnosis. When we talk of focusing on an issue, or illuminating a problem, we are using these concepts in a metaphorical rather than literal way. It could be argued that visual metaphors do not significantly contribute to our understanding of organisational processes. In effect, they primarily act as a form of literary embellishment. As such, they add weight to the school of thought which suggests that metaphors are merely 'dispensable literary devices' (Tsoukas, 1993).

Equally, it could be argued that the pervasiveness of visual language in the diagnostic phase of OD interventions perhaps indicates that it serves a different and more elaborate purpose; one which is more closely aligned to the notion that metaphors have a generative value (Schon, 1979).

Juxtaposing the fields of organisation development and ophthalmology is intended to stimulate a deeper understanding of the nature and complexity of diagnosis. In particular, visual metaphors are used as a vehicle for identifying and illuminating the intricacies and nuances of diagnostic problems.

DIAGNOSIS AS VISION

It is possible to think of the vision metaphor as operating at two levels. First, at a macro level the metaphor can be applied in a complete but necessarily broad fashion to OD. Second, it can move beyond this surface-level interpretation of metaphorical linkage and provide a more detailed analysis of the subject area by comparing and contrasting the sub-components of the visual and diagnostic processes.

The macro-level metaphor can be thought of as providing what Ortony (1975) has termed as vividness and compactness. This can be illustrated by the metaphor used by a comedian to describe his mother-in-law as looking like a 'bulldog chewing a wasp'. The image created is both compact and vivid in so far as it conveys a rich and detailed amount of information about the target (i.e. the mother-in-law) and manages to do so using only four words. It would be hard to generate the same level of insight using an equivalent volume of plain, rather than metaphorical, language. In a similar way, albeit not as colourfully, thinking of the diagnostic phase as merely constituting a way of seeing perhaps enables something of the Gestalt of the process to be understood. The eyes look at an object with a view to 'making sense of it'. At a broad level it is this process that the consultant seeks to apply to an organisation (or as it is more commonly termed in OD, the client system). It is possible to regard eyes as being analogous to an OD consultant and a visual target (or object) as comparable to a client system.

Similarities also exist between the visual image produced by the eye and the diagnosis made by a consultant. The eyes enable an image of the object to be produced which is processed by the brain. Both the eyes and the object are real in a physical sense, while the image is merely an interpretation of the object. A parallel process is found in OD. The consultant and the client system are real, but the diagnosis, like a visual image, is not real. It is effectively an intangible interpretation of something which does not materially exist.

It is this shift from the real to the interpretive which forms the basis for a secondary-level metaphorical analysis. Just as a visual image can become distorted or obscured, so too can a diagnosis. The inaccuracies and inconsistencies that can arise between an object and an image are attributable to physical defects and psychological impediments. In the field of ophthalmology these problems are acknowledged and well documented. For example, impaired or defective eyesight can be attributed to problems such as colour blindness, myopia, tunnel vision etc. In the field of OD diagnostic impediments are less well understood. In the remainder of this chapter the physiological and psychological aspects of vision are compared to aspects of the diagnostic process. This subsidiary level of analysis concentrates on matching various sub-components of the two disciplines; an approach which has been described as the application of 'second-order metaphors' (Alvesson, 1993). This is undertaken with a view to developing a better understanding of diagnostic issues and problems by drawing on areas of visual equivalence.

PHYSIOLOGICAL ASPECTS OF EYESIGHT AND THE OD PROCESS

Psychological aspects of eyesight relate primarily to the brain and the system of processing that it uses, including factors such as past experiences, values and attitudes – all of which can be applied to an object in order to arrive at a picture or image. Physical problems can relate to the brain (i.e. a lack of processing power), but are far more commonly located within the eyes. Table 9.1 provides a brief overview of the salient physical characteristics of eyesight and the corresponding diagnostic features, which are subsequently discussed in greater detail within this section.

Table 9.1 Physiological aspects of vision and diagnosis

Visual characteristics	Diagnostic attributes
Blind spot – an area in the eye where an image is not formed	*OD blind spot* – an area or aspect of the client system which is continually overlooked during diagnosis
Visual accommodation – ability to switch focus between near and distant objects	*OD accommodation* – the ability to recognise, and distinguish between, overt and covert organisational problems
Visual acuity – the end product of accommodation, a sharp image which is free from blurring	*Diagnostic acuity* – the objective of OD accommodation, a clear, sharp and complete diagnosis
Cones – part of the eye which enables sight in bright lights and provides coloured images	*Perceptual cones* – a consulting style used in situations of stability, high internal consistency or favourable circumstances
Rods – part of the eye which facilitates vision in dim light and provides black-and-white images	*Perceptual rods* – a consulting style suited to situations which are turbulent, hazy, ambiguous or adverse

OD blind spots

The existence of a blind spot in the eye can be equated to the diagnostic ability of the OD consultant, albeit that a visual blind spot is physical while an OD blind spot is primarily psychological. In visual terms a blind spot is located at the point where blood vessels and nerve fibres emerge from the optic nerve. It is effectively an area where an image is not formed, hence part of the visual object is not visible. Whenever the same viewing position is taken up the same portion of the object is unseen. In order to see the part of the object obscured by the blind spot it is necessary to adopt a different viewing position.

For the consultant, a blind spot can be described as an area of the client system which is consistently overlooked during the data-gathering phase of an OD intervention. Randomised inconsistencies in diagnosis are attributable to incompetence rather than a blind spot. It is the repeated failure to identify a specific area or avenue of investigation across a variety of assignments which constitutes a blind spot. For example, a consultant who has a strong inter-personal focus is likely to be very adept at identifying problems relating to interaction between various parties within the organisation (e.g. inter-group conflict, dysfunctional communication mechanisms, lack of team cohesiveness etc.). In addition, the consultant may be able to isolate other people-related problems which are in peripheral, but nevertheless related, domains of expertise (e.g. motivation, morale or culture problems). It is the inability to identify problems located in areas which are almost antipodal to the ones found in the area of expertise which creates a blind spot. In this instance, structural problems and technical difficulties (such as inappropriate lines of responsibility, overly narrow spans of control and poor job design) may well go unnoticed.

In short, just as all eyes have a blind spot so too do all consultants. OD blind spots are inevitable and somewhat unavoidable. It is impractical to expect any change agent to have a complete repertoire of skills and behavioural science knowledge. Every consultant will have some weaknesses and shortcomings and it is the most deficient of these areas which give rise to blind spots.

A further common facet of both optical and organisational blind spots is an accompanying lack of awareness of the problem. Atkinson et al (1993), when discussing the impact of blind spots on vision, have commented: 'we are not ordinarily aware of the blind spot. In effect, the visual system fills in the parts of the visual field that we are not sensitive to; thus, they appear like the surrounding field.' Arguably, this ability subliminally to 'fill in the missing bits' also extends to OD blind spots. Areas of the client system not put under the microscope are simply assumed to have the same, or at very least similar, problems as the areas which have been more thoroughly scrutinised.

It was suggested earlier that the only way to gain access to the part of the visual target hidden by a blind spot is to alter the viewing position. In a similar way, in order to overcome an OD blind spot the consultant has metaphorically to 'take up a new position'. This can be achieved by adopting a fresh approach or what Kuhn (1962) would describe as a 'paradigmatic shift'. An alternative is to take a step back from the immediate point of involvement and indulge in what the popular management literature has termed 'helicopter management'. The vertical take-off of a helicopter away from the ground enables a wider area of the ground to be seen. In a similar way, for a manager, or a consultant, a metaphorical movement upwards and away from immediate contact with a problem is suggested to provide a new viewing position. The problem can be viewed in a wider, possibly even different context and previously obscured problems can be observed.

Accommodation in vision and OD

Accommodation has been defined as a process by which the curvature of the eye lens is changed to enable the eyes to bring into focus objects positioned at varying distances. The primary purpose of accommodation is to provide visual acuity. If this process of switching from distant to near objects did not occur, either the objects close by or the ones far away would remain blurred, and therefore only a partial picture could be created. OD initiatives frequently require a form of accommodation to ensure diagnostic acuity, i.e. a sharpness, clarity and completeness of understanding of the prevailing organisational problems.

If we think of organisational problems as being close or distant, then a mechanism which facilitates organisational accommodation becomes essential. Clearly, the difficulty with this analogy is the notion of distance as a means of isolating and distinguishing between client system problems (or symptoms). However, it is possible to substitute distance for profile, i.e. near objects equate to overt problems and distant objects equate to covert problems. In effect we can locate all organisational problems on an overt–covert continuum.

The significance of visible and hidden problems is well established in the OD literature. For example, the 'organisational iceberg' model provided by Selfridge and Sokolik (1975) highlights 'above the surface' and 'below the surface' factors. If you are in a ship approaching an iceberg the part above sea level is clearly visible from a distance. Similarly, parts of a client system are immediately visible on entering an organisation (e.g. the physical layout, the organisational structure, and the rules and regulations). Like the submerged part of the iceberg, certain aspects of an organisation are less visible. These covert elements typically include the political system, the organisational culture and employee attitudes. There appears to be a correlation between the overtness and the nature of a problem – overt factors tend to be hard in so far as they are generally quantifiable and tangible, while the covert factors are inclined to be soft and behavioural, and therefore more subjective and intangible.

It is important for consultants to be able to distinguish between the profile and the significance of a problem. The most obvious problems are not necessarily the most important ones. A willingness to delve around below the surface is clearly required. An inability to apply the process of accommodation in organisational settings results in some problems remaining out of focus. Such a lack of diagnostic acuity means that the problems that are blurred are likely to be only partially understood. This has a 'knock-on effect' because it increases the probability that the diagnosis and the intervention will be inadequate, or even inappropriate.

Client system visibility

In order to explore the interaction between organisational visibility and consultant activity, it is first necessary to explain how a parallel process operates in the field of vision. The retina contains receptors which are sensitive to light. There are two different kinds of receptors, called 'rods' and 'cones'. Rods provide scotopic vision – vision in dim light. Cones provide photopic vision – vision in bright light. As the intensity of light is reduced cones cease to respond and the rods take over. Rods give monochromatic vision (black-and-white images), while cones contain three different visual pigments and offer trichromatic vision (coloured images).

Changes in the brightness of light have a direct impact on the visibility of an object and the internal processes of the eye. Nevertheless, variations in illumination are not physically part of either the object or the eye. Light is effectively an external intervening variable. Thinking of the eye as comparable with the consultant and the object as a client system permits a connection to be made between light and contextual factors in the client–consultant relationship. More specifically, light can be viewed as the environment; an object is surrounded by light just as an organisation is located within an environment.

At a slightly deeper level, variations in light are mirrored by environmental changes. An object in darkness can be compared to an organisation in an adverse or uncertain environment. Indeed, terminology such as 'being in the dark' has been used to describe situations of uncertainty. The reverse is true of the organisational counterpart to bright light, where the environment might reasonably be described as favourable, predictable or stable. Both light and the environment are in a state of flux. The dynamic nature of both constructs means that they are constantly shifting. Objects move within a range from being brightly lit to practically obscured by darkness. Environments alter on several dimensions, such as the degree of certainty driven by competition and technological change.

The major distinction between light and the environment is that the light which is cast on an object can modify the image that is produced, but in real terms it does not physically have any impact on the actual object. In contrast, changes in the environment typically have physical connotations for the organisation as well as perceptual repercussions for the consultant. Notwithstanding this subtle difference, it is still fruitful to juxtapose eyes, objects and light with consultants, client systems and their environments.

If rods and cones accommodate variations in object visibility, does a similar mechanism exist in OD that ensures organisational visibility in changing environmental circumstances? Arguably, consultants require perceptual rods and cones in order to maintain organisational visibility and diagnostic acuity. Perceptual rods and cones for a consultant might legitimately be described as representing two different consulting styles. One style is analytical, participative and non-confrontational and for use in situations of high visibility, strong internal consistency and generally favourable conditions. The other style demands a confrontational approach tempered with a mixture of charisma and creativity, to be used in circumstances which are more hazy, ambiguous and adverse. Ideally, the selection of either style should occur intuitively and should be contingent on the particular circumstances faced. Unfortunately, consultants often have a predisposition for one or other of the styles and consequently find it difficult to switch. For representatives of the client system this would suggest that when engaging a consultant it is important not only to consider a a particularly innovative approach has been adopted by Marr (1982). He has sought to explain the perceptual process by examining what purposes it serves. It has been suggested that the two primary problems which visual perception attempts to address are pattern recognition and spatial localisation. Pattern recognition involves identifying what an object is, and spatial localisation is used to determine where it is. Both of these components are essential for survival. We need to know what an object is before we can assess its characteristics and take action. For instance, if while out walking you see a long thin animal with no legs that is moving along the ground, you are likely to apply your powers of recognition to it. If you perceive the object to be a poisonous snake this is going to lead to a very different set of actions than if you think it is a worm. Equally, the implications of spatial localisation are easily understood if we imagine the difference between seeing a lion at a distance through binoculars while on safari, and being in a cage alongside a lion tamer with a lion only a few feet away.

The identification of problems or potential avenues for investigation in OD also requires the application of pattern recognition and spatial localisation. The recognition process can be thought of as determining the type of problem (e.g. technical, structural or inter-personal) and isolating its component parts. Spatially locating the problem is generally more difficult. It involves examining both the context of the problem and its inter-relationship with other areas. Consultants and client representatives often concentrate on problem recognition, but sometimes overlook the need for problem localisation.

Although a comparable term to spatial localisation does not seem to exist in OD literature, the need for a functional equivalent seems to have been implicitly recognised by several authors. Hence Tichy (1982) has talked of the linkage between the political, technical and cultural systems within an organisation and the need for separation and reconnection when dealing with system alignment and problems. A further example of the need for a form of organisational localisation is provided by Leavitt (1965). He identifies the four main components of an organisation as being the people, task, structure and technology. In his view the four areas are all inter-connected. As a consequence there are two significant implications for organisational change programmes. First, tackling a problem in one area will have repercussions in the other three areas. Second, it is possible to intervene in one area in order to solve problems which exist within another.

Recent developments in the study of pattern recognition indicate that processing does not occur in a haphazard or random manner (Bruce and Green, 1990). Instead it relies on a sophisticated system of interpretation. Biederman (1987, 1990) argues that recognition is based on assessing the features of an object as a series of geometric forms. He has identified a set of 36 basic three-dimensional shapes which he refers to as geons. Controlled experiments have shown that a subject's ability to recognise a series of pictures of objects is strongly influenced by the extent to which geons can be picked out.

The use of geons in visual recognition involves scanning an object for the presence of any of the 36 geometric shapes. Once a permutation of features is isolated, the pattern is compared to other combinations stored in memory in order to identify the object. The whole mental process is completed very quickly, and is largely subconscious.

If geons are used to 'make sense' of objects, does a parallel system operate in the field of OD? In other words, do consultants have a set of behavioural science geons which they apply during the diagnostic phase of OD interventions? If a functional equivalent to geons does exist for consultants, it is unlikely that the pattern would be exactly the same for each person. If, as suggested earlier, all consultants have OD blind spots, then it is doubtful that anyone possesses a full set of diagnostic geons. The diagnostic geons used by a particular consultant appear to be inextricably linked to what Hofstede (1991) has termed 'mental programming'. Psychological geons are put together within the minds of consultants and are a concoction of attitudes, values, past consulting experiences, dominant personality traits, main areas of behavioural science knowledge, natural aptitudes and preferred areas of skill.

The geons which exist as three-dimensional geometric shapes in vision can be interpreted and applied in a fairly objective manner, i.e. it is easy to distinguish between a cube and a cylinder. The same luxury does not often exist with geons when applied to OD. The matching of the geons present in an organisational setting with those stored in the consultant's memory is a highly subjective process. Arguably, the theory of diagnostic geons reinforces and supports some of the previously stated problems which arise in OD. For example, a lack of diagnostic acuity may be due to an inability to isolate specific geons which form what can be construed as a blurred image (or organisational problem). Equally, the inability to switch between perceptual rods and cones might be attributable to the possession of a limited set of diagnostic geons.

Imagery and OD

The use of imagery in OD is not an entirely new phenomenon and is distinct from the aforementioned perceptual processes. Imagery requires the construction of an imaginary ideal within the mind's eye. This goes some way to explaining why the execution of organisational change is often fundamentally dependent on the development of a strategic vision. Indeed, Bennis and Nanus (1985) define vision as 'a mental image of a possible and desirable future state of the organisation'. Imagery can be enlisted in a very meaningful and constructive way by consultants to help to provide solutions or guide intervention. However, its inclusion too early during the OD process can be problematic.

It is possible to think of the diagnostic phase of OD as being predominantly convergent in nature, attempting to isolate problems and causation. As such, it is analytical and corresponds to the 'making sense of it' objective of perception. By contrast, the prescriptive (or intervention) phase of OD tends to contain a divergent stage where a number of possible remedial courses of action are generated. This involves the application of the kind of creativity typically associated with imagery. In the field of OD the application of the equivalent of perception followed by imagery is necessarily chronological. This is illustrated by the OD technique of gap analysis (Harvey and Brown, 1992). The first stage of this approach involves asking; 'Where are we now?', which is primarily a perceptual question. The second phase asks, 'Where would we like to be?', clearly, a question requiring the application of imagery. It would be impractical to reverse the order of questioning in gap analysis, and so too in a wider sense with any OD initiative.

The problem with imagery in both the visual and the organisational context is that it can inadvertently happen at the wrong time. Imagery can cloud or distort the perception of an object. Similarly, having a premature picture of the desired organisational state can hinder the identification of organisational problems. An image of change prior to data collection can lead to bias. In extreme forms organisational imagery can be seen as identifying a solution and then looking for problems to fit it.

IMPAIRED VISION AND DIAGNOSTIC PROBLEMS

At a broad level we have equated eyes to OD consultants, objects to client organisations, and psychological and physiological features of sight to diagnosis. It is possible to refine the metaphorical interpretation further by specifically looking at the ability of the eyes (consultant) to construct an accurate, representative and meaningful image (diagnosis) based on an analysis of the object (client system). As highlighted in earlier sections, the ability to develop an accurate visual representation of an object is influenced by a variety of factors. However, more specifically it is possible to classify a particular set of diagnostic problems using various visual impediments as metaphorical descriptors. These problems are summarised in Table 9.3 and examined in greater detail below.

Blindness in OD

Blindness at one level can be described as a total inability to see objects and therefore distinguish between them. Here it is equated to a total lack of

Table 9.3 Visual impediments and diagnostic problems

Visual problem	Area of diagnostic equivalence
Blindness	*Diagnostic blindness* can be described as an inability to identify accurately organisational problems due to incompetence
Colour Blindness	*Diagnostic colour blindness* relates to a consultant's ability to spot the same problem against different organisational backgrounds (or contexts)
Blurred Vision	A *blurred diagnosis* occurs where an organisational problem appears to blend in with its surrounding field and other problems
Tunnel Vision	A *tunnel diagnosis* is attributable to a tendency to focus too heavily on data gathering in one area hence neglecting others
Short-sightedness	*Diagnostic myopia* arises in circumstances where the consultant concentrates on tackling the symptoms of an organisational problem and fails to address the underlying cause
Long-sightedness	The *long-sighted diagnosis* places an emphasis on intervention and the application of ready-made solutions, and tends to ignore data collection and problem definition as preceding stages of the OD process

understanding of OD as a process. A blind diagnosis results from deficient consulting skills and the possession of only very limited behavioural science knowledge. Diagnostic blindness is different from the presence of a blind spot. A blind spot refers to the small area of weakness that all consultants have. Diagnostic blindness is an affliction which hopefully applies to only a very small minority of OD consultants – a group which might reasonably be referred to as behavioural charlatans!

The precise measurement of diagnostic incompetence is very difficult. However, there are several classifications of areas of core consulting competence which provide a basis for identifying shortcomings and gaps in ability (see, for example, Lippitt and Lippitt, 1986; Menzel, 1975). Remedial action for areas of consulting weakness is not necessarily straightforward, as illustrated in a quote by Havelock (1973). He observes:

> **Most of the tactics or functions discussed [as interventions] cannot simply be picked up casually from a manual. They are skills which have to be learned. A good tactic badly executed may be worse than no tactic at all.**

Colour blindness

In an earlier section, the function of cones in facilitating trichromatic vision (coloured images) was explained. Colour blindness is due to a deficiency in one of the three different visual pigments (red, blue and green). The most common form of colour blindness is due to a lack of red cones which leads to an inability to distinguish between red and green.

Colour blindness in OD can be described as an inability to identify a particular kind of problem when located in a certain context. This is due to the deficiency of a specific category of perceptual cones. This diagnostic problem is similar to, but subtly different from, an OD blind spot. With a blind spot certain types of problems would never be easy to see in any context. With OD colour blindness red problems would be obscured in a green context, but highly visible in a blue one. For example, certain problems which pass unnoticed by a consultant working with blue-collar workers may become highly visible when located against a white-collar background. A consultant who competently diagnoses the interaction problems that exist within a team of senior executives may not demonstrate the same level of diagnostic acuity when confronted with a comparable problem within a shopfloor production team.

Blurred vision

Blurring effectively means that the outline and features of an object become hazy. This causes problems with the perceptual process of pattern recognition and can lead to an inappropriate interpretation of geons. As a result, an object can be wrongly labelled, e.g. mistaking apples for pears. The OD equivalent is misunderstanding the problem.

Blurred vision can also cause another kind of perceptual problem – the fuzziness of an image can mean that it is difficult to pick out against a background. In visual terms the object seems to merge, and blend into, the surrounding field. In effect, the resultant lack of clarity means that it is difficult to locate where the object begins or ends. Similarly, during the diagnostic phase of OD problems can become blurred. They seem to spill over into each other, and into the context in which they are located. The inability to segregate and place parameters on the problem often leads to a delusion that a multitude of problems exist. This manifests itself as a kind of 'kitchen sink' diagnosis – with problems being seen anywhere and everywhere. As a consequence a form of 'interventional overkill' is often applied to solve the perceived problems.

Tunnel vision

In ophthalmology tunnel vision is normally attributable to a hereditary condition called retinitus pigmentosa (Perkins et al, 1986). The condition involves a clear central field of vision, but surrounding this is a peripheral field of darkness. The effect is similar to wearing blinkers. Like tunnel vision, the approach adopted by OD consultants on occasions might reasonably be described as blinkered. An overly narrow focus when collecting data can lead to a number of potentially fruitful avenues of investigation being neglected.

Tunnel vision in diagnosis is perhaps attributable to the consultant's possession of a restricted set of diagnostic geons. For example, a consultant who specialises in structural interventions is likely to possess a set of geons which are particularly geared towards identifying structural problems. Hence, the insensitivity of the geons to other problems which remain in the peripheral field of vision means that they are therefore not 'picked out'. The tendency to 'see what we want to see' and the strong orientation towards a particular area of consultant expertise means that the end product is normally the application of the consultant's favourite diagnosis. Specialists in ergonomics are likely to identify the need for job redesign; experts in team-building are likely to highlight the need for increased teamworking; and so on. It is perhaps not surprising that there is often a correlation between a consultant's area of expertise and the recommended area of intervention. The onus is arguably on the client representative to ensure that a consultant is employed who has a breadth of expertise.

Short-sightedness

Short-sightedness (or myopia) can be described in simple terms as an inability to focus on distant objects. This arises where rays from a distant object are brought into focus in front of, rather than on, the retina.

In the OD context short-sightedness can be likened to a diagnosis which addresses the symptoms and misses the underlying cause. It is an inability to see beyond the immediate problem. The implications for intervention are that there is a short-term alleviation of the symptoms; but because the cause is not tackled the problems return and the intervention is ineffectual. This can be more fully explained by using a medical analogy. Imagine that you are feeling ill and therefore go to see your doctor. You explain that you have a sore throat, a cough, a runny nose, a fever, and you ache all over. The doctor, having heard your description, prescribes lozenges for your throat, linctus for your cough, an inhalant for your nose, cold showers for your fever, and paracetamol for your aches. In effect, the doctor has addressed the symptoms rather than identifying the underlying cause (i.e. flu). In a similar way, an OD consultant can make the mistake of assuming that a series of organisational problems (such as poor morale, high absenteeism, high labour turnover, low productivity) are unrelated. The independent treatment of the organisational problems, like the prescription for the medical symptoms, is likely to have only limited success because it fails to tackle the root cause.

Long-sightedness

Long-sightedness (or hypermetropia) is the reverse of short-sightedness. It is an inability to focus on near objects. A diagnosis can be long-sighted in so far as it is focused on intervention rather than more immediate tasks. It involves a neglect of the data-gathering phase of OD and a direct leap into the latter stages. The emphasis is on providing a solution and largely ignores problem identification as a necessary prerequisite. Ironically, a preoccupation with the intervention stage is likely to mean that it is not well directed, and is likely to fail in its efforts to secure organisational improvements.

This diagnostic affliction can often be attributed to a strong belief in the universal application of the prescribed solution. In effect, the consultant believes that the prevailing problems do not need to be isolated because whatever they are the consultant's panacea will work. Certain patterns emerge regarding panaceas. A particular panacea enjoys a wave of popularity and then gives way to a 'new pretender'. Quality circles and teamworking have both had spells in the limelight during the 1980s as 'cures for all ills'. At the moment 'empowerment' and 'total quality management' would appear to be just about holding off the advances of 'business process re-engineering'. Not all consultants are drawn into applying the kind of off-the-shelf standard solutions described here. However, there is perhaps a small caucus of consultants who move from organisation to organisation pedalling universal remedies, in a manner that we more commonly associate with the prairie doctors who roamed around in the wild west selling potions and elixirs which they claimed had numerous applications ranging from curing arthritis to enhancing sexual prowess.

CONCLUSIONS

The metaphorical exploration of the diagnostic stage of OD undertaken in this chapter does not attempt to offer prescriptive solutions to the diagnostic minefield which often confronts the client and the change agent. It is hoped that the vision metaphor has provided a worthwhile and meaningful vehicle for raising the general level of awareness of some common, but nevertheless frequently overlooked or misunderstood problems which can arise during the diagnostic phase. The intention has been to provide at one level a way of seeing organisational problems, and at another a way of thinking about diagnosis.

REFERENCES

Alvesson, M. (1993) 'The play of metaphors', in Hassard, J. and Parker, M. (eds) *Postmodernism and Organizations*. London: Sage.

Atkinson, R.L., Atkinson, R.C., Smith, E.E. and Bem, D.J. (1993) *Introduction to Psychology*. 11th Edition, Fort Worth: Harcourt Brace Jovanovich.

Bennis, W. and Nanus, B. (1985) *Leaders: The Strategies for Taking Charge*. New York: Harper and Row.

Biederman, I. (1987) 'Recognition by components: a theory of human image under-standing', *Psychological Review*, No. 94.

Biederman, I. (1990) 'Higher-level vision', in *An Invitation to Cognitive Science: Visual Cognition and Action (Vol. 2)*. Cambridge, Mass.: MIT Press.

Bruce, V. and Green, P. (1990) *Visual Perception: Physiology, Psychology and Ecology*. Hove: Lawrence Erlbaum Associates.

Buchanan, D. and Boddy, D. (1992) *The Expertise of the Change Agent*. Hemel Hempstead: Prentice-Hall.

Cummings, T.G. and Huse, E.F. (1989) *Organization Development and Change*. 4th Edition, St Paul: West Publishing.

Ebenoltz, S. (1977) 'The constancies in object orientation: an algorithm processing approach', in Epstein, W. (ed) *Stability and Constancy in Visual Perception*. New York: Wiley.

French, W.L. and Bell, C.H. (1990) *Organization Development: Behavioral Science Interventions for Organizational Improvement*. 4th Edition, Englewood Cliffs, NJ: Prentice-Hall.

Gibson, J.J. (1966) *The Senses Considered as Perceptual Systems*. Boston, Mass.: Houghton Mifflin.

Harvey, D.F. and Brown, D.R. (1992) *An Experiential Approach to Organization Development*. Englewood Cliffs, NJ: Prentice-Hall.

Havelock, J. (1973) *The Change Agent's Guide to Innovation in Education*. Englewood Cliffs, NJ: Educational Technology Publications.

Hofstede, G. (1991) *Culture and Organisations: Software of the Mind*. London: McGraw-Hill.

Kotter, J.P. (1978) *Organizational Dynamics: Diagnosis and Intervention*. Reading, Mass.: Addison-Wesley.

Kuhn, T.S. (1962) *The Structure of Scientific Revolutions*. Chicago: University of Chicago Press.

Lawrence, P.R. and Lorsch, J.W. (1969) *Developing Organizations: Diagnosis and Action*. Reading, Mass.: Addison-Wesley.

Leavitt, H. (1965) 'Applied organizational change in industry: structural, technolog-ical and humanistic approaches', in March, J.G. (ed) *Handbook of Organizations*. Chicago, IL: Rand McNally.

Lippitt, G.L. and Lippitt, R. (1986) *The Consulting Process in Action*. 2nd Edition, San Diego, CA: University Associates.

Marr, D. (1982) *Vision: A Computational Investigation into the Human Representation and Processing of Visual Information*. San Franscisco: Freeman & Co.

Menzel, R.K. (1975) 'A taxonomy of change agent skills', *Journal of European Industrial Training*, Vol. 4, No. 5.

Ortony, A. (1975) 'Why metaphors are necessary and not just nice', *Educational Theory*, Vol. 25. No. 1.

Perkins, E.S., Hansell, P. and Marsh, R.J. (1986) *An Atlas of Diseases of the Eye.* Edinburgh: Churchill Livingstone.

Pfeiffer, J.W. and Jones, J.E. (1976) 'A current assessment of OD: what it is and why it often fails', in Pfeiffer, J.W. and Jones, J.E. (eds) *The 1976 Annual Handbook for Group Facilitators.* San Diego, CA: Pfeiffer & Co.

Rock, I. (1975) *An Introduction to Perception.* New York: Macmillan.

Schon, D.A. (1979) 'Generative metaphor: a perspective on problem-setting in social policy', in Ortony, A. (ed) *Metaphor and Thought.* New York: Cambridge University Press.

Selfridge, R.J. and Sokolik, S.L. (1975) 'A comprehensive view of organizational development', *M.S.U. Business Topics*, Winter.

Tichy, N. (1982) *Managing Strategic Change.* New York: Wiley.

Tsoukas, H. (1993) 'Analogical reasoning and knowledge generation in organization theory', *Organization Studies*, Vol. 14.

CHAPTER 10

The use of metaphor in the client–consultant relationship: a study of management consultants

Timothy Clark and Graeme Salaman

INTRODUCTION

A number of studies have indicated the rapid increase in the use of management consultants by British industry (Keeble et al, 1994; Clark, 1995; Schlegelmilch et al, 1992). Commentators have suggested that there are two inter-related reasons for this increase in the use of management consultants (see, for example, Peet, 1988; Rassam and Oates, 1991; Tisdall, 1982). First, in response to what are perceived to be radical changes and increased pressures from their markets and competitors, organisations are increasingly likely to be embarking on programmes of profound organisational change or already to have done so. Second, by virtue of the nature of this actual or planned organisational change, managers are likely to believe that new skills, values and qualities are necessary and that these are currently lacking. Essentially, therefore, from all sides managers are being convinced, or at least persuaded, that traditional structures, systems and cultures will no longer do; that their organisations must change fundamentally. The inference is that they must change paradigms and that the designing and managing of this change, and working in the changed organisation, will require new skills. It is in the context of these pressures and demands that managers feel it necessary increasingly to seek external support by turning to those who offer some solutions to these dilemmas – management consultants.

Before proceeding with the main discussion the term 'management consultancy' must first be defined. We use a composite term derived from the definitions suggested by Argyris (1970) and Greiner and Metzger (1983). This draws a boundary around what does and does not, in our view, comprise management consultancy. On the basis of these definitions we see management consultancy as an advisory activity which necessitates intervention in an ongoing organisational system where the advisers are external specialists and so have no organisational responsibility, and where the aim of the activity is some adjustment to the organisational system.

The focus of this chapter is on examining, critiquing and ultimately replacing the ways in which the work of consultants and their relationships with clients have been commonly understood and conceptualised. We argue that there are two main approaches to examining the work of management consultants. The first approach encompasses a wide range of literature which focuses on the *problems* which beset the work of consultants. Yet these 'problems' are essentially second-order problems and where the literature concentrates on them it is in fact deficient. The deficiency centres on its accepting the values, priorities and promises of consultants, i.e. that consultants are authoritative, expert and skilled and therefore can provide assistance. Were this to be the case, problems would only arise, and therefore occur within a context, where the client has already accepted that management consultants have something of value to offer. Consequently, while this literature has its uses, it may not be the most useful approach to understanding the nature of consultancy work, since it distracts attention from the fundamental problems which consultants must resolve if they are to remain in business; i.e. how they demonstrate their value to clients.

The second approach to conceptualising the client–consultant relationship is via *metaphor*. As with the first approach, while this has contributed to our knowledge of the consultant's role it is still rather wide of the mark. We shall argue that this is because it highlights aspects of the client–consultant relationship which obscure its reality. This arises because much of this literature is grounded in a root metaphor of the consultant as professional helper. Ironically, this is a metaphor emphasising that element which is missing from the client–consultant relationship – an authoritative and distinctive body of knowledge.

To overcome the deficiencies in these two approaches, we suggest that the most appropriate way to analyse and understand the nature of consultancy work is to apply a metaphor which focuses on how consultants seek to resolve their major problem – convincing clients of their value. We argue that the metaphor of *consultancy as performance* achieves this.

In pursuing this argument the chapter is structured as follows. It begins by outlining the main features of the problem-solving literature. This literature is classified into four broad streams, each of which are summarised and their main deficiencies considered. We then turn to a discussion of the second approach. The relevant literature is briefly reviewed prior to consideration of its main weaknesses. Finally, on the basis of the previous discussion the key features of the metaphor *consultancy as performance* are elaborated and its advantages explored.

PROBLEM-SOLVING LITERATURE

A great deal of the existing literature which examines the work of management consultants is focused on identifying the sources of deficiencies and effectiveness in the intervention process. In essence it is concerned with solving problems. The problems are those that arise within the working relationship between clients and consultants. For example, writers in this category concentrate on identifying actual or potential shortcomings in the intervention exercise, and then propose solutions for overcoming these which will ensure future effectiveness. Essentially, this literature aims to identify ways of achieving effective consultancy interventions in the face of certain constraints which make this difficult. We identify four streams within the problem-solving literature: the consultancy process, intervention objectives, modes of consultancy and information asymmetries. Each is considered in turn. All are seen to suffer from the same limitations.

The intervention process/appropriate sequencing

This strand of the literature argues that failure of the intervention activity results from the misapplication of the intervention process. The intervention process is reduced to a number of discrete stages. These provide a framework in which all issues and problems are identified and overcome. Hence, problems arise not from the content of the intervention activity but rather from the manner or sequence in which it is conducted. The number of stages in the intervention process have been variously classified as four (Kakabadse, 1986; Lippitt and Lippitt, 1978), five (Beckhard, 1969; Blake and Mouton, 1983; Kubr, 1986) and seven (Kolb and Frohman, 1970). While there is little agreement on the precise number of stages, these writers jointly argue that effective consulting results from the correct application of each stage to the intervention activity. These models can be 'readily extended to any type of consultant with any large client system' (Kolb and Frohman, 1970: 51).

Much of the intervention process and appropriate sequence literature highlights three main problems which centre on the progression from one stage to another. Each of these is illustrated in Figure 10.1, which is in part based on Kolb and Frohman's (1970) 'developmental model of consultation process'. While this shows a five-stage model, the same problems apply regardless of the number of stages. The vertical axis refers to the sequence of stages followed by the client, whereas the horizontal axis indicates the progression of the consultant. The shaded boxes represent the client and consultant progressing and therefore working in harmony. Horizontal movement, indicated by arrow 1, represents the consultant moving to the next stage without resolving the issues of the previous

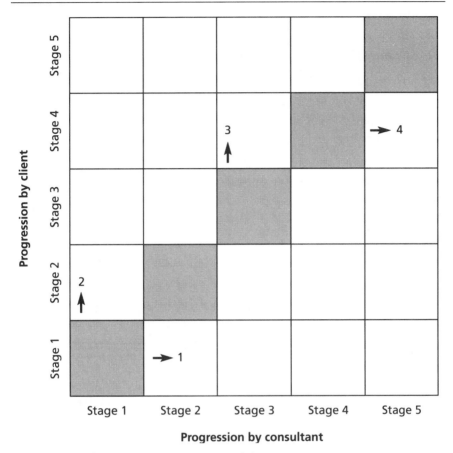

Progression by consultant

Figure 10.1 A five-stage intervention model

stage with the client. Vertical movement, shown by arrow 2, indicates the same deviation, but this time by the client. A final problem arises from either clients or consultants jumping to later stages without undertaking the earlier stages (arrows 3 and 4).

Intervention objectives/management learning

This strand in the literature is exemplified by the writings of Argyris (1970) and Turner (1982). Within this tradition, the consultant's work focuses on, and consists of, the encouragement of management learning, and the avoidance of defensiveness and denial. It differs from the above in that effective intervention is viewed as emanating from the mutual recognition and definition of the key intervention objectives. For example, Argyris (1970) identified three primary objectives to any intervention activity:

1 *Valid and useful information* – this highlights those factors which are creating problems for the client.
2 *Free choice* – the client is able to choose what action to take from the alternatives presented by the consultant. 'Through free choice the clients can maintain the autonomy of their system' (Argyris, 1970: 19).
3 *Internal commitment* – this implies that the course of action adopted by the client has to be internalised so that they feel a high degree of ownership and responsibility for the choice and its implications.

These aims are very ambitious. In order to achieve them the consultancy process, and therefore the role of the consultant, is focused on encouraging managers to step:

> outside their usual, taken-for-granted routines by adopting a strategic perspective on the interaction... where they are able, relatively dispassionately, to observe and reflect upon their everyday actions and the consequences of such actions for each other. (Mangham, 1978: 103)

This view of consultancy requires managers to recognise, confront and when necessary to modify their behaviour and the consequences of their behaviour (i.e. their responsibility for 'negative outcomes').

The difficulties are obvious. Argyris (1990) notes that it is common for senior managers deliberately and persistently to act in ways which have negative consequences for the organisation, and make any discussion of their behaviour difficult. Moreover, 'all of this is being done with the best of intentions. There is no evidence that the players intend to violate basic management rules or the fundamental values in managerial stewardship' (Argyris, 1990: 6).

Achieving success within these terms will be difficult. It will require unusual techniques if the transformation of managers' everyday habits and assumptions (and the consequences) is to be achieved. The goal is awesome: 'it is about making the undiscussable discussable, about not taking for granted what is taken for granted... so that the unmanageable can become manageable' (Argyris, 1990: 6).

Clearly managers may find it difficult, indeed may be unwilling, to depart from their conventional habitual attitudes, world views and behaviours. Achieving successful outcomes of such consultancy will require unusual and powerful techniques.

The implication of this literature is that if the intervention objectives are clearly identified and defined then potential misunderstandings are minimised. Therefore, the focus of the consultancy activity is on the nature of the client–consultant relationship and the extent to which this encourages managers' learning.

Intervention modes/contingency

This approach argues that effective intervention results from the matching of different consultancy modes to the focal problem. The problem is one of 'fit'. For example, Blake and Mouton (1983) identify five intervention modes:

1 *Theories and principles* – the consultant informs the client of relevant theories and principles.
2 *Prescription* – the consultant tells the client what to do.
3 *Confrontation* – the current way in which the client thinks is challenged.
4 *Catalytic* – the client is encouraged to think in new ways through a process which extends their knowledge base.
5 *Acceptant* – the client is encouraged to develop a basic sense of personal security so that they will feel free to express their thoughts without fear of recrimination.

Taking this approach means that no one kind of intervention mode is better than another. However, when confronted by a particular problem: 'There is one most effective way of handling it, but that way may be totally inappropriate for dealing with a different problem' (Blake and Mouton, 1983: 16).

Similar intervention roles have been identified by other writers (see Table 10.1). For instance, Schein (1969) identifies three modes of intervention, while Steele (1975) distinguishes nine. Underlying these is a basic assumption that a primary intervention objective should be matched by an appropriate intervention style. For example, if a consultancy is employed to communicate bad news, then in Steele's terms the relevant intervention mode is that of the 'ritual pig'.

Information asymmetries

This approach argues that effective intervention derives from an informational balance between the client and consultant (Clark, 1993; Holmstrom, 1985; Mitchell, 1994). It is argued that any successful intervention activity is based on the client's access to and understanding of relevant information. The argument suggests that the problems of information asymmetry associated with the client–consultant relationship are heightened by those characteristics which differentiate services from goods. Two unique and central characteristics of services are intangibility and perishability. These create special problems for the market provision of services such as management consultancy. In particular, they make for difficulties in assessing quality; whereas the supplier may know product quality, the client often does not. The asymmetry between sellers and buyers is of two types: 'adverse selection' and 'moral hazard'. Adverse selection occurs when the buyer cannot observe the relevant characteristics of the seller or the conditions under which they work. The problem of moral hazard is the buyer's

Table 10.1 Metaphors of consultancy work

Tilles (1961)	Schein (1969) (1978)	Lippitt and Lippitt	Steele (1975) (1983)	Blake and Mouton	Greiner and Metzger (1983)
Flow of information	Doctor–patient	Alternative identifier	Barbarian	Prescription	Generalist
Doctor–patient	Purchase	Positional advocacy	Detective	Theories and principles	Content
Purchase	Process	Technical expert	Talisman	Acceptant	Process
Reflector		Process specialist	Student	Catalyst	Specialist
		Fact finder	Clock	Confirmational	
		Collaboration	Monitor		
		Problem solving	Ritual pig		
		Methodological advocacy	Teacher		
		Trainer and educator	Advocate		

inability to observe the actions taken by sellers. Effective intervention is derived from overcoming these difficulties.

Weakness of the problem-solving approach

Each of the four streams detailed above undoubtedly contributes to our understanding of the nature, role and activity of management consultants. Their contribution to the *practice* of consultancy is obvious; and many of the authors whose work has been detailed above are, or were at one time, successful practising consultants themselves. Indeed, this problem-solving approach derives much of its value and purchase from practical experience. Nevertheless, a narrow concern with prescriptive and formulaic advice to clients and practitioners is, at the very least, limited in its contribution to a thorough conceptualisation and understanding of the consultancy role and process. This arises because this approach is located, as it were, inside the activity itself. It assumes that management consultants have convinced clients as to the value of their 'know-how'. This is problematic because, as Starbuck (1992: 731) argues:

> Clients often consult experts because they believe their own knowledge to be inadequate, so they cannot judge the experts' advice or reports mainly on substance. Clients may be unable to assess experts' advice by acting on it and watching the outcomes: the clients do not know what would have happened if they had acted otherwise and it is frequently obvious that outcomes reflect uncontrollable or unpredictable influences. Clients may not understand what their expert advisers are saying. Many experts – with awareness – use jargon that obscures their meaning.

As a result of these problems Starbuck argues that clients make their judgements as to the value of the service on the basis of 'generic symbols of expertise'. These include the qualifications of the experts, the quality of data and use of impressive statistical computations, credibility of analyses, and experts' dress, confidence and general demeanour. Hence, according to Starbuck (1992: 731), if we are truly to understand the success of management consultants we must 'pay attention to their symbolic outputs'.

Appreciation of these symbols is all the more pressing and relevant since management consultancy is one of the most intangible parts of the (business) service sector. This means that a client is unable to perceive a complete physical form. There is nothing which can be seen, touched, tasted, heard or smelt. In these circumstances Levitt (1981) argues that buyers are asked to purchase what essentially amount to no more than promises. According to Alvesson (1994: 544), this feature of services means that the expertise, skills and qualities of management consultancies 'do not talk for themselves'. Consultants must therefore convince clients that they have something of value to offer. The immaterial nature of consultancy work makes this neither obvious nor easy to demonstrate.

Thus the problems which are the focus of the literature elaborated above are therefore second-order problems. They only arise once it has been accepted – by clients – that consultants have something useful to offer. In this respect this literature misses the fundamental point that the real problem faced, and resolved, by consultants is how they demonstrate value to their clients in the first instance; i.e. how do they convince clients that they have something valuable to offer? As Alvesson (1993: 1007) notes: 'A management consultant is quite different from a bus driver. The latter is hardly in the business of rhetoric. The former, together with most of his knowledge-intensive colleagues, is.' This is what we should be addressing.

The alternative approach to the study of consultancy work seems to offer help with this more fundamental question, but is equally wide of the mark. This approach, via metaphor, claims to be useful precisely because it seeks to question and to raise problems about the nature of the consultants' role and activity. In effect, it refuses to accept the terms that consultants themselves take for granted. However, in a curious way this critical promise is also undermined since the metaphors used tend to accept the assumptions and priorities of consultants. Once again the full heuristic potential of the approach has been compromised.

METAPHORS IN MANAGEMENT CONSULTANCY

Metaphor consists of 'understanding and experiencing one thing in terms of another' (Lakoff and Johnson, 1980: 5). Thus metaphor proceeds from the assertion that A is (or is like) B, where A and B were previously classified and understood as different entities. This combination or juxtaposition of A and B creates new meaning which is absent until the two elements are joined. As Schon (1979: 259) writes: 'It is the restructuring of the perception of the phenomenon named by "A" and "B" which enables us to call "metaphor" what we might otherwise have called "mistake".'

A considerable amount of literature has conceived the activities of consultants in terms of a variety of roles, styles or metaphors. One of the earliest classifications was proposed by Tilles (1961), who distinguishes between three roles – seller of services, supplier of information and business doctor dispensing cures. The first is regarded by those involved in terms of a conventional sales–purchase transaction; the second in terms of the flow of information between the parties; the third in terms of patient and doctor.

Schein (1969) distinguishes between three types of consultancy which differ according to the roles of the consultant and client and the type of assistance sought; these are the purchase of expertise, doctor–patient and process models. Building on this classification, Margulies and Raia (1972) develop a model which locates the consultant's role along a continuum with the extremes of task orientation and process orientation. At the former end of the scale the consultant is a technical expert developing, recommending and implementing solutions to identified problems. In contrast, at the other extreme the consultant is a process facilitator working with the client in a collaborative manner so as to facilitate client learning in order to improve problem-solving processes within the organisation.

More briefly, Steele (1975) identifies nine roles that the consultant may adopt within a client system: teacher, student, detective, barbarian, clock, monitor, talisman, advocate and ritual pig. Ganesh (1978) identifies and elaborates two distinct consultancy styles – the human and systematic relations orientations. The former emphasises personal, inter-personal, or sub-system issues, while the latter is concerned with task, structure and total organisation– environment issues. Lippitt and Lippitt (1978) have developed a descriptive model which presents the consultant's role along a continuum with the two polar extremes of directive and non-directive. As a consultant becomes less and less directive they suggest that the role undergoes a number of changes which occur in the following sequence – advocate to informational expert, to trainer educator, to joint problem solver, to alternative identifier and linker, to fact finder, to process consultant, to objective observer/reflector. Sinha (1979) has produced an edited collection in which consultants use some of these roles to reflect on their own styles and approaches to consultancy. Blake and Mouton (1983) identify five 'consulting modes' which differ in terms of the way the consultant relates to the client, i.e. in terms of theories and principles, prescription, confrontation, catalytic and acceptant. Nees and Greiner (1985) identify and discuss the implications of five types of management consultant: mental adventurer, navigators, management physicians, systems architects, and friendly co-pilots.

An important feature of metaphor is its selective focus (Morgan, 1986; Ortony, 1975). Metaphor highlights certain aspects of a phenomenon and hides others. When we comprehend one phenomenon in terms of another we tend to develop a lopsided understanding. In highlighting certain features metaphor forces others into the background, or even conceals them altogether. As Ortony (1979: 6) writes: 'Metaphors result in a sort of cognitive myopia, in which some aspects of a situation are unwittingly emphasised at the expense of other, possibly equally important, ones.' For example, we might describe an athlete as being 'like a leopard on the track'. In choosing the term 'leopard' we draw attention to and conjure up specific images of an animal moving with explosive speed, power, strength and grace. At the same time this metaphor requires that the athlete possesses selected features of a leopard. We ignore the fact that a leopard is a wild animal with feline features, yellow and black spotted fur, four legs, claws and a tail. Instead, we concentrate on those features that the athlete and leopard have in common. In this way metaphor presents a partial truth. It gives a distorted image in which certain aspects of the phenomenon are selected in while others are selected out.

The four second-order problems outlined above rely on a broadly similar image of consultancy. They could be said to share a common root metaphor in which consultants are viewed as supplying assistance, guidance and support to clients, whereby the activity is conceptualised as part teacher, part therapist, part doctor.

Given the selective focus of metaphor, the problems detailed above are determined by, and derive from, the metaphor used to structure and understand the consultancy process. Hence a further major weakness in the problem-solving literature is the assumption that the identified problems are natural and inevitable because the nature and dynamics of the client–consultant interaction are clear, obvious and agreed – the consultant is concerned to help the client in complex and demanding ways, while the client accepts and understands the role and contribution of the consultant. In short, the problems faced by clients and consultants could be seen to arise not from the characteristics of the parties involved, nor from the consultant's work, nor even from the nature of the client–consultant relationship, but from the particular metaphor that is implicitly used to conceptualise and 'see' the consultant activity itself.

The problems identified above are technical problems that are seen to arise during the course of the consultant's activity. They presuppose the consultant's own view of this activity – the skilful helper struggling with complex and demanding tasks, seeking to achieve change, learning, progress. We would suggest that it is persuading clients of this conception of the consultant's activity and role that is actually the consultant's main and most pressing problem. The problems listed above are actually solutions to this larger problem. Once clients have been persuaded of the importance and value of the consultant intervention, their mastery at solving these second-order difficulties is simply further testimony to their skill and expertise.

Weakness of the metaphor approach

A major deficiency with much of this literature is its grounding in a root or structural metaphor of the consultant as professional helper. In part, this may arise since a number of these commentators, like many of those who have contributed to the problem-solving literature, are, or were at one time, active and highly successful consultants. The consultancy roles they seek to identify are therefore based in large part on their own activities and reflect their conceptualisations and understandings of their own consultancy activities. Many of these metaphors are flattering to the consultant, and it is likely that consultants, when possible, would seek to impose a conception of their role and function in terms analogous to the doctor or therapist. In general they appear to view their activities as synonymous, if not contermi- nous with, the role of professional helpers remedying illnesses, and it suggests a perception of 'the organisation as a human entity' (discussed by Kumra in Chapter 3).

Many of the consultancy roles identified above seek to highlight and reinforce professional status and professional autonomy, as well as assum- ing a major and acknowledged body of specialist knowledge. Therefore, these commentators invariably seek to impose and perpetuate a conception of the consultant role and function in terms analogous to the activities of a doctor, lawyer, therapist or other professional activity. It is our contention that these metaphors are inadequate in three main ways. First, many of them assume precisely what is *missing* from the relationship between con- sultant and client. This is an agreed, accepted, authoritative and relevant body of knowledge – in which the consultant is accomplished and expert, but which is denied to the client, and which can be used as a basis on which to build the nature of the client–consultant relationship. A number of commentators have noted that while there is consultancy knowledge which is deployed during the consultancy activity, it lacks the status and authority of other professional knowledge and so does not supply a basis for occupational qualification and certification (see Oakley, 1993; Whitely, 1991). This arises since management consultancies have failed to establish control over a distinctive domain of knowledge. Rather the management consultancy industry is characterised by a plethora of 'distinctive' bodies of knowledge. These include, among many others, Organisational Development (OD) models, or such models as the Boston Consulting Group matrix, transactional analysis, learning models, Gestalt theory, role theory etc. The very variety and diversity of these models and frameworks, which are the knowledge base of consultancy work, demonstrates that knowledge in the industry is actively contested.

This fluidity in the knowledge base of management consultancy is demonstrated by the consultant-driven, package-led orientation of certain types of consultancy work. Parts of the consultancy industry are to some extent fashion led, faddish and ephemeral. This is recognised by Gill and Whittle (1992) who argue that management consultants tend to peddle the latest in a long line of panaceas targeted at organisational improvement. Witness the emergence, initial enthusiasm, spectacular growth and then decline in popularity of such consultancy movements as conglomeration, intrapreneuring, the managerial grid, management by objectives (MBO), management by walking about (MBWA), T-groups and total quality management (TQM). The inherent cyclicality of such panaceas has the dual effect of expanding the knowledge base of consultancy work while at the same time destabilising and then refocusing the activities of many consultants as they seek to 'climb aboard' the latest fad. According to Oswick in Chapter 9, it can therefore impair the effectiveness of consultants.

In the absence of a clearly delineated and defendable formal body of knowledge, consultants' success is determined by their ability to appear authoritative via their manipulation of a knowledge base which is ambiguous, tacit and constantly under threat. In the face of competing knowledge bases, consultants have to appear authoritative by convincing prospective clients that their expertise is worth buying. Therefore, their skill lies in presenting themselves as experts and convincing clients that they provide the most relevant solution. They must persuade clients of their definition of the situation and to collaborate on the basis of this analysis. The creation, management and regulation of impressions and images is therefore a central feature of consultancy work. It therefore becomes necessary for management consultants to draw on various symbolic resources in order to convince clients of their inherent worth, their expertise, skills and talents. Through their actions consultants must generate images which are sympathetically received by clients, thereby leading them to value the service being offered and to recognise it as distinctive. Thus the work of consultants can be viewed as inherently symbolic.

Latour (1987) suggests that consultants are able to project their special and distinctive competencies to clients by 'bringing home' distant events, places, people. This is achieved:

- by rendering them *mobile* so that they can be brought back;
- by keeping them *stable* so that they can be moved back and forth without additional distortion; and,
- by making them *combinable* so that they can be cumulated, aggregated and manipulated.

Legge (1994: 3) writes that this is precisely what management consultants do 'when they make the experience of (distant) forms accessible and combinable through the development of (in Latour's terms) equations or packages – such as McKinsey's decentralisation package, HAY-MSL's job evaluation package or even Peters' eight rules of excellence'. Legge also notes that in order for these packages to achieve marketability and impact they need to be credible to potential clients and stakeholders. She identifies this issue as critical to the work of consultants. We shall return to the issue of understanding the achievement of impact below.

The second inadequacy of metaphorical analyses of the consultant's role concerns the way in which images of the client–consultant relationship are excessively focused on the rationality of modern organisations and modern industrial society. The metaphors assume the same 'celebration of rationality' within organisations. As Turner notes in his discussion of Weber:

> **When Weber wanted to contrast the organisations of industrial capitalism with those of other civilisations he identified their most distinguished characteristic as a belief that their affairs were conducted legally, reliably, consistently, calculatingly, and predictably, magic having been banished from their procedures.** (Turner, 1990: 83)

The views of the consultants' work and relationships mentioned earlier draw on the same rationalistic, utilitarian, formalistic, hard-headed assumptions. We suggest that the actual nature and focus of much consultancy activity deliberately oppose these values, and succeed because of it. This point will be developed further below.

The third inadequacy is that, in our view, the distinguishing qualities of the client–consultant relationship lie less in the currently available metaphors for institutionalised/professionalised assistance, counselling or exchange, and more in the nature of the *interaction* between these two parties. While supporting the value of metaphorical conceptualisations of the relationship between the parties (although wishing to move beyond the rational, secular, industrial context used by most commentators), we wish to use metaphor to capture the key features of what actually happens when clients and consultants meet and 'work' together.

This point needs emphasising. In our view the critical feature of consultancy that must be captured and highlighted by a metaphoric understanding is systematically overlooked by the majority of metaphors currently in use. These metaphors overstress the knowledge and professionalism elements of the consultancy activity and underestimate the role of client–consultant interaction. Oddly, despite the considerable emphasis in the OD literature on the importance of process in the consultants' task (e.g. Schein, 1969), relatively little attention has been paid to examining and understanding the dynamics of client–consultant interaction. Yet this interaction is critical. We agree with Legge (1994) that the key question to ask of consultancy is not 'what is consultancy knowledge?', but 'how do consultants develop a strong story?' That is, how do consultants convince clients that they are authoritative, competent, expert, knowledgeable and skilled. Legge (1994: 4) identifies a number of rhetorical techniques which involve the consultant 'developing a package that is self-fortifying and well positioned i.e., a product that not only clearly identifies its potential clients but which anticipates and answers their potential objections to the claims made in an on-going fashion.' She notes that this involves linking claims to statements which the client already believes and arranging statements hierarchically so that they support each other. In other words manipulating the client to arrive at a conclusion that they have already identified.

Attention to the processes whereby consultants demonstrate their value to clients is necessary, since as we noted earlier their value does not reside in the knowledge base of the activity. Oakley (1993) has usefully noted that a distinguishing feature of consultancy is that, unlike a profession, people cannot become qualified as consultants through 'rigorous and long training that leads to certification or licensure' (Blau, 1984, quoted in Oakley, 1993: 4). The point is not that such training is unavailable but that it is irrelevant, since the key to consultancy success lies more in the consultancy activity as a process of *construction of meaning* than in the mastery of any esoteric theory which might underlie it. Oakley (1993: 6) notes that one of the characteristics of 'knowledge industries', such as management consultancy, is that the knowledge which underlies success 'resists complete codification of a formal kind but... is dependent on the appreciation of complex relationships and the practice of craft skills embedded in systematic, reflective understanding.'

The focus of the consultant's activity must then be to overcome the inherent limitations of that activity. Great efforts must be made in order to persuade clients of their authority, expertise and skill. On this basis, it is fruitful to see consultancy work as symbolic action. Thus our metaphors of their work and their role must focus on how they make their claim to be of value clear, credible and distinctive. Our metaphors of their work must acknowledge their use of metaphors with their clients, i.e. their construction of myths and meanings by a process of persuasion. We must recognise that 'knowledge is inseparable from the rhetoric of persuasion and hence in a real sense. . . [management consultancies] might be seen, *par excellence* as "systems of persuasion"' (Legge, 1994: 6). It is not surprising 'therefore', that consultants have been regarded by those such as Czarniawska-Joerges (1990) as 'merchants of meaning'. Czarniawska-Joerges argues that consultants 'label' things so as to introduce 'order' and 'certainty' into organisations. Moreover, by then using metaphors to break through old labels, consultants create the expectancy of change; for while 'labels say what things are; metaphors say what they are like and could be like' (Czarniawska-Joerges, 1990: 144–5).

MANAGEMENT CONSULTANCY AS PERFORMANCE: AN INTERACTIONIST METAPHOR

Given the previous argument, we maintain that the most appropriate metaphor for understanding and analysing the activities of management consultants is one which focuses on the nature of the client–consultant interaction, and which draws attention to the ways in which this is manipulated by consultants in order to convey a sense of authority, insight and value to the client. An appropriate metaphor for consultants' roles, activities and relationships must not only focus on the issues addressed by both approaches within the literature, but must also overcome the limitations of both these traditions.

The most useful metaphor with which to view the consultant's role and activity is one which focuses on consultants' attempts to resolve their major problem – the creation and management of meaning within the client–consultant relationship. We must develop a metaphor which tries to catch and characterise the ways in which consultants typically resolve the real problem they face, i.e. the ways consultants effectively demonstrate their value, expertise and importance to clients when there is no obvious information or knowledge base on which to do this, when the services are intangible, when results are difficult for clients to evaluate, or when there is enormous competition from others.

The key to an understanding of consultancy and its success is to appreciate that successful consultancy, in its methods at least, recognises and indeed emphasises this aspect of client–consultant relations. In this respect consultancy can usefully be seen as if it were a performance. By considering the performance of the consultant we wish to draw attention to what happens when consultants and clients meet. What are the circumstances under which the consultant's 'promise' is offered, believed, sold?

This metaphor assists us to understand the consultant's actions. The focus is on *action*, on understanding what *actually happens*. Such a metaphor allows us to observe the client–consultant interaction not in terms of the technical complexities and problems of the activity, but in terms of the *achievement* of the activity itself. It allows us to show how consultants define and create a situation with clients where they are seen as and accepted as consultants, and where they are perceived to be people with particular skills and expertise to offer – people who can help.

A number of writers have looked at theatricality in organisational life – Goffman (1990) and Mangham (1978, 1986, 1990; Mangham and Overington, 1987), for example. Goffman (1990) uses the dramatic – or dramaturgical – metaphor somewhat statically for our purposes, focusing brilliantly on the heuristic advantages that accrue from conceptualising organisational and social life as if people were playing out roles, scripts and parts to audiences. We are not recommending a script-focused sense of performance, however, but are more concerned with the dynamics and implications of performance *per se*. Our interest is on seeing the consultant's work *as if it were* a performance.

When we talk of 'performance' we are not using this expression simply to refer to an occasion where individuals seek to present themselves to others in terms of certain roles (whether fixed, improvised, situational or personal), moods and attitudes. Although important, our sense of performance is not simply about *role play*. It owes more to Schechner (1977: 142) who describes it in the following terms:

> Performance originates in impulses to make things happen and to entertain;
> to get results and to fool around; to collect meanings and to pass the time; to
> be transformed into another and to celebrate oneself; to disappear and to
> show off.

By focusing on consultancy as performance we wish to draw attention to
the management – the achievement – of the performance itself as something critical to the successful 'bringing-off' of consultancy work. Any
performance is comprised of two regions – a 'front stage' and a 'back
stage'. According to Alvesson (1994: 558) symbolic resources are generated
in the 'back stage' of the supplier's organisation and then 'utilised in direct,
"front stage" encounters with customers and clients'. These two regions are
linked. The 'front stage' region refers to that part of the performance which
is visible to the audience and at which they are present. Burns (1992: 112)
notes 'some time and space for the preparation of procedures, disguises or
materials essential to the performance, or for concealment of aspects of the
performance which might either discredit it or be somehow discordant
with it.' This is the 'back stage' region. In this region the audience is
excluded, enabling the performer to 'drop his front, forgo speaking his
lines, and step out of character' (Goffman, 1990: 115). The conduct of any
performance is therefore characterised by a considerable degree of risk and
danger. Should the veil drop and the 'back stage' be revealed to the audience, the performer is exposed, with the consequence that the audience
reconceptualise the role of the performer. The outcome is total and very
public failure at the expense of acclaim.

We argue that the key to successful consultancy is the successful management of risk, promise and opportunity within a particular highly
demanding type of public performance. It has been suggested that the
value of consultants to organisations is their contribution to the reduction
of high levels of organisational uncertainty (Legge, 1994; Oakley, 1993).
What we are suggesting is that the work of consultants – bringing off successful consultant performances – is also inherently characterised by
uncertainty and risk, and that the successful ones use their ability to
manage this performance risk, to build their personal 'characters' or repu-
tations with clients and thereby convince clients of their inherent value.

But consultants' performance is not of the normal type. Their performance cannot simply be conceptualised as *theatrical*; it does not involve
performers performing at, and to, a largely passive audience. In the consulting performance the 'audience' is not merely an audience, it does not
simply listen and observe. Nor is it simply *involved* in the performance; it is
central to the performance itself. The audience *is* the performance, or at
least the *means* of the performance, its accomplice and its measurement.
Thus we wish to enlarge the concept to performance beyond its normal the-

atrical sense to include other sorts of performance where the focus is less on the performer complying with a script for and to an audience, and more on the 'performer' managing the whole event so that the audience actively contributes to the performance.

Consultancy is a performance. It is a performance within which the consultant manages meaning for the client – a meaning within which the consultant role is defined and valued. As is often the case with performances, it is an event that focuses on the irrational, emotional, sensual aspect of organisation. Successful consultants must lay claim to assisting the formal purposes of the organisation, but the ways in which they contribute are frequently via emotion and drama. Successful consultants not only use and develop emotion in their work, they also address the emotional, moral and symbolic aspects of organisation. The essence of performance is emotion. Performance depends on the development, arousal and focusing of emotion. It uses emotion; it addresses emotion. Even when a consultant performance is ostensibly concerned with cognitive, rational issues, the method is one of emotion. If a fuller understanding of the role and activity of consultants is to be achieved, we must focus our analyses of the masterful and accomplished ways in which consultants 'bring off' impressive performances with clients.

CONCLUSIONS

In this chapter we have sought to explore and develop our understanding of the relationship between management consultancies and their clients. The chapter has analysed and evaluated existing approaches to the study of management consultancy work. Two approaches were identified and considered: the problem-centred literature and the approach based on metaphor. It was argued that both impose constraints on the analysis of the client–consultant relationship.

Much of the literature on management consultancy is concerned with improving the effectiveness of intervention activities. It is also focused on identifying and solving specific consultancy problems, while recognising that these problems do not take the same form, or have the same potential of occurring, in every intervention activity. This 'technicist' literature can be classified into four broad streams – the intervention process, intervention objectives, intervention modes and information asymmetries. It was argued that it is limited in value because it assumes the very conditions that consultants themselves cannot take for granted – clients' acceptance of the value of consultancy services. The problem-focused literature is defective then because it deals with second-order technical problems and avoids the real consultancy problem – how consultants demonstrate and persuade clients that they have a useful and valuable role to play.

An alternative tradition is to conceptualise the activity of consultants in terms of some dominant metaphor. While the use of metaphors may offer illumination, it can also insidiously obstruct or distort perception. It was argued that the metaphor approach to consultancy work is flawed because this too has adopted as given the priorities and preferences of consultants themselves. If the metaphor approach is to be of use – and its value is supported here – the metaphor must focus on illuminating the ways in which consultants work to solve their major problem: how to prove and demonstrate their usefulness when they lack a credible or authoritative body of professional knowledge. The metaphor that can assist with this is one which characterises and describes the ways consultants manage and manipulate their interactions with clients to ensure their management of meaning; i.e. one which addresses their client management processes.

To conclude, we have offered a way in which to avoid the limitations of both the problem-centred and the traditional metaphorical approaches to examining management consultancy while acknowledging and preserving their respective advantages. Our prescribed route to achieving this is through the development of a metaphor which focuses on the management of meaning during client–consultant interaction.

REFERENCES

Alvesson, M. (1993) 'Organisations as rhetoric: knowledge-intensive firms and the struggle with ambiguity', *Journal of Management Studies*, Vol. 30.

Alvesson, M. (1994) 'Talking in organizations: managing identity and impressions in an advertising agency', *Organization Studies*, Vol. 15.

Argyris, C. (1970) *Intervention Theory and Method*. Reading, Mass.: Addison-Wesley.

Argyris, C. (1990) *Overcoming Organizational Defenses*. Boston: Allyn and Bacon.

Beckhard, R. (1969) *Organizational Development*. Reading, Mass.: Addison-Wesley.

Blake, R.R. and Mouton, J.S. (1983) *Consultation: A Handbook for Individual and Organizational Development*. Reading, Mass.: Addison-Wesley.

Blau, J. (1984) *Architects and Firms*. Cambridge, Mass.: MIT Press.

Burns, T. (1992) *Erving Goffman*. London: Routledge.

Clark, T. (1993) *Headhunters of Enterprise: Executive Search and Selection Consultancies*. Small Business Research Trust Business Services Research Monograph No. 1, School of Management, The Open University, Milton Keynes.

Clark, T. (1995) *Managing Consultants*. Buckingham: Open University Press.

Czarniawska-Joerges, B. (1990) 'Merchants of meaning: managing consulting in the Swedish public sector', in Turner, B. (ed) *Organizational Symbolism*. New York: Walter de Gruyter.

Ganesh, S.R. (1978) 'Organizational consultants: a comparison of styles', *Human Relations*, Vol. 31.

Gill, J. and Whittle, S. (1992) 'Management by panacea', *Journal of Management Studies*, Vol. 30.

Goffman, E. (1990) *The Presentation of Self in Everyday Life*. London: Penguin.

Greiner, L.E. and Metzger, R.O. (1983) *Consulting to Management*. Englewood Cliffs, NJ: Prentice-Hall.

Holmstrom, B. (1985) 'The provision of services in a market economy', in Inman, R.P. (ed) *Managing the Service Economy: Prospects and Problems*. Cambridge: Cambridge University Press.

Kakabadse, A.P. (1986) 'Consultants and the consultancy process', *Journal of Managerial Psychology*, Vol. 1.

Keeble, D., Bryson, J. and Wood, P. (1994) *Pathfinders of Enterprise: The Creation, Growth and Dynamics of Small Management Consultancies in Britain*. Small Business Research Trust Business Services Research Monograph No. 3, School of Management, The Open University, Milton Keynes.

Kolb, D.A. and Frohman, A.L. (1970) 'An organizational development approach to consulting', *Sloan Management Review*, Vol. 11.

Kubr, M. (1986) *Management Consulting: A Guide to the Profession*. 2nd Edition, Geneva: International Labour Office.

Lakoff, G. and Johnson, M. (1980) *Metaphors We Live By*. Chicago: University of Chicago Press.

Latour, B. (1987) *Science in Action: How to Follow Scientists and Engineers through Society*. Buckingham: Open University Press.

Legge, K. (1994) 'On knowledge, business consultants and the selling of TQM'. Unpublished paper, Lancaster School of Management, University of Lancaster.

Levitt, T. (1981) 'Marketing intangible products and product intangibles', *Harvard Business Review*, Vol. 59.

Lippitt, G. and Lippitt, R. (1978) *The Consulting Process in Action*. La Jolla, CA: University Associates.

Mangham, I.L. (1978) *Interactions and Interventions in Organizations*. Chichester: Wiley.

Mangham, I.L (1986) *Power and Performance in Organisations*. Oxford: Blackwell.

Mangham, I.L. (1990) 'Managing as a performing art', *British Journal of Management*, Vol. 1.

Mangham, I.L. and Overington, M.A. (1987) *Organisations as Theatre: A Social Psychology of Dramatic Appearances*. Chichester: Wiley.

Margulies, N. and Raia, A. (1972) *Organization Development: Values, Processes and Technology*. London: McGraw-Hill.

Mitchell, V.W. (1994) 'Problems and risks in the purchasing of consultancy services', *Service Industries Journal*, Vol. 14.

Morgan, G. (1986) *Images of Organization*. London: Sage.

Nees, D.B. and Greiner, L.E. (1985) 'Seeing behind the look-alike management consultants', *Organization Dynamics*, Vol. 14, No. 1.

Oakley, K. (1993) 'Management consultancy – profession or knowledge industry?'. Paper presented to Conference on *Professions and Management in Britain*, University of Stirling.

Ortony, A. (1975) 'Why metaphors are necessary and not just nice', *Educational Theory*, Vol. 25, No. 1.

Ortony, A. (ed) (1979) *Metaphor and Thought*. Cambridge: Cambridge University Press.

Peet, J. (1988) 'A survey of management consultancy: outside looking in', *The Economist*, February 13.

Rassam, C. and Oates, D. (1991) *Managing Consulting: The Inside Story*. London: Mercury.

Schechner, R. (1977) *Performance Theory*. New York: Routledge.

Schein, E.H. (1969) *Process Consultation: Its Role in Organization Development*. Reading, Mass.: Addison-Wesley.

Schlegelmilch, B.B., Diamantopoulos, A. and Moore, S.A. (1992) 'The market for management consulting in Britain: an analysis of supply and demand', *Management Decisions*, Vol. 30.

Schon, D.A. (1979) 'Generative metaphor: a perspective on problem-setting in social policy', in Ortony, A. (ed) *Metaphor and Thought*. Cambridge: Cambridge University Press.

Sinha, D.P. (1979) *Consultants and Consulting Styles*. London: Vision Books.

Starbuck, W.H. (1992) 'Learning by knowledge-intensive firms', *Journal of Management Studies*, Vol. 29.

Steele, F. (1975) *Consulting for Organizational Change*. Amherst, Mass.: University of Massachusetts Press.

Tilles, S. (1961) 'Understanding the consultant's role', *Harvard Business Review*, November–December.

Tisdall, P. (1982) *Agents of Change*. London: Heinemann.

Turner, A.N. (1982) 'Consulting is more than giving advice', *Harvard Business Review*, Vol. 60.

Turner, B. (1990) 'The rise of organisational symbolism', in Hasard, J. and Pym, D. (eds) *The Theory and Philosophy of Organisations*. London: Routledge.

Whitely, R. (1991) 'On the nature of managerial tasks and skills: their distinguishing characteristics and organization', *Journal of Management Studies*, Vol. 26.

CHAPTER 11

Organisational change interventions: a new set of beliefs?

Nic Beech

INTRODUCTION

This chapter will examine the intervention stage of organisational change through a metaphor of religious change. In taking this approach the chapter draws attention to certain aspects of change which are underplayed by rationalistic and technical approaches. It gives rise to a four-part typology of change. Each type has implications for management style and problem-solving approaches.

The intervention/implementation phase of organisational change can be seen as a process of conversion from one set of beliefs to another. This can involve a change in the 'way of seeing things', which has implications for the way things are done. It will be argued that the major changes which take place in Organisation Development involve an alteration in the dominant discourse. Discourses are not seen merely as patterns of language, but as ways in which limits are set specifying what concepts and expressions of those concepts are acceptable. For example, a person who is seen as a deity or messiah in one set of religious beliefs may be seen as a heretic or a false prophet from within another set of beliefs. Similarly, practices and ideas which are seen as positive in one organisational theory can be seen as negative in others. Power in organisations is implicit in the discourse (Foucault, 1974; Linstead, 1993). It relates to the ability to manipulate and structure rules and procedures. Manipulation of the rules of the discourse is not a trivial act, but is a manipulation of the way that meaning arises through the interaction of terms in the language game (Wittgenstein, 1958).

Therefore, a change in the paradigm or dominant discourse of an organisation is a change in the underlying beliefs and concepts of its members. A good example of this – one that will be discussed in more detail below – concerns total quality management (TQM). Under TQM the discourse of an organisation alters so that the customer takes pride of place. Moreover, the concept also involves members of the organisation regarding each other as 'internal customers'. Such a change will result in a very different perception of fellow members of staff and will influence relationships between people.

The metaphor of religious change is a useful one because it can illuminate the depth of the change indicated above. It helps us to see the change process as an essentially social process involving alterations to discourse that go on to affect behaviour. This is opposed to a view of change programmes as being essentially technical or rationalistic. Rationalistic approaches might introduce a new production process or service, but would de-emphasise the accompanying social changes. Successful implementation is more akin to conversion and a change in beliefs than a rational process such as accepting the outcome of a debate.

In order to expound this condensed argument the following will be examined: the nature of the intervention phase of organisational development, the process of change between paradigms/discourses, the application of the metaphor of religious change, and a critical examination of the value of the metaphor.

THE INTERVENTION PHASE OF ORGANISATIONAL CHANGE

The OD process can be seen as having three components: the diagnostic, the action (or intervention), and the process maintenance (French and Bell, 1984). The intervention phase is where the organisational system is altered in some way in order to make improvements. The intervention can aim to make changes in the total organisation, in teams, in increasing co-operation and problem solving, or it can relate to the roles employees have and the way they interact. OD interventions have been characterised as having five defining features (Beckhard, 1969). OD is planned, organisation-wide, managed from the top, concerned with increasing effectiveness, and usually involves changing the organisation's processes and attitude. A variety of methods can be used to bring about such changes, for example training and re-education, process consultation, data feedback and relationship and procedural interventions (Blake and Mouton, 1964). OD is then the phase at which there is an attempt to intervene in the organisational system to alter the way employees think and act. Examples include getting them to work co-operatively in teams, redefining the roles they have at work and introducing new techniques and skills. Such changes are not superficial and can be far-reaching in their consequences.

A number of factors can be identified as important influences on the level of success of the intervention. They include the process of encapsulating, strategic leadership, the role of the change agent and gaining organisational commitment to the new vision. These factors are part of a management style which sends messages to employees about what behaviour is acceptable, what the goals are, how success will be measured, and what the appropriate beliefs or approach are. In effect, the management style is vital to ensuring that the organisation as a whole falls into line with its leadership's newly acquired vision. (Management style and the use of metaphors to effect change are discussed by Broussine and Vince in Chapter 4.)

Formulating and applying leadership vision within an organisational setting can be broken down into a three-stage process: envisioning the image of the future state of the organisation, effectively communicating this to followers, and empowering the followers so that they can follow the vision (Westley and Mintzberg, 1991). The ability to carry out this process of empowering followers to act on the vision relies not only on informing them of the vision, but also on involving them in the vision. It is possible for employees to learn a set of behaviours which are seen as appropriate, but this would not be achieving change in the way required by Organisation Development. Learning sets of behaviours alone would lead to an inflexible set of responses, which is not desirable for organisations in environments which require the ability to adapt quickly (Kanter, 1989).

The way that vision is communicated is particularly important. As Kanter puts it:

> Martin Luther King's famous speech... personified this [leadership] as 'I have a dream'. He didn't say, 'I have a few ideas; there seem to be some problems out there. Maybe if we set up a few committees'. (Kanter, 1991: 56)

In order to gain commitment, communication needs to be 'energised' by conviction. Commitment is further gained by involving people in teams, forming coalitions, giving feedback, monitoring and evaluating the change (French and Bell, 1984).

Change agents can also play a role in the intervention. They can be a member of the organisation or, as discussed by Clark and Salaman in Chapter 10, can be an external consultant. A number of different styles can be adopted including being supportive of the emotional aspects of change, acting as a catalyst, making prescriptions, and helping organisation members to confront discrepancies between the values and beliefs they hold and their actual practice (Cockman et al, 1992). This role includes elements of inspiring change.

Intervention does not only lead to changes in the organisation. Analysis of narrative accounts from managers involved in change has indicated that individual interpretation is key to understanding change (Isabella, 1990). Four stages are revealed: 'anticipation', involving rumour and an attempt by individuals to piece together information; 'confirmation', which enables information to be fitted into stereotypical or conventional frames of reference (formed on the basis of the past); 'culmination', allowing the individual to amend their earlier interpretations and reconstruct history by moving out of the standard frames of reference (this is linked to symbolism and the search for new meanings); and finally 'aftermath', during which the events of the change are tested to confirm the new reality.

As an organisation goes through the intervention process, different individuals may be at different stages of this interpretive development at any one time. For example, managers may be at the stage of culmination where they are moving into a new frame of reference, while employees may be at the stage of confirmation where they are trying to fit information into the old frame of reference. This will have implications for the way that the vision can be expressed, and the appropriate management/consultancy style.

An examination of some organisation change interventions may serve to illustrate the nature of the intervention process. Earlier it was argued that satisfying customers' current and future needs and expectations can be seen as a central maxim of TQM and that this involves seeing other members of the organisation for whom a task is performed as internal customers (Dale and Cooper, 1992). The concept is that employees see themselves as suppliers for the next user of the service or product they are providing. There is a feedback loop between the suppliers and the internal customers in which expectations are expressed and requirements drawn up and catered for. For example, there may be change in the way that a finance department relates to line managers where there has been a process of devolving budgets and introducing the concept of internal customers. If the line managers are seen as internal customers, it implies that they are receiving a service over which they have some right to exercise demand. Therefore, the information they need in order to make budget decisions has to be supplied to them in a way which is non-technical and at a time when they need it. This represents a break with a controlling tradition of finance departments where spending departments have to check with them first and information may be stored and used in the form of technical language. With the introduction of the concept of the internal customer there is a change in the power of the relationship, and a change in the concepts which underlie the workings of the relationship. This has an impact on how decisions are made and by whom.

TQM can also be explicit about the role of concepts and frameworks of understanding. A three-part approach to managing TQM change (Dale, 1992) starts with understanding the cultural parameters which provide a basis for a common-level understanding throughout the organisation. The second stage involves measuring the fit of behaviour with these parameters. The final stage requires a plan of action (including training) to be drawn up that meets the requirements of the envisaged future situation.

A related form of change is the introduction of quality circles, which were popular during the 1980s. Quality circles are small groups (5–12 people) who meet to improve quality and productivity in their area. The concept was popularised in Japan, and is related to the idea of continuous self- and mutual development. The circles are led by team leaders, and they select work-based quality problems or issues and make suggestions on how improvements could be made. The aims are to increase the participation of workers in decision making, to increase job satisfaction and to stimulate personal growth (Hill, 1991). In some organisations they are restricted to relatively minor problems and issues (Schonberger, 1982), but in others there is a greater degree of devolvement of authority and responsibility.

This represents a shift in focus from traditional quality control (and the shift is even greater with the adoption of fully fledged TQM). The key difference is the role of the worker in quality control, and the conceptual framework which underlies the change. In extreme forms, traditional quality control is Tayloristic. The responsibility for evaluating output is in the hands of specialists, who have power over the workers who carry out production. This represents a separation of the 'thinking' aspects of work from the 'doing' aspects. In other words, it is a deskilling process (Braverman, 1974). The quality approaches discussed above are supposed to change responsibilities and reduce differentiation by including 'thinking' aspects of work in the job design. The significance of this is greater than merely changing a job description. It is indicative of a different conception of the way people are motivated (by having more control over their work, as opposed to being controlled or coerced into making effort), and of the nature of power relations in the work process.

Another form of organisational change which has recently gained prominence is business process re-engineering (BPR). BPR involves radical questioning of the way an organisation is working, with the aims of redesigning the processes and eliminating any non-central activities (Thomas, 1994). BPR frequently involves a change in the view of the way work is organised. Work can be organised around functional specialisms. In such cases a raw product (or service) will move from one department to another as they perform their specialisms to add up to a total finished product. In the case of Mutual Benefit Life (Hammer, 1990), new applications to the company were dealt with by a complex series of clerical processes in which the application went through 30 steps, 5 departments and the hands of 20 people. The process took between 5 and 10 days to complete. After a BPR intervention each application was dealt with by a single 'case manager' (apart from the most complicated cases). The case manager would work through a series of decisions about the case, supported by an expert system and database. The case has become central and forms of specialisation were brought to it via the expert system, rather than the functions being central and the case moving from one to the next. The time taken to process applications was reduced to 2–5 days, and there were major reductions in the number of staff involved.

This example indicates a move away from a departmentalised functional structure and a situation where the focus of organisation was the functional specialism of the employee, to a delayered individualised structure where the emphasis was on the case application.

Trends within currently popular change interventions such as quality and BPR approaches can be traced to more traditional OD. When the aim is total Organisation Development, the fundamental change is of concepts about the way things are understood and done. For example, a change to more organic forms of organisation (Burns and Stalker, 1961) can include elements such as teamworking. This challenges mechanistic ideas about the division of roles, hierarchies, authority and control, and encourages flexibility between members of a team. Members may expand their skills to be able to carry out a variety of tasks which fall under the remit of the team. This does not only involve different behaviours, but also different concepts of status, role, purpose and loyalty. The aim is to change and develop the meaning of work.

A common thread runs through the examples cited above. In each, a change in conceptual framework underlies a change in behaviour. In order to achieve genuinely effective OD interventions it is necessary for the individuals concerned to develop a new form of thinking, not just to change their behaviour at a superficial level. If behaviour alone is changed, then the modified form may occur in known situations where expected stimuli exist. However, in novel situations the individual may revert to their former mode of behaviour because their way of thinking has not changed. A worker who has learnt a new behavioural response to a stimulus (which is part of a new approach) can apply the new behaviour when prompted by the relevant stimulus. However, it is only the worker who has understood the underlying concepts who can produce an appropriate behavioural response when faced with stimuli for which they have not been directly trained. As organisations face increasingly complex and changing environments, a workforce is required which can apply principles in novel situations rather than relying on established behavioural patterns. Individuals are empowered when they are imbued with the new conceptual framework, so that in new situations they can act as if behavioural patterns had been established to meet that contingency from within the new model. That is, individuals become creators of the new model in the way they apply it.

CHANGING METAPHORS/PARADIGMS

The traditional view of the development of knowledge, particularly in the sciences, was that it was cumulative. Each new discovery was seen as adding to the sum of knowledge which existed previously. The result was progression thought to form a path towards the Truth. This view was challenged by Kuhn (1962, 1970). His argument was that while there were periods of cumulative growth, these only occurred when there were frameworks, or paradigms, which were generally accepted by the research community. Paradigms act as 'umbrella' theories which define the questions of interest, the appropriate methods of enquiry, and the boundaries of the on-going research process. Normal research is conducted into the implications of the paradigm, and is designed to solve 'puzzles' which it throws up.

The process of changing from one paradigm to another is not a smooth and evolutionary process, but occurs in an episode of revolution which involves irrational elements. Paradigms are incommensurable, so evidence which is significant in one theory may not be seen as important in another. Paradigms are different language games between which there is not a simple, rational debate. A rational debate presumes a set of common ground rules, but it is precisely the ground rules which are changed in a paradigm shift. Moving language games is like moving from draughts to chess; the rules change even though there are some resemblances (Wittgenstein, 1958). An example is the discovery of oxygen. This was not based on new evidence. Researchers had previously carried out the right processes to produce it, but as they had no concept of oxygen they had not perceived it. It is only when a different conceptual framework is embraced that the evidence is perceived in a new way.

Evidence for the new paradigm will not necessarily interact critically with the old paradigm. The change is more akin to a 'leap of faith' than the outcome of a rational argument between two positions within the same discourse. A key change agent in a paradigm shift has often been someone new to the field. This is significant because the innovator is not bound up with the rules and processes of the old paradigm. Kuhn acknowledges that in these aspects the study of science is similar to theology.

Morgan's (1986) treatment of metaphor is similar to the concept of paradigms. Metaphors are 'ways of thinking and seeing things' (1986: 12) which pervade the way the world is understood. Metaphors of organisations, for example as machines or as cultures, set out ground rules for further development. The machine metaphor is concerned with measuring output and the role of functions within the system. A metaphor of culture is concerned with norms of action and systems of belief. It is not that one is an improvement on the other in objective terms; rather each would reject the terms of the other. Although development of an organisation within a metaphor or paradigm would be incremental, change to a new metaphor or paradigm would be revolutionary.

Change approaches such as OD, TQM and BPR can involve fundamental changes in the framework of understanding which underlies behaviour, and it has been argued that this is desirable when organisations need a flex-ible responsive workforce to adapt to novel situations. It will be argued that these changes have important features in common with changes in reli-gious belief systems, and that this metaphor is a more useful way of explaining change intervention processes than a rationalistic (e.g. dialogue) explanation which assumes evolutionary development within a discourse, rather than revolutionary change.

CHANGE AND THE METAPHOR OF RELIGION

Figure 11.1 shows how religious changes may be characterised along two scales: macro–micro, and revolutionary–incremental. The introduction of a new religion would be macro-revolutionary change as it affects the whole community of members in a drastic way. An alteration to the rules of a com-munity, for example the introduction of the ordination of women in the Church of England, is a macro-incremental change as it affects the whole community but is a modification (albeit a significant one) rather than a rejec-tion of the conceptual framework. An individual's conversion to a religion is a micro-revolutionary change, whereas gaining a new understanding of a rule and acting accordingly is a micro-incremental change.

Macro-revolutionary changes have a fundamental effect on the conceptual framework of the community. Such changes frequently involve a charismatic leader who has a message which people need or are willing to hear. The propensity to accept the message may arise from a need to have an under-standing of, or a way of dealing with, unexplained or poorly explained phenomena. This indicates that the previously held beliefs need to be able to give answers to key problems, but a factor of importance is their ability to provide a way forward, a way of seeking solutions in new situations.

Macro-incremental changes will have a far-reaching effect and may inter-act with fundamental principles, but they indicate a framework adapting,

Macro-revolutionary	Macro-incremental
Micro-revolutionary	Micro-incremental

Figure 11.1 The metaphor of religious change

rather than being replaced. Examples within the Anglican and Roman Catholic traditions in Britain would be the ordination of women, and the use of contraception. Both of these issues have been the subject of intense debate, because it is not unequivocally clear from basic principles whether or not women should be ordained, or contraception be seen as acceptable. As such, these macro problems are dealt with by high-status members of the community, leaders, members of synods and so on. They are concerned either to create a rule where one does not exist, or to clarify an existing rule. In either case, the rules add on to the existing body of beliefs, rather than fundamentally challenging it.

Religious belief systems frequently establish purposes. Metaphysical beliefs about why the world and people were created relate to ideas of individual purpose and function such as serving a greater good, acting out the purposes of God and so on. In addition to encoding purposes, various forms of action are proscribed and prescribed. Clearly, however, some actions will fall outside the overt rules governing behaviour. In such circumstances the depth of the embeddedness of the individual comes into play. People who are a member of a particular religion have a religious 'attitude'. This means that their way of thinking is inherently linked to the conceptual framework. In situations where there is no clear rule, this allows them to act in the way a rule would prescribe if it had been written. This level of absorption can be related to the highest level of ethical development of post-conventional reasoning (Kohlberg, 1981, 1984; Snell, 1993). At the post-conventional level people have moved past acting properly (because of fear of punishment or because of their social roles) into a phase of fully adopting principles of action, and developing new forms of practice to express those principles. At the most developed level the individual both follows from and inputs to the basic principles. Acts of individual conscience can add to the sum view of what constitutes appropriate behaviour within the community. What has occurred is not a religious conversion but a revised and socially acceptable interpretation of existing beliefs by the individual. This would constitute an example of micro-incremental change.

Micro-incremental change can also arise when an individual experiences problems in the interpretation of a rule. They may seek advice from written sources, or sources (such as priests) in the structure of the community. The questions being addressed are not about their fundamental beliefs, but about how they enact those beliefs.

Micro-revolutionary change relates to a fundamental change in the system of beliefs held by an individual. This may be a conversion process, where a new vision is received. The acceptance of a new paradigm enables the individual to 'see the light'. In particular, life events or experiences which create a propensity to accept the new set of beliefs may be important contextual factors. Normally there will be ceremonies (such as baptism) to symbolise the change.

When one thinks of the process of paradigm change outlined by Kuhn (1970), it can clearly be related to this classification of change in religion. There is then a fundamental similarity between the two – the replacement or adaptation of framework or thought.

APPLYING THE RELIGIOUS METAPHOR OF CHANGE

Certain lessons can be drawn from an analysis of the religious metaphor of change. Change which is incremental assumes stability in the framework (either at macro or micro levels), and takes place in different conditions to revolutionary change. In contrast, a revolution is not just a very big version of incremental change, it is something quite different in nature as it assumes a basic instability in the framework of thought. Such differences explain why when applying the revolutionary/incremental dimension to organisational change we can see a variety of approaches to the intervention process.

Similarly, change at both micro and macro levels take place in OD, and this too implies the need for different management consultancy styles. In addition, and to demonstrate the use of the religious metaphor a little further, attention should be paid to the use of ceremonies, rituals and symbols. These can involve, for example, a change in corporate name and logo (as with the change of polytechnics to universities), or a public relations event to launch a new product.

The role of rationality is also important. Some models that look at decision making related to the organisation are rationalistic in nature. For example, Porter (1980, 1985) advocates decisions based on an analysis of the environmental forces operating on an organisation. Similarly, strategic management texts encourage the use of analytical techniques to assess the strengths and weaknesses of the organisation, and to deduce the appropriate direction in which to go (Johnson and Scholes, 1984). However, a number of criticisms have been voiced about these models. It has been argued that decisions made by managers are not necessarily fully rational in that they have limited information (Lindblom, 1968), that direction emerges from experimentation (Quinn, 1989), and that strategy can be emergent rather than deliberate (Mintzberg and Walters, 1989).

Application of the religious metaphor supports the view that rationality is limited in deciding on the direction of organisational change. However, it goes further, in that it is seen as desirable that non-rational elements are stressed in the intervention phase if it is to be successful.

An example of an attempt to make a macro-revolutionary change is the series of interventions carried out in British Airways (BA) throughout the 1980s. The circumstances were right for paradigmatic change as there was a degree of crisis in 1981. Money was being lost at the rate of £200 per minute, there were poor industrial relations, over-staffing and bureaucratic management (Hopfl, 1993). In addition there were external (political) forces for change. In the circumstances the existing paradigm had reached a point of breakdown. It cannot be proved that prolonged bureaucratic manage-ment (the existing paradigm) would not have served to bring about recovery in BA; however, it was sufficiently doubted to bring about a crisis of faith.

A new chairman and a new chief executive were appointed. These key figures brought with them a different view of the way things should be understood and done – a new vision of what BA could look like. This not only involved a major cutting exercise (staff numbers were cut from 60 000 to 38 000), but also a new focus on the customer. The vision was clear and distinct for those involved, and this was important in order to start the process of macro-revolutionary intervention.

In order to support the change in the long term, a more supportive intervention is also needed. In the case of BA this involved a series of training and development events which were cumulative. In 1983 12 000 customer-contact staff went through a two-day training event, 'Putting People First'. This aimed to increase their self-esteem and confidence and to improve the way they dealt with other people (principally customers). 'Customer First Teams' using quality circle techniques were established in 1984, and subsequent training interventions included 'Managing People First' which aimed to increase the openness and vision of managers in establishing trust-based relationships.

These interventions represent a process of macro-incremental change aimed at substantiating and supporting the revolutionary change. They indicate a change in management style and an increase in involvement. This is important in facilitating individuals' progress through the micro-incremental change of developing customer awareness, working in a quality-oriented way, and fulfilling the various aspects of the framework.

It is notable that there was a concerted attempt to alter the discourse of the organisation. Some employees found this difficult, experiencing con-flicts between caring values and the need to generate profits. This meant that the interventions during the 1980s were 'emotionally charged' (Hopfl, 1993). The interventions, changes in senior management and reductions in the levels of staffing were all important symbols of the new paradigm. The interventions also have an element of ritual about them in that a large pro-portion of the staff went through them and they symbolised a change from the old to the new.

A different approach to change, which can also be analysed using the metaphor, is exemplified by Business in the Community. Business in the Community (BITC) was established in 1982 as a not-for-profit organisation with the aim of increasing ethical investment by business and public sector organisations in the communities within which they operate. BITC functions as a change agent, a campaigner and a catalyst, carrying out interventions in a wide range of organisations (Beech and Moore, 1994).

BITC's strategies for eliciting change have been successful and by the end of 1993 there were 450 member organisations and an annual turnover of £5 million. The strategy has been one of subtle evangelism, aiming for significant but not revolutionary change. It is not revolutionary (and is therefore incremental) because it still accepts the basic precepts of business (such as the need to make a profit). Nevertheless, it represents significant change because it is seeking to widen the framework and incorporate other (social) needs such as those relating to equal opportunities, regional development and investment in the community.

BITC has developed a series of methods for gaining converts. When targeting an organisation it identifies individuals who hold key positions and may be sympathetic to its ideas. This is done through examining organisational charitable giving, using personal contacts with existing members and so on. Thus the aim is to target individuals for whom involvement with BITC would not be micro-revolutionary, but micro-incremental change. The BITC change agents gain access to the individuals identified by entering business, and relating BITC activities to business aims such as team building and enhancing reputation.

There is also a conscious use of symbols and rituals. For example, the 'seeing is believing' campaign can be seen as a ritual-centred form of evangelism. Business leaders are invited to attend an event which is chaired by the Prince of Wales. They are asked to select a project to visit, and to report back saying how they can contribute. Projects have included the regeneration of a housing estate, building links between business and schools and addressing homelessness projects. The campaign has been successful in gaining considerable commitment. One campaign leader claimed it has the 'Heineken effect' as it reaches the parts other approaches could not.

The outcomes which BITC has achieved are grouped under various campaign headings. 'Employees in the Community' has been a significant campaign. It aims to facilitate the employees of organisations volunteering to undertake activities which will benefit their local community. Employees give their time and enthusiasm, and organisations give resources and sometimes staff time. Projects have included ecological work to help with the regeneration of woodlands, providing sea-going activities for disadvantaged children and building a playground for disabled children. The concept is sold to organisations as a way of helping with team building and staff morale. Many participants have reported finding out new things about the people with whom they work and feeling good about contributing something. Once organisations become involved they typically maintain their commitment, and often become evangelists themselves.

A number of different management and change agent styles are used in the evangelical intervention process. BITC starts with a clear vision which is communicated in the dominant discourse. Once it achieves micro change in key decision makers, it makes use of high status, symbols and rituals to gain commitment. Once commitment is gained the approach changes to a more facilitative one. For example, in employee volunteering the employees themselves are encouraged to generate ideas for projects.

Although the aim is not to subvert the dominant discourse, significant changes do occur when businesses start to talk of a wider range of stakeholders and expend energy on projects which do not relate to their main goal of creating a profit. It is also notable that employees give their time and effort for no remuneration. The changes tend to be long term, but to return to our earlier religious examples, they are probably more similar to the ordination of women than conversion to Christianity.

In general the metaphor implies that in cases of macro-revolutionary change particular emphasis should be placed on vision and the introduction of a new paradigm, either through key individuals making micro-revolutionary changes or, as in the case of BA, by introducing new individuals who already hold a new paradigm. Such periods need to be supplemented by periods of macro-incremental change, in which a more facilitative style of management is appropriate as employees work through what is involved in acting out the new paradigm. This leadership role is akin to the priest's role of encourager and interpreter of the rules of the paradigm. Change under the religious metaphor can then be dramatic and sudden, but is not necessarily so. It can be a gradual process as under micro-incrementalism. Such a process was seen in the interventions carried out by BITC where employees were encouraged to become involved and to contribute their own ideas and projects. It can lead to a level of development, as noted by Kohlberg (1981), where in effect the members of the organisation are interacting with the paradigm, and are applying it in new situations. At this stage flexibility of response has been achieved through commitment.

It should be noted that the metaphor of religious change does not assume or guarantee smooth conversions. In particular, difficulties can arise when a change is generally perceived as fitting one category, but some individuals perceive it as another. For example, the acceptance of the ordination of women in the Church of England was managed as if it were a macro-incremental change. A rational debate was carried out within what was assumed to be an accepted framework. The proponents of women's ordination were arguing for what they saw as the best possible interpretation of the basic concepts of the Church. They were not arguing for a revolution to destroy the basic concepts. However, some members did perceive the change as revolutionary. They did feel that it altered the fundamental framework and as a result left (the social grouping of) the Church.

The issue here is not whether the change can be judged objectively to be revolutionary or incremental. Rather, the concern is that for some members it was revolutionary and for others it was incremental change. As was discussed earlier, it follows that if the change is to be successful, different members will need different styles of change management. Rational debate may work for those who perceive it as incremental, but for others a leap of faith is required to alter their basic concepts. Where this did not occur there was 'micro fallout'; that is, some members left the organisation.

Within business organisations this type of conflict can result in individuals leaving. However, where easy mobility to other organisations does not exist, the individuals may remain but be alienated from the new approach.

LIMITS TO THE USE OF THE METAPHOR

Although the metaphor of religious change can be used to illuminate Organisation Development interventions, limits to the utility of the metaphor can be identified. Technological factors do not feature strongly in the metaphor, but some aspects of change are generated or facilitated by advances in technology. Many cases of BPR entail the introduction of new information technology, and would not be possible without it.

Intuition, emotion and non-linear forms of thought are important in the way people form beliefs and are converted to 'ways of seeing things', but there are also rational elements. In the organisational setting, SWOT analyses and other rational measures of problems and potential solutions are both useful and important. These aspects may be underplayed in the metaphor, however, when the concentration is on the intervention phase of OD. It is often the emotional, belief-oriented areas of human thinking which can strongly influence the success or failure of a project – an issue investigated by Broussine and Vince in Chapter 4.

A third limitation is that while religious belief systems encompass whole ways of life, organisational paradigms are less pervasive, and probably less deeply held by individuals. Therefore change in the organisational sphere is less difficult than in the religious sphere. However, given the great amount of attention paid to resistance to change in organisations, it could be concluded that beliefs are deeply held in organisations.

CONCLUSIONS

The metaphor of religious change can be used as an analytical tool in assessments of OD interventions. Its particular strengths are the emphasis on ritual, discourse, style of leadership, visioning, and the revolutionary nature of fundamental OD. It must also be acknowledged that there are important rational and technical aspects to OD interventions. However, in the literature on change and strategic interventions considerable attention has been paid to these factors. Tools of analysis have been devised to help decision makers to be as objective and rational as possible, and irrational elements are seen as problems to be eradicated. The religious change metaphor seeks to provide some balance to this view. Sets of beliefs and emotional attachments are not just irritating impediments to change. They are what an organisation needs to develop if it is to have a genuinely adaptive workforce who can apply concepts in novel situations.

Achieving such a change is similar to achieving a shift in paradigms or religious beliefs. Changes in this arena can occur in a number of ways: macro-revolutionary, macro-incremental, micro-revolutionary and micro-incremental. Different change management styles are appropriate in these different classifications. Visioning and directive charismatic leadership may be appropriate in revolutionary change, whereas debate and involvement can be more appropriate where there is incremental change. Use of an inappropriate style can lead to major problems, including individuals leaving the organisation. A key difficulty for management is that at any one time different individuals may be going through different types of change. An awareness of these difficulties, combined with an ability to adopt the appropriate style of management change, is therefore necessary if they are to be overcome.

REFERENCES

Beckhard, R. (1969) *Organizational Developments: Strategies and Models.* Reading, Mass.: Addison-Wesley.

Beech, N. and Moore, K. (1994) 'Business in the community', in Scholes, K. and Darwin, J. (eds) *Exploring Public Sector Strategy: A Casebook.* Sheffield: PAVIC Publications.

Blake, R.R. and Mouton, J.S. (1964) *The Managerial Grid.* Houston: Gulf.

Braverman, H. (1974) *Labour and Monopoly Capital.* New York: Monthly Press.

Burns, T. and Stalker, G.M. (1961) *The Management of Innovation.* London: Tavistock.

Cockman, P., Evans, B. and Reynolds, P. (1992) *Client-Centered Consulting.* London: McGraw-Hill.

Dale, B.G. (1992) 'Continuous quality improvement: why some organizations lack commitment', *International Journal of Production,* Vol. 27, No. 1.

Dale, B. and Cooper, C. (1992) *Total Quality and Human Resources.* Oxford: Blackwell.

Foucault, M. (1974) *The Archeology of Knowledge.* London: Tavistock.

French, W.L. and Bell, C.H. (1984) *Organizational Development: Behavioral Science Interventions for Organizational Improvement.* 3rd Edition, Englewood Cliffs, NJ: Prentice-Hall.

Hammer, M. (1990) 'Re-engineering work: don't automate, obliterate', *Harvard Business Review,* July–August.

Hill, S. (1991) 'Why quality circles failed but total quality management might succeed', *British Journal of Industrial Relations,* Vol. 29, No. 4.

Hopfl, H. (1993) 'Culture and commitment: British Airways', in Gowler, D., Legge, K. and Clegg, C. (eds) *Case Studies in Organizational Behaviour and Human Resources Management*. 2nd Edition, London: Paul Chapman.

Isabella, L.A. (1990) 'Evolving interpretations as a change unfolds: how managers construe key organizational events', *Academy of Management Journal*, Vol. 33, No. 1.

Johnson, G. and Scholes, K. (1984) *Exploring Corporate Strategy*. 3rd Edition, London: Prentice-Hall.

Kanter, R.M. (1989) *When Giants Learn to Dance: Mastering the Challenge of Strategy, Management and Careers in the 1990s*. London: Unwin.

Kanter, R.M. (1991) 'Change-master skills: what it takes to be creative', in Henry, J. and Walter, D. (eds) *Managing Innovation*. London: Sage.

Kohlberg, L. (1981) *Essays in Moral Development, Volume One: The Philosophy of Moral Development, Vol 1*. New York: Harper and Row.

Kohlberg, L. (1984) *Essays in Moral Development, Volume Two: The Philosophy of Moral Development, Vol. 2*. New York: Harper and Row.

Kuhn, T.S. (1962) *The Structure of Scientific Revolutions*. Chicago: The University of Chicago Press.

Kuhn, T.S. (1970) *The Structure of Scientific Revolutions*. 2nd Edition, Chicago: The University of Chicago Press.

Lindblom, C. (1968) 'The science of "muddling through"', in Etzioni, A. (ed) *Readings on Modern Organizations*. Englewood Cliffs, NJ: Prentice-Hall.

Linstead, S. (1993) 'Deconstruction in the study of organisations', in Hassard, J. and Parker, M. (eds) *Postmodernism and Organisations*. London: Sage.

Mintzberg, H. and Walters, J.A. (1989) 'Of strategies, deliberate and emergent', in Asch, D. and Bowman, C. (eds) *Readings in Strategic Management*. Basingstoke: Macmillan.

Morgan, G. (1986) *Images of Organization*. London: Sage.

Porter, M.E. (1980) *Competitive Strategy*. New York: Free Press.

Porter, M.E. (1985) *Competitive Advantage*. New York: Free Press.

Quinn, J.B. (1989) 'Managing strategic change', in Asch, D. and Bowman, C. (eds) *Readings in Strategic Management*. Basingstoke: Macmillan.

Schonberger, R. (1982) *Japanese Manufacturing Techniques*. New York: Free Press.

Snell, R. (1993) *Developing Skills for Ethical Management*. London: Chapman and Hall.

Thomas, M. (1994) 'What you need to know about business process re-engineering', *Personnel Management*, Vol. 26, No. 1.

Westley, F. and Mintzberg, H. (1991) 'Visionary leadership and strategic management', in Henry, J. and Walker, D. (eds) *Managing Innovation*. London: Sage.

Wittgenstein, L. (1958) *Philosophical Investigations*. 2nd Edition (translated by G.E.M. Anscombe), Oxford: Basil Blackwell.

PART IV

Management strategies and development

INTRODUCTION

The three chapters contained in this part of the book respectively address human resource management (HRM), outdoor management development (OMD), and small business development. At a surface level these areas do not appear to share much common ground. Arguably, the most striking similarity is the manner in which these important issues have been neglected by OD consultants and ignored in most of the mainstream OD textbooks. If we think of OD as a journey, we can regard the areas tackled in this section as being analogous to 'major sites of interest' which are frequently overlooked by tourists and visitors to the OD domain.

It is perhaps worthwhile briefly elaborating on the relevance of the three chapters before outlining their contents. HRM and OD share a number of similar features, particularly in terms of their humanistic orientation. The relative status of HRM and OD is rather hazy. Some commentators would suggest that HRM is a subset of OD activity or that it represents an extension of the discipline. It could equally be argued that HRM is a distinct and separate field of enquiry. No matter which of the viewpoints is adopted, it is clear that HRM warrants inclusion and consideration within the OD literature.

There is also a paucity of research which applies OD principles to small businesses. If OD is primarily concerned with increasing organisational effectiveness and health, should it not apply to all organisations regardless of size? If we turn to OMD, there can be little doubt that OMD qualifies as a form of OD intervention. However, its existence is rarely acknowledged in the core texts. OMD is frequently used as a means of team building. It is also used as a medium for inter-personal interventions such as 'T' groups, and this area of application is reflected in the recently coined term of 'outdoor labs'.

In Chapter 12 Grant suggests that HRM has often been described using a type of metaphor which creates something which is highly desirable and of great value while at the same time being imprecise, and perhaps most importantly unobtainable. The root metaphor which pervades the HRM literature is a *becoming* metaphor and is most commonly portrayed as a journey. In particular, HRM has been described as analogous to a pioneering wagon train in the American West, aiming to move beyond existing frontiers into new and uncharted territory. Grant reassesses this root metaphor and its recent influence on the way employees are managed. This leads him to discuss how under HRM, internalised forms of control are used by management so as to bolster external control mechanisms. It is argued that in terms of the journey metaphor there is a definite homecoming for management in so far as they have made significant gains in the battle for control of the workplace.

The existence of a unique metaphorical link between the activities and processes which constitute OMD and those found within organisations is explored in Chapter 13. Jones argues that much of the support for the effectiveness of OMD is largely based on anecdotal evidence. The claims that outdoor training is a 'great leveller' and exhibits 'high process reality' are investigated. It is posited that although OMD may improve managerial skills and performance, a further area of application relates to the formation of learning skills. The author concludes that one of the principal benefits of OMD lies in its ability to help participants in learning how to learn and hence the development of learner autonomy.

Chapter 14, by Perren, uses a series of biological metaphors to investigate small business behaviour and development. Six categories of biological metaphor are explored in relation to small businesses, namely classification, evolution, stage models, disease, symbiosis, and genetic engineering. A synthesis of the insights provided by the various biological metaphors is undertaken and the resultant implications for future research are discussed. Finally, the limitations of the metaphor are examined, including a consideration of the danger that it becomes an 'intellectual cage' which restricts rather than enables understanding.

CHAPTER 12

Metaphors, human resource management and control

David Grant

INTRODUCTION

The way in which human resource management (HRM) links the management of employees to business strategy has been the focus of considerable discussion (see, for example, Armstrong, 1987; Beer and Spector, 1985; Boxall, 1993; Guest, 1987, 1989a, 1991; Hendry et al, 1988; Noon, 1992; Storey, 1989, 1992). Under HRM, employees are recognised as a key resource – one that is vital to ensuring an organisation's competitive advantage. To this end, the organisation places considerable value on an integrated package of policies and practices related to employee training, development and motivation.

As this chapter will go on to show, attempts by organisations to move towards more HRM-oriented workplaces can be portrayed as a journey. It is consultants, as practitioners of Organisation Development (OD), who often assist organisations in making this journey. Hence, reading HRM case study literature it is common to find OD consultants involved in the design and implementation of HRM policies and practices (see, for example, the discussions of Rover and ICI in Storey, 1992). Their involvement comes as no surprise. After all, there is a considerable overlap between HRM and OD.

The overlap between HRM and OD can be interpreted in two ways. Both interpretations suggest that OD consultants have significantly contributed to the growth of HRM. First, it can be argued that it is inevitable that OD consultants, as change agents, are likely to use what they consider to be the best tools to effect change. Often these tools will be akin to HRM policies and practices and this reflects the apparent similarities between OD and HRM. The argument can be taken further in that many HRM policies and practices could be seen as a subset of existing OD techniques, or that the roots of HRM can be traced back to OD, i.e. HRM policies and practices were available as OD techniques some time before HRM itself arrived on the scene. The second interpretation of the overlap is that HRM appears as something new and innovative and that it has a potential to improve competitiveness. Accordingly, it has not taken consultants long to perceive that these attributes make HRM highly attractive to organisations and they have therefore been quick to market and apply it. For further discussion of the overlap between OD and HRM see, for example, Hallier (1993).

Where HRM is put into operation it is essential to analyse the nature of workplace control. From a management perspective workplace control is an economic necessity – without it an organisation cannot be regarded as economically viable (Huczynski and Buchanan, 1991: 577–605). The importance of this issue is implicit in most studies of control and often, as in the case of Salaman's work (1981: 164), explicit. Consequently, and as this chapter will demonstrate, management never, even under HRM, abdicates control of the workplace in any meaningful sense.

In what follows it is argued that an evaluation of the type of metaphor used to describe HRM leads to an understanding of the nature of workplace control under HRM. We shall also see that management is able to manipulate the metaphor in its favour and that this exposes the control mechanisms in use under HRM in a new light.

THE ROOT METAPHORS OF OLD INDUSTRIAL RELATIONS AND HRM

To begin with it is necessary to look at the recent UK debate concerning 'old' and 'new' industrial relations. One of the most influential articles on this issue has been provided by Dunn (1990). He identifies 'root metaphors' for the old and new industrial relations. For the purpose of clarification, two points need to be made. First, to Dunn, new industrial relations is synonymous with HRM – the subject of this chapter. Second, by 'root metaphor' he is talking about the key metaphor on which knowledge about a subject is based and which is used to start off thought processes that expand that knowledge.

For Dunn the root metaphor of old industrial relations is Goodrich's (1975, first published 1920) 'frontier of control'. He sets out to demonstrate that Goodrich provided an extraordinarily powerful and pervasive metaphor – one that provides the perfect starting point for an understanding of British industrial relations up until the 1980s. The frontier it describes reflects the point where workers resist management's exercising their prerogative in order to attain or retain control over certain issues at the workplace. There is not always agreement on whether there should be unilateral control by one party or the other. In such instances the outcome – achieved through a process of bargaining, compromise or conflict – is a set of rules or procedures designed to allow either formal or informal joint control (see, for example, Batstone, 1988; Edwards, 1979; Edwardes and

Scullion, 1982; Storey, 1980). Dunn (1990: 9–10) goes on to argue that the image presented by Goodrich 'readily translates' into a system of 'trench warfare' reminiscent of the 'Great War'. Each side attempts to shift the frontier of control in its favour. There are skirmishes and there are major assaults, but little ground is ever really gained by either side.

Taken at its most literal Goodrich's root metaphor of old industrial relations describes the employment relationship (what occurs where employees exchange their labour in return for pay and other terms and conditions of work) in deeply pessimistic terms. It is characterised by low trust, conflict and most importantly 'it does not sell hope' (Dunn, 1990: 17). The stalemate of trench warfare means that nothing changes, there is no progress, nothing to look forward to in the future except more of the same.

On this basis it is small wonder that the root metaphor offered by HRM in the 1980s and 1990s has been so keenly grasped by management and workers, for as we shall see it provides an apparent escape route from the sterility of the old industrial relations. And this, says Dunn, is its attraction. It is a metaphor that is 'much more open, expansive and even heroic' than that which is applied to old industrial relations (Dunn, 1990: 17).

Dunn's analysis of the root metaphor of HRM leads him to conclude that it is about organisations embarking on a journey that takes them away from old industrial relations towards HRM. It seems that this is indeed the case. A quick sweep through the growing number of texts devoted to HRM reveals the journey metaphor in terms such as 'from personnel management to HRM' and 'on the road to HRM' (Storey, 1989, 1992); 'the road to Nissan' (Wickens, 1987); and 'routes' to attitude change under new industrial relations (Kelly and Kelly, 1991). However, to Dunn the most appropriate type of journey to apply to HRM is that of the pioneering wagon train in the American West, aiming to move beyond existing frontiers into new and uncharted territory. In this context and in line with Guest's (1990) assertion, HRM even when practised in the UK can be seen as congruent with the 'American Dream'. With this in mind, Keenoy and Anthony (1992: 236) point to HRM in the UK placing emphasis on a number of policies and practices such as individualism and unitarism that are major components of the enterprise-oriented social and economic structure which exists in the US. Moreover, Dunn and others such as Wood (1989) are quick to point out that much of the early management literature that discusses HRM is American (see, for example, Beer and Spector, 1985; Beer et al, 1984a; 1984b; Foulkes, 1980; Kochan et al, 1986; Robbins, 1978; Skinner, 1981; Walton, 1985). This in itself may have contributed to the apparent suitability of the American metaphor. Dunn (1990: 19) himself goes so far as to say that: 'reading many such books, by academics and consultants I was struck by their style... they were so full of prairie philosophising that I could almost smell the wood smoke from the campfire'.

ASSEMBLING THE HRM WAGON TRAIN

Three points need to be made about the HRM wagon train. The first is that, as Dunn points out, unlike traditional journey metaphors it offers no prospect of a homecoming – no return to the sterile comfort of old industrial relations and the battle for control of the workplace. The expectation is to start afresh somewhere else, building a new relationship between management and workers that is free from existing norms; to create an environment where in line with HRM individuals can make a success of themselves.

Second, HRM is actually unobtainable. The journey towards it is never ending; 'there is no arrival... to travel hopefully is the crux of the metaphor' (Dunn 1990: 21). On this basis, HRM can be likened to the horizon. The closer you get to it, the further away it becomes. Similarly, Keenoy and Anthony (1992: 252) have argued that to be properly understood HRM must be 'recognised as a fantasy' and divorced from the 'real'. These analyses are not as odd as they may sound. To understand what they are driving at, try imagining the policies and practices underpinning an ideal model of HRM. We all have such a model in our minds – the theoretical construct supplied by the considerable literature on the subject (see, for example, Armstrong, 1987; Beer and Spector, 1985; Boxall, 1993; Guest, 1987, 1989a, 1989b, 1991; Noon, 1992; Storey, 1989, 1992). But as Guest has pointed out: 'HRM is a term widely used but loosely defined', accounting for us all having different ideal models (Guest, 1989a: 48) and we cannot be sure which is correct. HRM-oriented companies are no different. While they may strive to achieve HRM, they are unsure of what it would look like in its ideal form at their organisation. Few would therefore claim to have reached the end of the wagon train. It is hardly surprising then that few companies actually claim they are thoroughbred HRM – witness the paucity of such case studies in the British and, as Guest has noted (1990: 333), the US literature. This brings us to the third point.

If it is true that organisations see the necessity of making a journey towards something that is unobtainable, what are their motives for taking the journey? After all, it appears to represent a period of considerable change and upheaval within an organisation. Why depart from the comfort – albeit sterile comfort – of old industrial relations? The answer to this question concerns the catalysts of the change.

In the UK one can link the growth of HRM-oriented practices over the last 15 years to a number of economic-related factors. Old industrial relations offers no solutions to managers faced with issues such as recession, the globalisation of markets, or new technology. Conversely, they see the journey towards HRM as doing just that. Is arrival so important?

The journey itself is what matters. It is a process which offers the chance to implement important changes in the workplace – changes which would have been difficult, if not impossible, to implement under old industrial relations.

Management commitment to making the HRM journey is one thing, but it is valueless unless employees are persuaded of the merits. There seem to be two ways to achieve this. First, Dunn's pioneering wagon train metaphor ('open, expansive and even brave') may be highly attractive to employees. It may, as management at Jaguar suggest, allow them to 'win the hearts and minds' of employees (Storey, 1992: 59). Couched in unitarist terms the idea of everyone making the same journey, undergoing the same hardships and sharing the same values might well encourage employees eagerly to jump into the wagon with a set of positive expectations as at 'greenfield' sites (see, for example, Grant, 1993, 1994, 1995; Guest and Rosenthal, 1993; Trevor, 1988; White and Trevor, 1983; Wickens, 1987).

Second, potential employee resistance to the changes that occur under HRM are ameliorated by the 'communication of gloom and doom' (Wilkinson et al, 1994: 131). HRM can be portrayed to workers as offering the company salvation from competitive pressures and/or recession. It becomes attractive to employees, appearing to be a lifeline, staving off the threats of closure and unemployment. They go along with management's suggested changes and clamber into the wagon because there seems to be no other feasible option. HRM is shown to be their only hope. They are told the journey may be hard and require sacrifice. Some may lose their jobs, but without pain there will be no gain – no reward of the company's survival and eventual prosperity (see, for example, Cressey et al, 1985; Oliver and Wilkinson, 1992: 90–123; Smith, 1988; Turnbull, 1986; Wilkinson et al, 1994).

A journey that on the one hand appears an attractive proposition for both employer and employees (and therefore unitarist) may then on the other have repercussions that work primarily in the employer's favour. HRM may be unobtainable, but for the company it is the potential rewards to be picked up as the wagon train *progresses towards* HRM that make it attractive. These rewards have been described by Guest (1989a: 50) as 'positive outcomes'. Positive outcomes directly attributable to HRM are commitment, flexible working, quality, customer orientation and the integration of employee management with business strategy. These in turn are said to lead to organisational outcomes variously described as organisational effectiveness, competitiveness, cost effectiveness, high job performance and increased productivity, a high degree of problem solving, change and innovation, and low levels of absenteeism, turnover, grievance and workplace conflict (Beer et al, 1984a, 1984b; Beer and Spector, 1985; Guest, 1987, 1989a; Noon, 1992; Storey, 1992; Tichy et al, 1982). Small wonder then that companies have been willing to embark on the HRM journey.

To expand the wagon train metaphor further, there is considerable baggage that needs to be thrown into the wagons in order to assist in the journey and which facilitates the achievement of the HRM outcomes discussed above. In effect, what we are talking about are key HRM practices.

This argument – that HRM places emphasis on internalised control mechanisms as opposed to external ones – is fine as far as it goes, but there is more to the story than that. To illustrate what is meant, take this quote from Singh:

> **Conflict does not originate inside the structures in organisations practising HRM; when it does appear – as it nearly always does – solutions are focused on the problems of individuals. It is the individual that has to be dealt with not the organisation.** (1992: 140)

Singh's quote suggests that under HRM there is no longer a need for structural (external) control mechanisms. Rather, the need is for internalised control mechanisms that deal with the possibility of the individual being out of kilter with the organisation's goals and aims. In this respect Singh seems to be demonstrating the movement away from external control mechanisms towards those that are internal. But Singh's quote highlights (one suspects inadvertently) the fact that the old external forms of control have not been replaced by internal forms of control. *They are still in operation.* What has happened, however, is that they are no longer questioned. When conflict arises at the HRM workplace, it is not the fault of the external control mechanisms breaking down at the organisation; the blame for the conflict is shifted to the individual who deals with it using internalised control mechanisms along the lines of 'it cannot be the organisation's fault, it must be mine'.

This process is akin to the use of 'insidious controls', for it means that the employee's attitudes and behaviour have been influenced, without management having to resort to any overt forms of control or manipulation (Blau and Schoenherr, 1971). The value of insidious controls is that because they are self-enforced they appear democratic in nature. They are not, for example, reliant on external controls such as direct supervision or personal authority. Furthermore, where external controls are enforced they meet with little employee resistance because insidious controls mean that they are accepted as legitimate. The external forms of control as existed under old industrial relations are then still in place. There has been not so much a movement away from these forms of control in HRM-oriented workplaces as an overlaying of a package of internalised control processes.

'WAGONS ROLL!': CONTROL AND THE HRM JOURNEY

This section of the chapter has two aims: to identify and discuss those internalised control mechanisms that exist in an HRM-oriented workplace and to illustrate how, in an HRM-oriented work environment, internalised controls bolster the effectiveness of any external controls that may be present. These aims are achieved by using a combination of primary and secondary data. The primary data is drawn from two case studies (referred to in the subsequent discussion as Company A and Company B). Interviews were conducted with management and employees at each company. Both are Japanese manufacturing transplants in the UK consumer electronics sector. At the time of the study Company A employed 230 people, Company B 90 people.

The secondary data is drawn from a number of other studies of control in an HRM environment. Several of these studies discuss internalised forms of control. None of them addresses the issue of internal control mechanisms bolstering those that are external. Nevertheless, they are of considerable value in that they provide some supportive evidence and corroborate the primary data.

A number of internal control mechanisms are summarised in Table 12.2. Four points need to made. First, any combination of these mechanisms could be in operation in an HRM-oriented workplace. They are not regarded as mutually exclusive. Second, there is a degree of overlap among

Table 12.2 Internal control mechanisms

1. Organisational commitment
- identification with goals and values of organisation
- strong desire to remain a member of the organisation
- creation of psychological contract

2. Reductions of them and us
- increased contact across group boundaries
- creation of a superordinate goal
- changes in management behaviour

3. Workplace culture
- pervasive company mission/shared values and goals with management
- emphasis on management–employee co-operation and partnership
- creation of stretch objectives
- hegemonistic taint to workplace culture induces conformity
- fear of punishment/sanctions by employer and/or co-workers due to failure to comply with workplace culture

4. Peer group pressure
- need to conform with norms and values of co-workers
- public display/knowledge of performance
- threatened or actual imposition of penalties and sanctions by co-workers

5. Empowerment
- use of empowerment techniques to enforce worker accountability rather than encourage responsibility
- fear of public failure reinforces conformity to use of empowerment

Sources: Argyris, 1960; Delbridge and Turnbull, 1992; Guest, 1987, 1991; Mowday et al, 1982; Ogbonna, 1992; Sewell and Wilkinson, 1992a, 1992b

some of the mechanisms. For example, compliance with workplace culture may, in part, be achieved through peer group pressure. Third, it is acknowledged that the list of mechanisms may not be complete. Fourth, the effectiveness of these internal controls may be enhanced where HRM-oriented organisations adopt selection processes that identify candidates best suited to the absorption and use of such mechanisms. It has been suggested by some that this may go some way to explaining the emphasis placed on selection under HRM (Sewell and Wilkinson, 1992a: 152; Keenoy and Anthony, 1992: 239).

One internal control mechanism is organisational commitment. This is expressed through the employee's 'strong acceptance of and belief in an organisation's goals and values; willingness to exert effort on behalf of the organisation; and a strong desire to maintain membership of the organisation' (Mowday et al, 1982).

One can argue from Walton's (1985) work that in an HRM-oriented workplace management should be battling for employee commitment rather than workplace control. Committed employees offer no threat to the economic effectiveness of the organisation. They have entered into a 'psychological contract' (Argyris, 1960) with the organisation and therefore the application of external controls ought not to be necessary. Commitment under HRM can therefore be seen as an internalised control mechanism. It has a positive impact on employee attitudes and behaviour, yet its attributes will remain unchallenged by workers because they may never regard them as forms of managerial control. This may go some way to explaining the importance which management attached to commitment at Companies A and B. As the personnel manager at Company A put it:

> We want them [employees] to have pride in the quality of their work, and their team; a recognition that these aims are good for the company and good for them. Those qualities display a potential for the development of a long-term commitment to staying with us. After all, quality work is an expression of commitment.

Commitment is only one facet of the internalised control structure that exists under HRM. A further facet concerns the issue of 'them and us'. A social psychological definition of 'them and us' in the workplace is given by Kelly and Kelly (1991). They argue that it stems from a perception that there exists a clear division between management and workers and that the two groups have conflicting interests.

Kelly and Kelly's theoretical framework is based on the argument that a narrowing of the divide between management and workers may be induced by HRM practices such as financial participation, new forms of job design, influence in decision making, and communication (Kelly and Kelly, 1991: 27–33). The practices (what we have defined as baggage for the HRM wagon train) use any one, or a combination, of three mechanisms to reduce 'them and us' attitudes among employees. In line with this chapter's argument, achieving such a reduction could be seen as a form of internalised control. A movement 'from them and us to just us' (Wickens, 1987) ought to mean that employees no longer need to be subject to intensive external controls.

The first of Kelly and Kelly's three mechanisms to attitude change concerning 'them and us' is inter-group contact. Increased contact between the two groups of management and workers supposedly results in a reduction of the importance of group membership and the development of inter-personal relationships (Allen, 1985; Allen, 1986). Through the use of practices such as consultation or quality circles the two groups begin to find common interests, realising that the negative perceptions they hold of each other are inaccurate.

The second mechanism is the creation of superordinate goals. These supersede the sectional goals of opposing parties and cannot be achieved unless the two groups co-operate with each other (Sherif, 1966). A unitarist outlook is adopted whereby the interests of the worker and the employer merge into one based on the profitability or success of the company. By virtue of its title, British Rail's 'Partnership for Progress' campaign signalled the pursuit of just such a superordinate goal (for a discussion of this campaign and its impact on 'them and us' attitudes, see Guest et al, 1993).

The third mechanism is based on the possibility of altering worker attitudes by changes in management behaviour at the workplace. For example, a Japanese manager at Company B argued that their use of co-operative and participative practices aimed to promote a 'positive and harmonious relationship between the Company and members of staff'. Such an approach would conflict with traditional worker perceptions of the management/worker relationship being adversarial. This conflict leads to a state of dissonance, which is resolved by employees altering attitudes so that they are aligned with the new behavioural requirements (Cooper and Fazio, 1984).

For management at Companies A and B a reduction of 'them and us' attitudes was a key objective. Hence a senior UK manager at Company A talked of the search for a 'community spirit'. He clearly regarded this as an important internal control mechanism, arguing that workers would accept the regime under which they worked, 'because they will feel part of a community to which they have a responsibility'. For their part, employees at Company A talked of an atmosphere in which management and workers were, to quote one operator, 'all part of the same team'. They had an awareness of and a willingness to strive for the superordinate goal of managers and workers alike, working to make the company successful because its success was in workers' as well as management's interests.

Another facet of internalised control under HRM is related to the creation of a workplace culture that is centred on employees adopting and sharing common values and a mission with management (Guest, 1987, 1990, 1991; Ogbonna, 1992; Storey, 1992; Keenoy and Anthony, 1992). As Keenoy and Anthony (1992) have pointed out, values, missions and goals construct meaning and purpose for employees. In this respect, they represent powerful 'stretch objectives' (Walton, 1985) and therefore internal controls for employees.

The use of missions, values and goals to construct a workplace culture that acts as an internalised control mechanism is well demonstrated in Ogbonna's (1992) work. He describes supermarket cashiers who feel compelled to smile to all customers as part of their employer's push towards quality customer service, even where they do not wish to conform with this behaviour (Ogbonna, 1992: 92). Child (1984: 159) has labelled this a process of workplace 'cultural control'. A failure to comply with company culture may place the worker in a tricky position on two counts. First, to appear to undermine the wagon train's journey towards HRM could result in punishment by the employer. Second, it could result in ostracism by fellow workers.

On the first count, it appears that HRM missions, goals and values have a hegemonistic taint. This may well account for the 'acceptance and legitimation' among employees of external control mechanisms that exist in the workplace (White and Trevor, 1983: 46). As an example, take operators at Company B. Their performance was closely monitored and where they failed to achieve acceptable performance levels related to absenteeism, quality and output, management would invoke disciplinary procedures. On the one hand operators disliked these external control mechanisms as and when applied to them. On the other hand they accepted them as an inevitable and legitimate feature of their workplace, arguing – as did the company – that an individual's poor performance ought to be punished since it harmed the company's success and therefore the interests of their co-workers.

On the second count those such as Delbridge and Turnbull (1992) have suggested that HRM can create peer group pressures in the workplace. They and others (Sewell and Wilkinson, 1992a, 1992b; Oliver and Wilkinson, 1992), assert that where the individual fails to comply with the norms and values of their co-workers, they are seen to be letting others down and face exile from the group. This too can be seen as a form of internalised control. Sewell and Wilkinson have noted how in a team-based organisation the public display of performance indicators such as absenteeism, quality of work and output may be used to create:

a climate where horizontal disciplinary force, based on peer scrutiny, operates throughout the team as members seek to identify and sanction those who may jeopardise its overall performance. (Sewell and Wilkinson, 1992a: 109–110)

Such peer group pressure was highly visible at Company B. Its influence over employee attitudes and therefore its role as a control mechanism were particularly apparent where individual performance indicators were available for quality and output. Operators frequently talked with great pride about the figures they had achieved and were publicly disparaging of those who could not reach the minimum targets or were too lazy to do so. They often saw such individuals as letting the team down and were consequently unsympathetic towards them where, as a result of poor performance, they were subject to disciplinary proceedings.

Empowerment may also contribute to a degree of internal control. Under empowerment employees are expected to manage themselves, either as teams or as individuals, and are given greater responsibility for their performance at work. However, there appears to be considerable concern that there is a very fine dividing line between what constitutes empowerment and what constitutes accountability. Empowerment has been accused of leaving employees totally accountable for their failures and of making them even more susceptible to external controls such as surveillance techniques that closely monitor performance (Fuller and Smith, 1991; Oliver and Wilkinson, 1992; Ogbonna, 1992; Sewell and Wilkinson, 1992a, 1992b, 1992c; Singh, 1992). Again, fear of very public failure and therefore peer censure may also play a role here. In a variation of a similar theme, Fuller and Smith (1991) discuss an organisation whose stated aim is for every employee to 'internalise responsibility' for customer service. This is stretched to the point where customers are sometimes involved in disciplinary proceedings (Fuller and Smith, 1991: 14).

CONCLUSIONS

In this chapter it has been suggested that under HRM the relationship between management and employees is no longer characterised by conflict arising through management's use of external control mechanisms. Instead, HRM is reliant on internal control mechanisms. It is these mechanisms that bring the employee's attitudes and behaviour into line with management's expectations and requirements.

The use of internalised control mechanisms seems inextricably linked to a root metaphor that portrays management and workers embarking on a journey (a pioneering wagon train) that takes them to a new conflict-free management/employee relationship. There is considerable baggage necessary to undertake this journey – in the form of HRM practices. Internalised control mechanisms can be seen to offer potential penalties where employees do not adhere to these practices and are in effect endangering the success of the wagon train as it progresses through the inhospitable terrain of competition and recession. For example, there is the prospect of the company failing and resultant job loss. There is also the possibility of public humiliation and of ostracism by co-workers.

While much of the HRM literature suggests a movement away from external controls towards the use of internalised mechanisms, this is inadvertently wide of the mark. What seems to happen is that the internalised controls discussed in this chapter can be seen as eliciting employee compliance towards, legitimation of, or acceptance of, the externalised control mechanisms that remain a significant feature of HRM-oriented workplaces. In using the root metaphor of HRM to construct internal control mechanisms, management has discovered a way of avoiding conflict and resistance related to those external control mechanisms that they wish to operate.

We know that management sees control as an economic necessity for the organisation. It appears that management is able to manipulate the root metaphor of HRM in a way that helps them achieve this. This manipulative aspect of the metaphor is best explained by focusing on a particular facet of Dunn's (1990) work which was mentioned earlier. Dunn argues that part of the attraction of HRM is that the journey metaphor of a pioneering wagon train does not involve a homecoming. In the case of employees, this attraction may be true. They are encouraged by management to embark on a journey towards HRM – a journey that is very real – on the basis that HRM offers them the prospect of a new beginning in a different environment.

In management's case, the idea that there is no homecoming under the HRM metaphor is highly questionable. The journey towards HRM offers managers the use of internalised controls as a means to securing external controls in the workplace. The irony is that these are the very external controls that led to the type of conflict so perfectly captured by the root metaphor of old industrial relations. It seems then that for management there is a very definite homecoming with regard to the HRM metaphor. By taking workers on a journey towards HRM, they have won a very significant gain in the battle for control of the workplace. They have, in acting out the root metaphor of HRM, been able to advance under the terms of the root metaphor of old industrial relations – an advance made at the expense of workers.

REFERENCES

Allen, P.T. (1985) 'The relationship of inter-group understanding and inter-party friction in industry', *British Journal of Industrial Relations*, Vol. 23.

Allen, P.T. (1986) 'Contact and conflict in industry', in Hewstone, M. and Brown, R. (eds) *Contact and Conflict in Inter-Group Encounters*. Oxford: Basil Blackwell.

Argyris, C. (1960) *Understanding Organisational Behaviour*. London: Tavistock.

Armstrong, M. (1987) 'Human resource management: a case of the emperor's new clothes?', *Personnel Management*, Vol. 19, No. 8.

Batstone, E. (1988) 'The frontier of control', in Galle, D. (ed) *Employment in Britain*. Oxford: Basil Blackwell.

Beer, M. and Spector, B. (eds) (1985) *Readings in Human Resource Management*. New York: Free Press.

Beer, M., Spector, B., Lawrence, P., Quin Mills, D. and Walton, R. (1984a) *Human Resource Management: A General Manager's Perspective*. Illinois: Free Press.

Beer, M., Spector, B., Lawrence, P., Quin Mills, D. and Walton, R. (1984b) *Managing Human Assets*. Illinois: Free Press.

Blau, P. and Schoenherr, R. (1971) *The Structure of Organizations*. New York: Basic Books.

Boxall, P.F. (1993) 'The significance of HRM: a reconsideration of the evidence', *The International Journal of Human Resource Management*, Vol. 4, No. 3.

Child, J. (1984) *Organisation: A Guide to Problems and Practices*. 2nd Edition, London: Chapman.

Cooper, J. and Fazio, R.H. (1984) 'A new look at dissonance theory', in *Advances in Experimental Social Psychology*, Vol. 17.

Cressey, P., Eldridge, J. and MacInnes, J. (1985) *Just Managing*. Milton Keynes: Open University Press.

Delbridge, R. and Turnbull, P. (1992) 'Human resource maximisation: the management of labour under Just-In-Time manufacturing systems', in Blyton, P. and Turnbull, P. (eds) *Reassessing Human Resource Management*. London: Sage.

Dunn, S. (1990) 'Root metaphor in the old and new industrial relations', *British Journal of Industrial Relations*, Vol. 28, No. 1.

Edwardes, P. and Scullion, H. (1982) *The Social Organisation of Industrial Conflict*. Oxford: Basil Blackwell.

Edwards, R. (1979) *Contested Terrain*. London: Heinemann.

Foulkes, F. (1980) *Personnel Policies in Large Non-Union Companies*. Englewood Cliffs, NJ: Prentice-Hall.

Fuller, L. and Smith, V. (1991) 'Consumers' reports: management by customers in a changing economy', *Work Employment and Society*, Vol. 5, No. 1.

Goodrich, C. (1975). *The Frontier of Control: A Study in British Workshop Politics*. London: G. Bell (first published 1920).

Grant, D. (1993) *Japanese Manufacturers in the UK Electronics Sector: The Impact of Production Systems on Employee Attitudes and Behaviour*. PhD Thesis, London School of Economics and Political Science.

Grant, D. (1994) 'New style agreements at Japanese transplants in the UK: the implications for trade union decline', *Employee Relations*, Vol. 16, No. 2.

Grant, D. (1995) 'Japanization and new industrial relations', in Beardwell, I. (ed) *New Industrial Relations?* Oxford: Oxford University Press.

Guest, D. (1987) 'Human resource management and industrial relations', *Journal of Management Studies*, Vol. 24, No. 5.

Guest, D. (1989a) 'Personnel and HRM: can you tell the difference?', *Personnel Management*, Vol. 21, No. 1.

Guest, D. (1989b) 'Human resource management: its implications for industrial relations and trade unions', in Storey, J. (ed) *New Perspectives on Human Resource Management*. London: Routledge.

Guest, D. (1990) 'Human resource management and the American dream', *Journal of Management Studies*, Vol. 27, No. 4.

Guest, D. (1991) 'Personnel management: the end of orthodoxy?', *British Journal of Industrial Relations*, Vol. 29, No. 2.

Guest, D. and Rosenthal, P. (1993) 'Industrial relations in greenfield sites', in Metcalf, D. and Milner, S. (eds) *New Perspectives on Industrial Disputes*. London: Routledge.

Guest, D., Peccei, R. and Thomas, J. (1993) 'The impact of employee involvement on organisational commitment and "them and us" attitudes', *Industrial Relations Journal*, Vol. 24, No. 3.

Hallier, J. (1993) 'HRM as a pluralistic forum: assumptions and prospects for developing a distinctive research capacity', *International Journal of Human Resource Management*, Vol. 4, No. 4.

Hendry, C., Pettigrew, A. and Sparrow, P. (1988) 'Changing patterns of human resource management', *Personnel Management*, November.

Huczynski, A. and Buchanan, D. (1991) *Organisational Behaviour: An Introductory Text*. London: Prentice-Hall.

Keenoy, T. and Anthony, P. (1992) 'HRM: metaphor, meaning and morality', in Blyton, P. and Turnbull, P. (eds) *Reassessing Human Resource Management*. London: Sage.

Kelly, J. and Kelly, C. (1991) 'Them and us: a social psychological analysis of the new industrial relations', *British Journal of Industrial Relations*, Vol. 29, No. 1.

Kochan, T., Katz, H. and Mckersie, R. (1986) *The Transformation of American Industrial Relations*. New York: Basic Books.

Mowday, R., Porter, L. and Steers, R. (1982) *Employee–Organisation Commitment: The Psychology of Commitment, Absenteeism and Labour Turnover*. New York: Academic Press.

Mullins, L.J. (1993) *Management and Organisational Behaviour*. 3rd Edition, London: Pitman.

Noon, M. (1992) 'HRM: a map, model or theory?', in Blyton, P. and Turnbull, P. (eds) *Reassessing Human Resource Management*. London: Sage.

Ogbonna, E. (1992) 'Organisation, culture and HRM', in Blyton, P. and Turnbull, P. (eds) *Reassessing Human Resource Management*. London: Sage.

Oliver, N. and Wilkinson, B. (1992) *The Japanization of British Industry*. Oxford: Basil Blackwell.

Robbins, S.P. (1978) *Personnel: The Management of Human Resources*. Englewood Cliffs, NJ: Prentice-Hall.

Salaman, G. (1981) *Class and the Corporation*. London: Fontana.

Sewell, G. and Wilkinson, B. (1992a) 'Empowerment or emasculation? Shopfloor surveillance in a total quality management organisation', in Blyton, P. and Turnbull, P. (eds) *Reassessing Human Resource Management*. London: Sage.

Sewell, G. and Wilkinson, B. (1992b) 'Human resource management in "surveillance" companies', in Clark, J. (ed) *Human Resource Management and Technical Change*. London: Sage.

Sewell, G. and Wilkinson, B. (1992c) 'Someone to watch over me: surveillance, discipline and the Just-In-Time labour process', *Sociology*, Vol. 26, No. 2.

Sherif, M. (1966) *Group Conflict and Co-operation*. London: Routledge and Kegan Paul.

Singh, R. (1992) 'Human resource management: a sceptical look', in Towers, B. (ed) *The Handbook of Human Resource Management*. Oxford: Basil Blackwell.

Skinner, W. (1981) 'Big hat, no cattle: managing human resources', *Harvard Business Review*, Vol. 59.

Smith, D. (1988) 'The Japanese example in south west Birmingham', *Industrial Relations Journal*, Vol. 19, No. 1.

Storey, J. (1980) *The Challenge to Management Control*. London: Kogan Page.

Storey, J. (1989) 'Introduction: from personnel management to human resource management', in Storey, J. (ed) *New Perspectives on Human Resource Management*. London: Routledge.

Storey, J. (1992) *Developments in the Management of Human Resources*. Oxford: Basil Blackwell.

Tichy, N., Fombrun, C. and Devanna, M.A. (1982) 'Strategic human resource management', *Sloan Management Review*, Vol. 23, No. 2.

Trevor, M. (1988) *Toshiba's New British Company*. London: Policy Studies Institute.

Turnbull, P. (1986) 'The Japanization of production and industrial relations at Lucas Electrical', *Industrial Relations Journal*, Vol. 17, No. 3.

Walton, R. (1985) 'From control to commitment in the workplace', *Harvard Business Review*, Vol. 64, No. 5.

White, M. and Trevor, M. (1983) *Under Japanese Management*. London: Heinemann.

Wickens, P. (1987) *The Road to Nissan*. London: Macmillan.

Wilkinson, A., Marchington, M., Ackers, P. and Goodman, J. (1994) 'ESOP's fables: a tale of a machine tool company', *The International Journal of Human Resource Management*, Vol. 5, No. 1.

Wood, S. (1989) 'Researching the new industrial relations', *Employee Relations*, Vol. 8, No. 5.

CHAPTER 13

Outdoor management development: a journey to the centre of the metaphor

Philip J. Jones

> . . .this seems so outlandish a thing that one must needs go a little into the history and philosophy of it. (Melville, 1851: 358)

INTRODUCTION

The use of the outdoors as a means for the development of managers has grown rapidly during the past decade. A survey of 120 employers found that 49.5 per cent were current users of outdoor-based development training (IRRR, 1992b: 2). Outdoor management development (OMD) interventions are routinely depicted as resulting in both training and development outcomes. That is, they are involved with the achievement of effective performance in participants' present jobs, and at the same time they are concerned with preparing the same individuals for future changes. When used as part of a wider organisation development intervention OMD is portrayed as not only improving the effectiveness of individual managers, but as being capable of improving organisational effectiveness as a whole. Hence McGraw (1993: 61) argues:

> OMD has the proven capacity to stimulate significant improvements in the way that individuals orient themselves to their work. It also has the capacity to make a profound impact on the moral, managerial and, ultimately, financial health of organisations.

Many published articles proclaim the beneficial outcomes of this form of training, despite the dearth of valid and reliable studies in support of these claims. Work by Jones and Oswick (1993: 10) notes that over 200 different benefits have been attributed to OMD, but that: 'Supporting evidence is most commonly in the form of the personal testimony of those providing the training, or selective, positive accounts from participants.'

The views of those who write in this area appear to be highly polarised: 'For advocates. . . [OMD] appears to hold an almost mystical power to promote revolutionary, performance-enhancing changes for those experiencing it' (Jones, 1993: 12). For the sceptics OMD is at best a series of contrived, irrelevant and superficial attempts to create organisational metaphors away from the workplace; and at worst, OMD represents a highly discriminatory form of training fraught with unjustifiable physical and psychological danger.

Management training using the outdoors has been the subject of little comprehensive and/or controlled investigation, consequently limited evidence about its utility, effectiveness or appropriateness as a training intervention exists (the work of Lowe, 1991; Bronson et al, 1992; Wagner and Rowland, 1992; and Burnett, 1994 represent notable exceptions). As a result, both advocates and critics have remained largely free to engage in unhindered speculation about the advantages and disadvantages of these techniques. Advocates of OMD have increasingly made claims for the utility of OMD based on the existence of unique metaphorical links between the activities and processes which constitute this form of training and the activities and processes which constitute managerial work within contemporary organisations. Supporters argue that the isomorphic resemblances (structural and/or process similarities) that link OMD training and work scenarios are sufficient to allow this form of training to act as a metaphor for processes found in the workplace. This metaphorical bridging is seen as the means by which learning and knowledge acquired during participation in course activities are subsequently transported into the workplace. A comprehensive review of published literature relating to OMD reveals that these claims have not been examined in any critical or systematic manner. This chapter seeks to address this gap and explore the relationship between OMD, metaphor and learning.

OMD: PROBLEMS OF DEFINITION

Any examination of OMD, regardless of perspective, requires us at some stage to indicate what is being included within this term, and what lies outside the scope of the investigation. One major problem inherent in any examination of OMD lies in defining or describing the term in a way that allows it to be systematically investigated. No universal, comprehensive definition of OMD exists. Even the term OMD is not in universal usage, but is used interchangeably with terms such as development training, outdoor-based development training, and outdoor-based experiential training.

An additional complication is derived from the fact that training interventions, all of which could be reasonably described as 'OMD programmes', on closer inspection vary across an extensive number of dimensions. Many heterogeneous forms of training are being collectively grouped under the single label of 'OMD'. The term 'OMD' may describe three weeks of survival training in the Highlands of Scotland, or three hours of activity on a school playing field. Variance in some or all of the dimensions that constitute this form of training (the 'who', 'what', 'where', 'why' and 'how') may be critical in bringing about the desired training outcomes. The wide variance within these dimensions may explain in part the multiplicity of outcomes which are routinely claimed to be the result of OMD training programmes. In order to recognise this diversity, it might be appropriate to think about the concept of 'OMD' in a way similar to that commonly used when thinking about the concept of 'sport'. Both terms represent a wide variety of heterogeneous forms of activity and experience which are united under a single broad heading. Our day-to-day exposure to the variety of activities which we recognise as constituting the concept of 'sport' makes us aware of the variety of dissimilar forms which exist. We are conscious that each form is associated with its own idiosyncratic combination of inputs, processes and outcomes. As a result, we quite readily recognise and accept that training for, and participating in, different sports exposes people to different training inputs and processes, and as a result, different training outcomes are elicited.

The same does not appear to hold true of OMD. Substantially different forms of training intervention are described by using the term 'OMD'. As a result, it is not surprising that 'beyond some broad and largely uninformative generalisations about enhanced self-development, team-building, leadership and communication' (Jones, 1993: 12) it is unclear exactly what management development programmes using the outdoors can generally be expected to achieve. Because the various forms of OMD differ in respect of the inputs and processes experienced by participants, they may genuinely result in the wide variety of different training outcomes reported in the literature. Difficulties in defining these programmes do not appear to be unique to the UK. There is evidence to suggest that similar problems exist within the North American literature: 'Some of the controversy over outdoor training stems from the confusion over the different types of training available. . . Confusing the different types obscures the potential benefits and liabilities without increasing our understanding of outdoor training' (Wagner et al, 1991).

Jones and Oswick (1993) have attempted to avoid this semantic confusion by describing some of the attributes of the 'paradigm example' of OMD. They argue that their definition, although not exhaustive or comprehensive, is useful because it describes OMD sufficiently well to allow systematic investigation to take place. In addition, they claim that it describes this form of training in a way which is consistent with the experiences and views of the majority of providers, sponsors, participants and writers in the field. That is, it describes a form of training which it would be very difficult to argue is not OMD. Jones and Oswick (1993: 11) claim that extensive review and structured analysis of the published OMD literature suggests that the 'paradigm example' of OMD in the United Kingdom is described by the following three criteria:

1 The outdoors as a *Means-to-an-end* criterion: the outdoors is used as a training medium for a substantial part of the course. A task is completed in the outdoors as a means to an end, rather than as an end in itself. The purposive ends of the training are concerned with management development, not with the development of skills to be used in outdoor settings.

2 The *Managerial* criterion: the recipients of training are, or expect to be, formally responsible for achieving organisational goals by working with, and through, other people.

3 The *Developmental* criterion: the desired outcomes of training (at least from the point of view of the sponsors and providers of the event) are implicitly or explicitly concerned with bringing about changes within the participants which are thought to cause increases in the effectiveness and/or efficiency of participants' work behaviours. That is, participants will, as a result of the training, be more able to do their job after training than before.

OMD: AFFECT V. EFFECT

Jones and Oswick (1993) define OMD by describing the 'where', 'who' and 'why' of the paradigm example of this form of training. The 'why' and the 'how' of paradigm OMD interventions are justified by claims that OMD is an unusually effective form of training which is capable of accelerating the learning process (Alder, 1990; Arkin, 1991; Calder, 1991; Campbell, 1990; Kirk, 1986; Long, 1987; Petrini, 1990; Ryan, 1993; Schofield, 1985; Scott, 1988). Providers and sponsors state that one of the primary aims of OMD is to improve managerial effectiveness and organisational performance, and that this is achieved through the successful transfer of learning from the training event into the organisational setting.

OMD programmes are described as being highly experiential, comprising the whole person and all of their sensory modalities in a process of learning; course activities involve participants in learning by thinking, feeling and doing (Alder, 1990; Cacioppe and Adamson, 1988; Calder, 1991; Crawford, 1988; Elkin, 1991; Everard, 1988; Everard, 1991; Kirk, 1986; Long, 1987; Reeve, 1982). These exercises are thought to be more vivid and memorable than non-OMD activities which typically exhibit these experiential learning characteristics to a much lesser extent. OMD programmes are thus suggested to be unique among management development techniques in the extent to which this complete learning process is invoked. Learning theory suggests that this holistic, experiential approach results in the enduring images of the training being generated. In addition, the physical and mental stress, and the subjective risk experienced by participants, are suggested to combine and elevate the memorability of the experience (Campbell, 1990; Crawford, 1988; Evans, 1988; Gall, 1987; Long, 1987; Lowe, 1991; Schofield, 1985; Scott, 1988; Sewell, 1991). It is alleged that the combination of these factors results in an increased probability that what is learnt will be remembered and transferred to the workplace. By employing Kolb's Model of Learning (Kolb and Fry, 1975) it is argued that if events are remembered they have the potential to be incorporated into a process of reflective thinking, the end result of which is an idiosyncratic conceptual model of the world. It is suggested to be this model which provides the rational basis for subsequent problem-solving action plans. Thus it is concluded that, since OMD is a more memorable form of training than the available alternatives, it is more likely to provide a rich source of memories which will facilitate learning from subsequent experiences.

There is much anecdotal evidence to support the claim that OMD is a highly affective and therefore memorable form of training: participants, whether they enjoyed or hated the experience, are usually affected by it in some way. Both advocates and critics of OMD appear to accept this premise. However, in order for OMD to result in increased work performance, it must be both memorable and relevant. That is, the changes resulting from the training must be capable of being transferred into the organisational setting. It is this second premise – the relevance of this form of management development technique to the workplace, and its potential for transfer – which is highly disputed.

In response to commentators who suggest that OMD is affective rather than effective, proponents claim that there are unique metaphorical links between the activities and processes which constitute OMD and those found in organisational settings. These metaphorical links are implicitly and explicitly cited as the mechanism by which the transfer of relevant learning from the training event and into the organisational setting can and does take place:

> **Managers apply their skills to a range of tasks which are quite different to those they face at work but which are challenging and real. The results of their actions are immediately apparent, providing clear evidence of their performance. . . Although the outdoor tasks are not 'normal' they are inescapably 'real'. Managing an outdoor situation is like managing life . . . the underlying management processes are laid bare.** (Creswick and Williams, 1979)

Experience-based activities are real problem-solving tasks that take place in real time, and which have real and clear-cut consequences. There is no ambiguity about success or failure; the participants receive immediate feedback about the efficacy of their decisions and actions. The task does not try to replicate the worksite-specific situation. Instead it is selected to represent or have a metaphorical relationship to the issues and processes that come into play in managerial efforts. The many distracting and extraneous aspects of the worksite are eliminated or diminished, giving the salient aspects clarity and focus. (Neffinger, 1990: 28)

by placing managers in a situation of unfamiliarity, the outdoors provides a living workshop for managing uncertainty or change – something textbooks and lectures just cannot emulate. As a vehicle for learning it can be more powerful than classroom simulations, in that real consequences are produced by the actions (or inactions) of those involved. (Dainty and Lucas, 1992: 107)

Proponents of the use of the outdoors as a training medium argue that the outdoors resembles managerial reality to a much larger extent than any classroom environment. (Burnett, 1994)

It may be true that many of the tasks within OMD courses are presented or framed as metaphors of organisational structures and activities. However, superficial links between almost any object or process and some aspect of organisational life can quickly and easily be conjured up by a skilled metaphorist. This leads Wilson (1992) to suggest that:

Today the role of the traditional researcher has arguably been usurped by the wordsmith, in particular by the wordsmith who has mastery of the pithy phrase and who can fashion a colourful metaphor. In a remarkably short time the language used by practising managers, by many management trainers and by many researchers has coalesced into a diorama of metaphor. . . Virtually everything that moves within an organisation is subject to metaphor.

The problem is to distinguish between activities which, although presented as metaphors of organisational structures and processes, may be quite irrelevant in achieving the stated aims of OMD training, and those activities which through their metaphorical links with the workplace have the potential to make a significant contribution to the performance of managers and their organisations. Crawford (1988), using concepts developed by the Centre for the Study of Management Learning in Lancaster University, has advanced a plausible hypothesis which explains how OMD activities have the potential to act successfully as metaphors of organisational situations and lead to relevant and transferable learning being achieved.

Crawford advances the view that three dimensions of reality exist within the training event:

- Task – what must be done.
- Process – how it is to be done.
- Environment – the context in which it is done.

The successful manipulation of these three dimensions of reality is seen as critical in determining what is learnt and what can subsequently be transferred into the work environment:

> **The model proposes that where reality on all three is high (such as on-job training), the learning will be primarily about the task. It suggests that it is only when the reality of both the task and environment are low that there will be significant process learning.** (Crawford, 1988: 18)

By applying this model to analyse paradigm examples of OMD training, it can be seen that course designers endeavour to create conditions of high process reality (the outdoor activities employed on OMD courses attempt to replicate the processes and skills necessary for successful workplace performance) together with low task and environmental reality when compared with organisational situations. This is taken to indicate that the primary outcome of learning in this context is liable to be about process issues. Adopting this line of argument leads advocates of outdoor training to conclude that OMD activities, as a result of their metaphorical resemblance to managerial and organisational processes, allow meaning and understanding to be transferred from the training activities to the workplace. It has been suggested that it is this transference that offers:

> **the possibility of participants discovering the processes lying beneath the outdoor activities: how people behave, interact and achieve, regardless of whether they are abseiling or undertaking a work role. This is the key to the effective use of the outdoors: first designing a course strong in isomorphs – the similarities between behaviours at work and in the outdoors – and then enabling participants to discover the relevance and transfer their learning back to the workplace. This is known as isomorphic transfer.** (IRRR, 1992a: 16)

If memorable and relevant experiences form the basis of future actions, then paradigm OMD activities appear to have the potential to provide the building blocks of managerial and organisational learning and behaviour. Thus, claims that OMD, through metaphorical modelling of managerial processes, can act as an effective management development medium appear plausible. However, other claims commonly made by advocates about the unique properties of OMD training, also supported by reference to the metaphorical links between the training and workplace processes, appear less credible.

LEVELLING, NEUTRALISING AND FREEDOM TO LEARN

It is frequently claimed that OMD has the rare training property of being a 'great leveller'. Because of the novelty of the activities, all participants start from the same learning base. This argument is used by various commentators to justify the conviction that OMD provides a freedom to learn not present in alternative forms of training:

> We use the outdoors. . .because it's an environment which most of our participants aren't used to. It has perceived risks and produces a significant experience for them. . . It's also a good way of 'stripping off the pinstripes'. (Evans, 1988: 20)

> The outdoors allows many options for devising the distilled and original tasks that are important for clarity and for 'levelling' or neutralising prior experience. (Neffinger, 1990: 28)

> the conventional training programme and the management retreat retain the trappings of the work environment. . . Those with the greatest seniority are expected to make the largest contributions and take the greatest responsibility. In outdoor programmes participants are placed in unfamiliar environments where a greater sharing of knowledge and abilities is necessary for optimum results. . . The formal hierarchy is replaced with a dynamic set of working relationships in which each participant is more likely to contribute according to her or his abilities. (Miller and Rooke, 1991: 76)

> it is believed that in unfamiliar surroundings managers are stripped away from using learned 'organisational behaviour' and fall back on behaviours that are undisguised by hierarchical or 'classroom' norms. (Dainty and Lucas, 1992: 107)

> The tasks are usually unfamiliar to delegates and consequently everyone is starting from a similar knowledge position. Where delegates do have some previous experience this is rarely to the level of genuine technical expertise. (Dainty and Lucas, 1992: 114)

> The outdoors, as a training environment, offers some unique advantages not found in the typical training setting. The outdoors appears to be a very therapeutic setting which strongly motivates most people to participate actively in the training programme. The outdoor environment tends to eliminate much of the role conflict so common in office settings, and tends to give both managers and subordinates a fresh and unbiased view of one

another. **Outdoor-based activities require making decisions and solving problems in an ambiguous setting, where previous experience is generally not available to help participants deal with the situations they encounter.** (Wagner and Campbell, 1994: 4)

The claims and assertions in these and similar quotes from the OMD literature raise a number of questions:

- What is meant by 'levelling' or 'neutralising' knowledge?
- What sort of knowledge is allegedly being levelled or neutralised?
- How can this 'levelling' or 'neutralising' effect be explained?

A review of the published literature in this area provides the following answers. Terms such as 'levelling' or 'neutralising' are used by authors to suggest that certain aspects of participants' prior learning will not affect their subsequent performance within the OMD training arena; and as a result, at the commencement of the training course, no single individual has any significant knowledge advantage over any other individual. There appears to be a wide acceptance of the notion that both task/technical knowledge and process knowledge are levelled or neutralised by the application of OMD training. The mechanism by which this occurs is suggested to be an attribute of the novelty of the training tasks and activities. At first glance such arguments may appear plausible; many of the tasks within an OMD course are certainly novel and unlike those faced at work. However, closer examination raises significant doubt about the existence of the levelling or neutralising phenomenon.

To what extent is it credible to suggest that participants' prior task/technical experience can have no significant effect on the learning that may result from their participation in an OMD programme? Even though OMD tasks may be novel, and participants may not possess significant technical knowledge in these areas, it is difficult to justify the intuitive leap required to conclude that differences in participants' pre-course knowledge will have no significant effects on the outcomes of the training intervention. This inference is difficult to support, because actual or perceived differences between participants in task/technical knowledge, however small, have the potential significantly to distort the power relationships within a group and hence have an impact on the individual and group processes experienced by participants. For example, if a group is given a task, such as raft building, which requires them to tie knots, individuals with even a slight technical knowledge in this area, however incomplete or outdated, can find themselves thrust into a leadership role. This may happen because their knowledge, even though it is recognised by their peers as limited, may nevertheless be perceived as significant in aiding the group successfully to complete its allocated task. In such a case, it is not necessary for participants to have knowledge which amounts to genuine technical expertise for their prior technical experiences to have a significant impact on the processes within the OMD training event, and hence on the resulting learning outcomes.

Since the utility of OMD as a training intervention is largely justified by reference to its alleged ability to bring about process learning in participants, casting doubt on its capacity to level or neutralise prior task/technical knowledge might be considered a minor criticism. However, a lack of support for the claims that OMD levels or neutralises participants' prior process knowledge would substantially undermine the claims that this form of training presents participants with a unique freedom to learn.

Several hypotheses can be formulated to explain how participants might start from the same position in relation to the process knowledge required to complete the tasks which make up an OMD training course.

> i) *Participants on OMD courses have no process knowledge of any sort at the commencement of the training. There is therefore no relevant knowledge to transfer into the training event and, as a result, all participants start from the same learning base*

If it is accepted that all OMD participants will have had a lifetime of social interaction during which time they will have developed some process knowledge and skills, then the premise that participants on OMD courses have no prior process learning or knowledge is false and this hypothesis can be rejected.

> ii) *Participants on OMD courses arrive with identical non-OMD process knowledge*

In order for this to be true, OMD courses would have to be filled with individuals who have had identical learning experiences throughout life and have learnt the same lessons. However, participants on OMD courses are clearly heterogeneous in their past learning experiences and resulting process knowledge. It follows that this hypothesis can also be rejected.

> iii) *Participants arrive at OMD courses with differences in their process knowledge. OMD process knowledge and non-OMD process knowledge are different to the extent that transfer between the two does not or cannot occur. Therefore, when participants arrive on OMD courses differences in non-OMD process knowledge cannot transfer into the OMD training event and affect the learning outcomes*

If transfer between OMD and non-OMD process learning and knowledge cannot occur, OMD training cannot positively affect participants' subsequent work-based performance. The validity and utility of OMD as a training intervention are largely supported on the basis that significant transfer of process learning and knowledge occurs between OMD training and the workplace. If this hypothesis is accepted, then OMD's utility as an effective management development tool is rejected.

iv) *Participants arrive at OMD courses with differences in their process knowledge. Prior non-OMD process knowledge cannot transfer into an OMD training event. OMD process knowledge can transfer to non-OMD situations. Thus, all participants start from the same learning base, but the transfer of knowledge from OMD training courses into the workplace is possible*

This position is implied by much of the published literature which deals with OMD and the transfer of knowledge via metaphor. In order for this view to be sustained, it requires the existence of some mechanism within the model which acts like a 'non-return valve'. This valve allows the transfer of process learning from OMD situations into non-OMD situations to occur, but prevents transfer in the opposite direction; that is, from prior experience into the OMD training event. The existence of this hypothetical non-return valve is not discussed, argued for or even recognised by the OMD literature. Yet without it, or some equivalent device, it is difficult to admit the claims of those who advocate that OMD training levels or neutralises prior process learning and knowledge and yet still allows learning acquired on a course to be transferred into the work environment.

In the absence of any compelling arguments or evidence for the existence of the implied non-return valve, it might be prudent to conclude that any metaphorical bridge is probably capable of carrying two-way traffic: work activities can act as metaphors of OMD activities *and* facilitate a transfer of process learning and knowledge from the organisational situation into the OMD activity. Participants will not all start from the same point. The environment and task may be equally unreal for all concerned, but the high process reality claimed to be present in this form of training will allow inequalities resulting from prior managerial, organisational and life experiences to transfer into the OMD arena. This is a point expressed particularly clearly by Boud et al (1993: 8):

Learning always relates, in one way or another, to what has gone before. There is never a clean slate on which to begin; unless new ideas and new experience link to previous experience, they exist as abstractions, isolated and without meaning. The effects of experience influence all learning. What we are attracted towards, what we avoid and how we go about the task, is dependent on how we have responded in the past. Earlier experiences which had a positive or negative effect stimulate or suppress new learning. They encourage us to take risks and enter new territory for explo-

ration or, alternatively, they may inhibit our range of operation or ability to respond to opportunities.

Prior learning will inevitably affect the ways in which an individual perceives, responds to and learns from participating in an OMD course. If there were no metaphorical links between OMD activities and participants' prior learning, the OMD activities would be perceived by those taking part as abstract, isolated and without meaning. If participants were unable to make sense of their experiences, it is unlikely that any significant learning could result. Consequently, if it could be demonstrated that OMD has the capacity to level or neutralise participants' prior process experience and knowledge, such an effect would appear to reduce the likelihood of individuals learning from their experience rather than, as suggested, providing them with a unique freedom to learn.

In a further contradiction of popular belief, it can be contended that high process reality, a stressful environment and novel tasks (stated virtues of management training using the outdoors) may not result in any significant change, but may paradoxically conspire to reinforce the individual and organisational *status quo*. OMD activities which require participants to perform novel tasks under stressful conditions while being evaluated by peers and trainers will tend to increase the likelihood that the performer's existing dominant behaviours are elicited. If these existing behaviours (imported into the training event via metaphorical links) are perceived by the performer as appropriate or successful in solving their problem, then they will be strengthened by the experience. In this way, OMD training activities may reinforce participants' existing attitudes and behaviours rather than weakening, revising or replacing them.

This process of reinforcement and entrenchment of existing attitudes and behaviours may be even more pronounced when whole work teams are sent on OMD programmes. If an OMD programme is presented to an intact work team as a metaphor of the workplace, then there is a great potential for the existing power structures and hierarchies to transfer wholesale into the training event. Such transfer may act to promote and sustain a self-confirming reality which reinforces the self-evident truth that the existing organisational power structures and hierarchies represent the commonsense, natural order of things. Thus, OMD as a metaphor of the organisation may act to prevent organisational change and development through its role in creating and sustaining a system of hegemonic control. If reinforcement of the organisational *status quo* is the aim of the OMD intervention, then this training outcome may be perceived as an asset. OMD is, however, more usually employed as part of a wider organisational change and development programme, and in this context, the reinforcement of existing attitudes and behaviours can be regarded as counterproductive.

OMD, METAPHOR AND MANAGERIAL LEARNING

By drawing on Crawford's (1988) work, it can be asserted that paradigm examples of OMD, when compared with organisational situations, exhibit high process reality and low task and environmental reality. The low task and environmental reality of the intervention are used to support the conclusion that participants' learning will be about process issues. OMD is thus seen to represent a viable way of developing the process skills thought necessary for effective managerial performance. It is unclear, however, exactly what process learning will take place as a result of training. The general supposition implied by a large proportion of the literature is that significant process learning will be limited to management, team and/or inter-personal issues. The possibility that alternative, unplanned, but nonetheless significant learning outcomes may result from these training interventions is largely ignored.

Although OMD activities have been widely claimed to represent metaphors of managerial and organisational processes, their potential to act as metaphors of managerial learning processes does not appear to have been explicitly recognised or explored. An examination of the published literature on OMD suggests that a variety of different process learning outcomes may be experienced and exhibited by participants as a result of paradigm OMD interventions. Among these process outcomes are a number which appear to correspond closely with the 14 managerial learning skills identified by Mumford (1981: 37):

- Ability to establish effectiveness criteria for oneself.
- Ability to measure one's own effectiveness.
- Ability to identify ones own learning needs.
- Ability to plan one's learning.
- Ability to take advantage of learning opportunities.
- Ability to review one's learning process.
- Ability to listen to others.
- Ability to accept help.
- Ability to face unwelcome information.
- Ability to take risks and tolerate anxieties.
- Ability to analyse what other successful performers do.
- Ability to know oneself.
- Ability to share information with others.
- Ability to review what has been learned.

Mumford (1981) suggests that these skills are essential for managers to learn from experience, adapt to change and continually improve their own work performance. An analysis of the process learning outcomes described in the published OMD literature using Mumford's 14 managerial learning skills reveals that a high proportion of articles cite learning outcomes which closely match those listed by Mumford. This invites the speculation that OMD training may result in an increase in participants' learning skills as well as changes to specific management skills.

Learning to learn

How might OMD training result in participants learning to learn? If the processes which constitute OMD programmes were able to act as metaphors of the learning process, then they might conceivably result in OMD participants learning to learn. An explanation of how this could happen is outlined by Gass (1985, 1991) who suggests that the transfer of learning occurs on one of three levels: specific transfer, non-specific transfer, and metaphoric transfer:

> *Specific transfer* occurs when the *actual products* of learning (e.g., skills such as canoeing, belaying, reading) are generalised to habits and associations so that use of these skills is applicable to other learning situations. *Non-specific transfer* occurs when the *specific processes* of learning are generalised into attitudes and principles for future use by the learner (e.g., co-operation, environmental awareness). *Metaphoric transfer* occurs when *parallel processes* in one learning situation become analogous to learning in another different, yet similar situation. (Gass, 1991: 6)

OMD could result in learning to learn via specific transfer: paradigm examples of OMD activities commonly require participants consciously and deliberately to pass through all four stages represented in Kolb's model of experiential learning. Participants may be taught how to apply this model in order to learn from their experiences. After leaving the course they may, as a direct result of this training, consciously apply the stages of this model when faced with a new learning opportunity or problem-solving situation.

OMD may bring about learning to learn via non-specific transfer: attitudes and principles outlined by Mumford and thought necessary for autonomous managerial learning to occur could be acquired as part of the course. Participants may, for example, have their attitudes and ability to ask for and provide help changed by the OMD experience.

Metaphoric transfer of learning autonomy may occur if learning to learn in the work situation closely parallels learning to learn in the OMD situation. Gass (1991: 7) states that:

> Isomorphism... occurs when two complex structures of different situations can be mapped on to one another so that similar features can be linked together. Once the connection of these features is made, the similarity of roles they play in their respective structures create a medium for change.

> This medium provides possible connections for the transfer of valuable
> information learned in one environment for future use in another.

The processes by which we learn to learn are not situation specific but universal. Any learning autonomy developed during OMD training will give individuals the potential for increased learning autonomy in the workplace. The process of learning to learn, which might start within an OMD course, has the potential via isomorphic transfer to be continued within the workplace.

If OMD has the potential to increase participants' learning autonomy, OMD participants might become increasingly capable of defining learning outcomes, setting learning agendas and pursuing their personal, idiosyncratic learning goals. The training/learning needs of the participants would be expected to vary according to personal differences. Therefore, any given sample of individuals who have completed an OMD course might report a multiplicity of training outcomes resulting from the same intervention, each having used the course to learn what was personally important to her or him. In this way the 'learning to learn' hypothesis may be used to provide a partial explanation of the wide variety of training outcomes commonly attributed to this form of programme.

CONCLUSIONS

It has been argued here that OMD activities, although traditionally presented as metaphors of managerial and organisational processes, may additionally act as metaphors for managerial learning processes, resulting in participants learning how to learn. The principal benefit of OMD as a training intervention may consequently lie in its potential to increase the learning autonomy of participants and thus act as a precursor to other learning events. There is much evidence that writers on OMD have selectively examined the metaphorical links between this form of training and the workplace. This has resulted in a number of distorted or internally inconsistent arguments. Continued exploration of the links between OMD, metaphor and learning may be fruitful in furthering our conceptual understanding of this widely used, but under-researched and poorly understood form of training.

REFERENCES

Alder, A. (1990) 'Going back to the woods', *Transition*, Vol. 89, No. 11.
Arkin, A. (1991) 'An open approach to retail training', *Personnel Management*, Vol. 22, No. 8.
Boud, D., Cohen, R. and Walker, D. (1993) 'Understanding learning from experience', in Boud, D., Cohen, R. and Walker, D. (eds) *Using Experience for Learning*.

Buckingham: The Society for Research into Higher Education and Open University Press.

Bronson, J., Gibson, S., Kichar, R. and Priest, S. (1992) 'Evaluation of team development in a corporate adventure training program', *Journal of Experiential Education*, Vol. 15, No. 2.

Burnett, D. (1994) 'Exercising better management skills', *Personnel Management*, January.

Cacioppe, R. and Adamson, P. (1988) 'Stepping over the edge: outdoor development programs for management and staff ', *Human Resource Management Australia*, Vol. 26, No. 4.

Calder, H. (1991) 'Outdoor training: is it training?', *Institute of Personnel Management Journal (South Africa)*, Vol. 10, No. 1.

Campbell, J. (1990) 'Outdoor management development: a fad or a phenomenon?', *Training Officer*, Vol. 26, Nos. 7–8.

Crawford, N. (1988) 'Outdoor management development: a practical evaluation', *Journal of European Industrial Training*, Vol. 12, No. 8.

Creswick, C. and Williams, R. (1979) 'Using the outdoors for management development and team building'. Internal paper, Food, Drink and Tobacco Industry Training Board.

Dainty, P. and Lucas, D. (1992) 'Clarifying the confusion: a practical framework for evaluating outdoor development programmes for managers', *Management Education and Development*, Vol. 23, No. 2.

Elkin, G. (1991) 'Outdoor challenge programmes: employee development in New Zealand', *Training Officer*, Vol. 27, No. 7.

Evans, J. (1988) 'The boulder-strewn path to the top jobs', *Transition*, Vol. 86, No. 10.

Everard, B. (1988) 'The growing pains of development training', *Transition*, Vol. 88, No. 2.

Everard, B. (1991) 'Effective use of the outdoors', *Transition*, Vol. 91, No.7.

Gall, A. (1987) 'You can take the manager out of the woods, but...', *Training and Development Journal (USA)*, March.

Gass, M.A. (1985) 'Programming the transfer of learning in adventure education', *Journal of Experiential Education*, Vol. 10, No. 3.

Gass, M.A. (1991) 'Enhancing metaphor development in adventure therapy programs', *The Journal of Experiential Education*, Vol. 14, No. 2.

IRRR 514 (1992a) 'Using the outdoors: 1. Background', *Industrial Relations Review and Report*, No. 514, Employee Development Bulletin No. 30.

IRRR 522 (1992b) 'The role of outdoor-based development: a survey of 120 employers', *Industrial Relations Review and Report*, No. 522, Employee Development Bulletin No. 34.

Jones, P.J. (1993) 'OMD: guidance for sponsors', *The Mentor: Management Digest*, Vol. 2, No. 3.

Jones, P.J. and Oswick, C. (1993) 'Outcomes of outdoor management development: articles of faith?', *Journal of European Industrial Training*, Vol. 17, No. 3.

Kirk, P. (1986) 'Outdoor management development: cellulose or celluloid?', *Management Education and Development*, Vol. 17, No. 2.

Kolb, D.A. and Fry, R. (1975) 'Towards an applied theory of experiential learning', in Cooper, C.L. (ed) *Theories of Group Process*. London: Wiley.

Long, J.W. (1987) 'The wilderness lab comes of age', *Training and Development Journal (USA)*, Vol. 41, No. 3.

Lowe, J. (1991) 'Teambuilding via outdoor training: experiences from a UK automotive plant,' *Human Resource Management Journal*, Vol. 2, No. 1.

McGraw, P. (1993) 'Back from the mountain: outdoor management development programs and how to ensure the transfer of skills to the workplace', *Asia Pacific Journal of Human Resources*, Vol. 31, No. 3.

Melville, H. (1851) *Moby-Dick, or The Whale*. London: Oxford University Press.

Miller, E. and Rooke, S. (1991) 'Journeys towards excellence: the design and facilitation of outdoor management development programmes', *Human Resource Management in Action*, Vol. 29, No. 4.

Mumford, A. (1981) 'What did you learn today?', *Personnel Management*, Vol. 13, No. 8, August.

Neffinger, G.G. (1990) 'Real learning in unreal circumstances', *Journal of Managerial Psychology*, Vol. 5, No. 4.

Petrini, C. (1990) 'Over the river and though the woods', *Training and Development Journal (USA)*, Vol. 44, No. 5.

Schofield, P. (1985) 'Outdoor development training', *Personnel Executive*, Vol. 4, No. 9.

Scott, A. (1988) 'Outward appearances', *Accountancy*, Vol. 102, No. 1140.

Sewell, C. (1991) 'Learning from the outdoors', *Transition*, Vol. 91, No. 7.

Reeve, D. (1982) 'Revitalising managers by training outdoors', *Personnel Management*, Vol. 14, No. 4.

Ryan, B. (1993) 'Outdoor leadership and team-building (a slightly different perspective...)', *Transition*, Vol. 93, No. 2.

Wagner, R.J., Baldwin, T.T. and Roland, C.C. (1991) 'Outdoor training: revolution or fad?', *Training and Development Journal (USA)*, Vol. 45, No. 3.

Wagner, R.J. and Campbell, J. (1994) 'Outdoor-based experiential training: improving transfer of training using virtual reality', *Journal of Management Development*, Vol. 13, No. 7.

Wagner, R.J. and Roland, C.C. (1992) 'How effective is outdoor training?', *Training and Development (USA)*, Vol. 46, No. 7.

Wilson, D.C. (1992) *A Strategy of Change: Concepts and Controversies in the Management of Change*. London: Routledge.

CHAPTER 14

Small business development: explorations using biological metaphors

Lew Perren

INTRODUCTION

Small firms are often overlooked in the mainstream Organisation Development (OD) literature. Nevertheless, they face considerable organisational challenges and must confront similar change issues to larger firms.

The purpose of this chapter is to use the notion of biological metaphors to investigate small business behaviour and development. This leads to an integration of concepts around various metaphors, rather than being constrained by previous categorisations in the literature. It suggests which biological metaphors have not been fully exploited and how they may offer new areas for research. Assessment is made of how useful biological metaphors are at increasing our understanding of small firms.

The chapter begins with an introduction to biological metaphors and an overview of previous applications. The following metaphors are then explored:

- *Classification*: the debate surrounding classification of small business owners is investigated by comparing it with attempts by early biologists to classify organisms. The need for stable and observable features in order to achieve successful classification is discussed.
- *Evolution*: since Darwin's theory of evolution biologists have considered organisms as being part of a dynamic environment to which they need to adapt. The extensive use of Darwin's ideas in the study of Organisation Development will be explored. Darwinian and Lamarckian theories of evolution are compared to see if any further insights can be drawn into the development of small organisations.
- *Stage models*: the dominant use of the evolutionary metaphor in small business research has been in stage models. These models attempt to describe the stages of evolution of an organisation. The limitations of the life cycle metaphor are explored.

- *Disease*: various diseases are compared to problems experienced by developing organisations. The treatment of disease is investigated to see if there are any insights for managing organisational difficulties.
- *Symbiosis*: the characteristics of natural symbiosis are compared with similar relationships between firms. The growing literature on owner–manager and small firm networks will be examined in the context of this comparison.
- *Genetic engineering*: genetic engineering is likened to external intervention by consultants into the operation of small firms. The appropriateness of interventions and issues surrounding the reluctance of owner–managers to accept help are discussed.

The conclusion offers a synthesis of the insights and suggests what implications they might have for further research. The limitations of biological metaphors are examined, including the risk of a particular metaphor becoming a 'cage' (restricting rather than enabling understanding) and the use of biological metaphors being confined by the current knowledge of the natural world.

BIOLOGICAL METAPHORS

The use of metaphor is powerful, pervading not only our modelling but potentially our design of organisations. The metaphor is often implicit and may not be recognised by the user. It is likely that most managers consider their firm as struggling for survival in a hostile environment, but unlikely that many would consider this as a biological metaphor which likens their firm to an organism existing in an eco-system.

Morgan (1986) suggests comparison of organisations with a range of metaphors, including machine, biological, brain, cultural, political, psychic prison and domination. This chapter will concentrate on the comparison of small firm development with various biological metaphors. It was felt that biological metaphors might well be the 'root metaphor' of small business development. In Chapter 12, Grant suggests that a 'root metaphor' is the key metaphor which lays the foundation on which knowledge about a subject is built (Grant himself cites Dunn's (1990) work on 'root metaphors' in industrial relations). Certainly, it appears from the discussion below that biological metaphors are at the origin of much of the research associated with small businesses.

It may be that 'root metaphors' do more than just lay the foundation of knowledge, they may also influence what is being studied. In the case of small firms, some owners may well have been influenced by the media and politicians' implicit use of biological metaphors associated with growth and

Darwinian notions of survival. The use of a 'root metaphor' to describe a situation can result in a 'self-fulfilling prophecy'.

CLASSIFICATION OF ENTREPRENEURS AND SMALL BUSINESS OWNERS

There has been much debate about the classification of small business owners and entrepreneurs. Daryl Mitton (1989) described this research as 'the entrepreneurship theory jungle' – a metaphor which conveys well the complexity and false tracts that exist in the literature. It is possible to draw comparison between the eighteenth-century biological classifiers and the twentieth-century classifiers of entrepreneurs. *Pears Cyclopedia's* (1987) introduction to the classification of organisms could equally be introducing the classification of entrepreneurs:

> **The early workers saw that some species were similar to one another while others were obviously dissimilar. Systems of classification based on the similarities and differences were drawn up. . . The dividing line between different groups at all levels is always difficult and in the final analysis somewhat arbitrary.** (Pears Cyclopedia,1987: F35)

Linnaeus put forward a classification system for organisms in the 1730s. He grouped organisms according to common features and created a hierarchical system extending through Kingdom, Phylum, Class to Species (Roberts, 1986). If a similar classification is made for entrepreneurs, then the overall Kingdom could perhaps be people, one of the Phyla could be business people and one of the Classes could be entrepreneurs.

Linnaeus's successful classification of organisms relied on common features around which groupings were formed. These features needed to be easily observable and stable throughout the generations. For example, the Class 'birds' is distinguished by all birds possessing feathers, wings and a beak.

Unfortunately, research into the classification of entrepreneurs and small business owners is not based around easily observable or stable features. A list combined from summaries provided by Gibb and Davies (1992) and Chell et al (1991) suggests that the features of being entrepreneurial include:

- risk taking (Cantillon, 1755);
- initiator of new risky activities (Sombart, 1950);
- planning and organising (Say, 1964);
- innovation and creation of new productive means (Schumpeter, 1934);
- alertness to profit opportunities (Kirzner, 1982);
- better judgemental decisions due to imagination (Casson, 1982);
- high need for achievement (McClelland, 1961);
- belief in personal control over events (Rotter, 1966).

None of the above features is likely to be displayed continuously by an individual and all could potentially be affected by environmental factors. Attempts to establish measures of innate traits that could potentially be stable have yielded inconclusive results (Chell et al, 1991; Stevenson and Sahlman, 1989). This leaves a perplexing task of trying to classify with features that are difficult to observe and potentially unstable. In addition, there is no current consensus on which factors are key to the definition of entrepreneurship.

Perhaps the way forward is to stop trying to classify individuals as entrepreneurs and to view entrepreneurship as a behavioural state that business people may display for varying periods. The behavioural state of 'entrepreneurship' may be shared between different Classes of business people in the same way that the behavioural state of 'hunting' is shared between some birds and some mammals. It also links well with Gartner's (1989) proposition that entrepreneurship is an impermanent role that individuals undertake to create organisations.

This releases the classifier to search for common features in the Phyla 'business people' which are observable and stable. Searching for stable features which are constantly with the 'business person' – in the same way that feathers, wings and a beak are with a bird – is rather unhelpful. It suggests physical features which are observable such as sex and height, or innate psychological features which are difficult to measure with certainty. Perhaps including features which are *relatively* rather than *totally* stable will give a way forward. Even Linnaeus's classification will have to change slowly as evolution progresses.

If *relatively* stable and observable features are allowed for classification purposes, then a much more useful set of possibilities is available, including type of function (specialist or multi-skilled), educational level, family background, educational background, size of company and type of company. For example, a Class 'small business owner' might be defined as people who have full ownership and control of a business with under a certain number of employees. The Class could be divided into various Orders – perhaps by the nature of the business offering. It may be that investigating innate psychological traits within these more tangible classifications will result in more conclusive findings in the future.

EVOLUTION AND THE ORGANISM IN ITS ENVIRONMENT

There has been an extensive use of evolutionary metaphors in the study of Organisation Development. Since Darwin's theory of evolution biologists have considered organisms as being part of a dynamic environment to which they must adapt or die. Morgan (1986) outlines the metaphor well:

And as we look around the organizational world we begin to see that it is possible to identify different species of organization in different kinds of environment. Just as we find polar bears in Arctic regions, camels in deserts, and alligators in swamps, we notice certain species of organization are better 'adapted' to specific environmental conditions. (Morgan,1986: 39)

The idea that an organisation has a life cycle has been a particularly popular version of evolutionary metaphor (see Chapter 3 for a broader discussion of this metaphor in relation to organisations). After all, one can speak of and conceptualise organisational 'birth', 'life' and 'death'. Organisations, like organisms, are affected by the early phases of growth and the external and internal forces that impinge on them.

It is interesting to explore whether Lamarckian or Darwinian evolutionary theory is the most appropriate metaphor for the creation and development of firms. Darwin's theory suggests that variation between the parents and offspring naturally occurs and that some offspring will by chance be better suited to the environment they face than others. These more successful organisms will have a greater chance of passing their genetic material onto the next generation. In this way the species constantly adapts and becomes better suited to the environment (Rothschild, 1992).

Lamarck's theory takes a different view. He suggested that during its life the organism adapts to its environment as best it can and these beneficial adaptations can be passed on to its offspring (Rothschild, 1992).

If the Darwinian perspective is taken, then parallels can be drawn between the genetic material transferred to an organism at inception and the past experience and psychological make-up of the owner being transferred to the firm at start-up. Implicit in the Darwinian metaphor is the starting of many other firms at the same time and that the fittest would survive while the others perish. This perspective emphasises the importance of the foundation genetic material; whereas the Lamarckian metaphor emphasises the firm's responsibility to adapt to the environment as best it can and its potential to pass on beneficial experiences to future firms.

Therefore the key difference between the Darwinian and Lamarckian metaphor is the degree of self-will. The Darwinian example stresses the power of the environment and the inevitability of the firm's circumstances, while the Lamarckian approach stresses the power of self-will to adapt to the environment. Penrose (1952) believes that organisations have self-determinism which sets them apart from organisms. She states:

We have no reason whatsoever for thinking that the growth pattern of a biological organism is willed by the organism itself. On the other hand, we have reason for thinking that the growth of a firm is willed by those who make the decisions of the firm and are themselves part of the firm... We know of no general laws predetermining men's choices, nor have we as yet

any established basis for suspecting the existence of such laws. By contrast ... we have every reason for thinking that these matters are predetermined by the nature of living organisms.

The Lamarckian metaphor appears to be the most appropriate comparison with the birth and development of the firm. It stresses self-determination and choice, which are characteristics successful small business owners certainly possess and must believe in to remain motivated. It also explains the firm's development of core competencies that can be transferred to spin-off firms in the future.

STAGE MODELS

The dominant use of the evolutionary metaphor in small business research has been in stage models. These models attempt to describe the stages of evolution of an organisation. Their dominance merits closer examination of the way they are applied and their appropriateness.

The chief variables in stage models are the size and age of the firm. The common theme is that as the organisation grows it will pass through stages of development, and that emphasis will shift from the owner–manager in the early stages towards more formal and bureaucratic structures in the latter stages.

Perhaps the first stage model was developed by McGuire (1963). He suggested five stages: traditional small company, planning for growth, take-off, drive for professional management, and mass production marked by 'a diffusion of objectives and an interest in the welfare of society'. A large number of stage models have been developed on the same theme (Christensen and Scott, 1964; Steinmetz, 1969; Greiner, 1972; Lievegoed, 1973; Churchill and Lewis, 1983; Kanzanjian, 1984; Flamholtz, 1986; Dodge and Robbins, 1992).

Greiner's (1972) model is often referenced. He proposes five phases of growth in the transition from small to large (in turnover or number of employees). He suggests that smooth evolution is not always inevitable and that periods of revolution may be needed. The periods of revolution are when substantial organisational turbulence and change occur. Each of the evolutionary phases is identified by a particular management style and each revolution is caused by a critical management problem.

Biological organisms tend to pass through reasonably clear and predictable stages of development, from simple to more complex (Kimberley and Miles, 1980). However, there is nothing inevitable about a small firm passing through all or any of the stages suggested by these models (Churchill and Lewis, 1983; Kimberley, 1980). In fact the vast majority of firms remain very small, with only 9 per cent of UK firms growing beyond

10 employees (Stanworth and Gray, 1991). Therefore the stage models proposed will only be applicable to a small percentage of firms.

Kimberley and Miles (1980) suggest that biological organisms begin to die the minute they are born. Death is an inevitable feature of biological life. The same cannot be said of firms; there is nothing about organisational life in itself which implies inevitable death. It could be argued, without entering into religious debate, that death may be just another state, a quantum leap into another dimension. Perhaps an organism's death represents a stage of transition to a new state, a reincarnation. If this is the case a parallel can be drawn between reincarnation and the large revolutionary organisational changes suggested in some of the literature (Greiner, 1972).

DISEASE

It is appropriate to commence examination of this metaphor and how it relates to small businesses with a quote from Stafford Beer's (1989) discussion of pathology and the viable systems model:

> In medical practice, there is such a thing as post mortem examination. Much knowledge of viable systems has been gained by the study of those that are viable no more. I have done some work of this kind, but only as the result of being fortuitously present at the deathbed. The suggestion would be that a small team of organisational pathologists should be informed, ready to rush to the scene of any incipient organisational demise. Of course, these people would not be loitering about, waiting for something to happen – they would be organised more like a lifeboat crew. The first imperative would be to resuscitate the moribund victim. Failing that, however, a post mortem would be performed before rigor mortis had set in, and before those nearest to the deceased had closed in like vultures they often emulate. I have certainly noticed many times how history is rewritten in these circumstances with breathtaking speed. It happens with people too. (1989: 29–30)

Taking the type of approach adopted by Beer allows comparison of various human ailments and diseases with the problems experienced by developing organisations. Here, the treatment of disease will be investigated to see if there are any insights for managing organisational difficulties in small firms.

Addiction

Addiction is the dependence on a drug. The treatment of addition includes analysis, group therapy, and the prescription of less harmful drugs to relieve withdrawal symptoms (Reference International, 1984). Owners of small firms can be considered as having a dependence on the drug of power, with a reluctance to lose direct control even though the way the firm is organised may need to change if it is to grow successfully (Mintzberg, 1979, 1983; Greiner, 1972; Flamholtz, 1986). As the firm becomes larger it will need to become more formalised, and the owner–manager will need to give up the drug of power and delegate to key individuals or growth may be inhibited through lack of control (Handy, 1985; Mintzberg, 1983; Ritchie et al, 1982).

There may be lessons in the treatment of drug addiction that could be applied to owners addicted to power. First, similar techniques to those employed in psychotherapy and group therapy could be used to help the owner address the addiction and perhaps alleviate the problem. This may involve counselling sessions where the owner is able to obtain relief through non-critical 'confessions', which may allow emotional discharge and anxieties to be brought into the open. It may also be possible to 'desensitise' the owner by referring repeatedly to the problems of power and delegation and to define the owner's feelings by exploring them. Interestingly, similar techniques are suggested by texts on Organisation Development interventions (see, for example, French and Bell, 1990). Second, a less harmful 'drug' may be used to relieve the owner's withdrawal symptoms, perhaps by suggesting that the owner retains power and 'hands-on' control of a small number of functions while delegating responsibility for others.

Hormones

These are complex chemicals secreted by glands which act as blood-borne 'messengers' which regulate cell functions in the body. They form a communications system which can bring about amazing changes in the body's cell activities, for example an immature child is changed by the influence of growth and sex hormones to become a sexually mature adult (Reference International, 1984). Deficiencies in growth hormone can cause severely restricted growth. Hormone disorders may be treated through hormone replacement therapy using synthetic compounds resembling the natural products (Reference International, 1984).

The deficiency of growth hormones in an infant can be compared to the owner of a firm not having an orientation towards growing the firm. A number of researchers have suggested that the growth orientation of the owner–manager may be an important driver of a firm's growth (Stanworth and Curran, 1986; Chell et al, 1991; Scase and Goffee, 1980). Stanworth and Curran (1986) suggest two types of owner–manager: the artisan with low growth orientation and the entrepreneur with high growth orientation. Loss of control as the business grows is seen by many researchers to be a potential barrier to growth for the artisan, while growth opportunity provides the *raison d'être* for the entrepreneur (Gill, 1985; Stanworth and Curran, 1986).

Perhaps it is possible to convert 'artisans' with low growth orientation into 'entrepreneurs' with high growth motivation through some mechanism similar to hormone replacement therapy in medicine. The equivalent of a synthetic growth hormone is required that can be administered to artisan owners to increase their growth orientation. The 'synthetic growth hormone' might be some form of incentive that is directly linked to the growth of the firm, perhaps performance-related grants or tax incentives.

Schizophrenia

This severe mental disturbance is characterised by disordered thought processes, bizarre actions and incapacity to maintain normal inter-personal relationships (Briggs, 1989). The causes of schizophrenia are uncertain but neuro-chemical imbalance is frequently displayed, hereditary factors are thought to make some individuals susceptible and stress may well act as a trigger. Bateson and Laing have hypothesised that 'double-bind situations', where an individual has contradictory commands made on them, may account for both the causes and experiences of schizophrenic illness (Briggs, 1989). Treatment often involves tranquillising drugs and perhaps psychotherapy.

Parallels can be drawn between Bateson and Laing's 'double-bind situations' and the considerable role ambiguity which may be experienced by individuals trying to be the owner of a firm and also the member of a family. The role ambiguity is likely to cause most stress during the start-up and growth phase of the business, which is unfortunately liable for many owners to coincide with family matters such as bringing up children and caring for elderly relatives. The accounts by Scase and Goffee (1980) illustrate the importance of the family and the role ambiguity felt by the owner–manager. They conclude:

> There are, then, heavy social and personal costs born by the 'self made' man and his family. Married women in particular, and the family in general, provide a hidden but necessary investment during the initial stages of the business. Further, family life continues to suffer as the business grows because family and business are inextricably interconnected. . . But are the costs worthwhile? This is something which only the individuals, themselves, can decide. Certainly, some of the proprietors we interviewed make conscious decisions to stop at various stages of business growth if only because the costs for personal satisfaction, life-styles and social relationships are too great. (Scase and Goffee, 1980: 107–8)

Scase and Goffee (1980) and Gill (1985) all state the importance of the owner–manager's relationship with their family if successful growth is to occur. Gill suggests that family conflicts, lack of a successor and the involvement of too many family members can all reduce the owner–manager's interest in the business and motivation for growth.

Research by Lambshead and Levy (1989) suggests that owner–managers of small firms have higher degrees of stress than managers in larger organisations. They suggest that the main difference in stressors are those concerning the home–work interface and relationships. They cite Khan et al (1964) to suggest that there are high inter-personal skill demands on owner–managers, especially in supporting 'boundary-spanning' relationships such as with bank managers, suppliers and customers. The role conflict that exists between the owner–manager as successful business person and as family person may well result in stress in the individual.

The stress and role ambiguity for the owner–manager may well act as a barrier to growth, especially through the early stages when the organisation probably relies solely on the owner–manager for direction and control. It appears that the medical treatment of schizophrenia offers little enlightenment here as it just suppresses the symptoms. Perhaps a preventative approach would be better for owners of small firms. Possible suggestions include scheduling the firm and family developments together to try and reduce potential conflicts, reducing the rate of the firm's development to give time for the family, or taking on partners to help with the early development of the firm.

SYMBIOSIS, RELATIONSHIPS AND NETWORKS

It is possible to juxtapose the characteristics of natural symbiosis with the relationships which exist between small firms. In older biological classifications the term symbiosis was used for mutually beneficial associations only; recently it has been used more generally to cover three types of association (Roberts, 1986):

1 *Parasitism:* an association between two organisms in which the parasite lives on the other and obtains benefit while causing harm to the host.
2 *Commensalism:* an association between two organisms in which the commensal gains without harm to the host organism.
3 *Mutualism:* an association between two organisms where both gain from the relationship.

The parasitism metaphor highlights how many owner–managers use their old employer's contacts and resources to help set themselves up. The benefits gained are very analogous to the biological situation, as are the potential consequences to the host firm. This is an area that does not appear to be particularly well researched from the literature and is certainly worth attention.

Completely commensal relationships seem quite rare in the small firm sector. An example might be where a large firm leaves a gap in its service that is continuously filled by a small firm. Relationships which are potentially mutualism can develop into commensalism or even parasitism; for example, a referral system between a bank and an accountant where referrals only go one way. Relationships that are pretending to be mutualism and become commensalism or parasitism tend to break down unless they are very cleverly managed by the covert parasite.

The mutualism metaphor encompasses many of the associations which occur with small firms. In this situation both parties benefit through the use of buyer–supplier relationships and collaborations.

The symbiotic metaphors link well with the developing literature on small business owners' networks, much of which currently concentrates on mutualism, suggesting that further research into commensal and parasitic relationships may well be worthwhile (Johannisson and Nielsson, 1989; Birley, 1985; Cromie and Birley, 1990; Aldrich and Zimmer, 1986; Blackburn et al, 1990).

GENETIC ENGINEERING

Comparing the process of genetic engineering with the support for small firms provides further insights. Genetic engineering is where a specific segment of deoxyribonucleic acid (DNA), which carries the organism's hereditary material, is either altered or transferred to another cell. It is possible that in the future humans will control the genetics of all organism's including themselves (*Encyclopaedia Britannica*, 1993).

At first examination, the genetic engineering analogy might include any intervention into the organisation of a small firm. If this very broad perspective is taken the metaphor is too imprecise and adds little value. It is more useful to view the core competencies of the firm as being equivalent to the DNA in an organism and providing the blueprint of how it will develop. The equivalent of genetic engineering would become very careful interventions that alter specific core competencies of the firm, rather than imprecise broad interventions.

This metaphor offers insights for external agencies that try to help small firms such as banks, consultants and accountants. It suggests that intervention needs to be specifically targeted at altering a defective core competence (part of the DNA). If the intervention is too broad it may alter the DNA to such an extent that a non-viable mutant firm will try to develop.

The reluctance of some owner–managers to allow broad intervention is understandable in this context. Many people would accept some form of genetic engineering to remove a clear defect which threatens their life; few would accept wholesale alteration of their DNA which would alter characteristics such as personality or intellect.

These ideas have relevance to the extensive literature on support for small firms that was sparked by the 1971 Bolton Committee Inquiry on Small Firms (example publications include Barber et al, 1989; Bhalla, 1991; Flamhotz, 1986; Jacobs and Pons, 1993; Jennings and Banfield, 1993; Lindsay et al, 1993; Stanworth and Gray, 1991; Vyakarnham and Jacobs, 1993). Where perhaps the genetic engineering metaphor brings insight is that it emphasises the requirement for specific profiling of needs of individual firms, rather than broad competence areas being offered as support. This suggests that further research should be directed towards designing better processes for profiling the specific weaknesses in individual firm's core competencies, so that support can be targeted.

CONCLUSIONS

The use of biological metaphor provides some interesting insights. The comparison between classifying entrepreneurs and classifying organisms suggests the need to treat entrepreneurship as a behavioural state and to search for more easily observable and stable features. This may well give a firmer platform for psychologists to investigate innate traits.

The section on evolutionary metaphors found the Lamarckian metaphor to be more appropriate to small firm development than the Darwinian metaphor. The Lamarckian metaphor emphasised the importance of self-will, the power the firm has to adapt to its environment and the potential to pass useful core competencies on to spin off firms.

The use of evolutionary metaphors to form stage models was examined. While these models were potentially useful for understanding some firms, they were not appropriate for the majority of small businesses, as it was far from inevitable that firms would pass through all or any of the stages suggested.

Various diseases were compared to problems experienced by developing organisations. The treatment of disease suggested some potential approaches to managing the organisational difficulties of small firms.

The metaphor of symbiosis highlighted the lack of emphasis placed on parasitic and commensal relationships within the literature on small business owners' networks. It also suggested the potential for managing relationships so they appear to be mutual but are in fact commensal or even worse parasitic. This may suggest some interesting research into the different strategies which owners employ to manage and possibly exploit the stakeholders in their network.

The genetic engineering metaphor gave insight into the importance of core competencies ('DNA') that will determine how the firm develops. It also highlighted reasons why some owner–managers are reluctant to allow broad intervention by consultants into their businesses. Further research was suggested into designing better processes for profiling the specific weaknesses in the core competencies of firms and targeting help directly.

There is a risk of a particular metaphor becoming a 'cage' and restricting rather than enabling understanding. Overcommitment to a metaphor can lead to it being inappropriately stretched to fit the object being investigated. The author found it important to remain flexible about the use of a particular metaphor and not to put too much investment into any particular comparison in its early stages. This reduced the risk of a 'cage' forming. For example, the following metaphors were experimented with but not investigated further as they were not found by the author to be useful: small firm growth as a viral infection, immune systems and small firm survival, nutrition and feeding as a metaphor for small firms obtaining resources, and rheumatism compared to formalisation of the organisation. This does not suggest that other researchers will not be able to gain insight from these rejected metaphors, simply that they were not found useful by the author in the preparation for this chapter.

The use of biological metaphors is confined by the current scientific understanding of biological systems. Some metaphors which seem to break down when compared with small businesses may do so not because they are inappropriate, but because of limitations in our current knowledge of the natural world.

REFERENCES

Aldrich, H. and Zimmer, C. (1986) 'Entrepreneurship through social networks', in Sexton, D. and Smilor R. (eds) *The Art and Science of Entrepreneurship*. London: Ballinger.

Barber, J., Metcalfe, J.S. and Porteous, M. (1989) *Barriers to Growth in Small Firms*. London: Routledge.

Beer, S. (1989) 'The viable systems model: its provenance, development, methodology and pathology', in Espejo, R. and Harnden, R. (eds) *The Viable Systems Model: Interpretations and Applications of Stafford Beer's VSM*. London: Wiley.

Bhalla, A.S. (1991) *Small and Medium Enterprises: Technology Policies and Options*. London: Greenwood.

Birley, S. (1985) 'The role of networks in the entrepreneurial process', *Journal of Business Venturing*, Vol. 1, No. 1.

Blackburn, R.A., Curran, J. and Jarvis, R. (1990) 'Small firms and local networks: some theoretical and conceptual explorations'. Paper presented at the 13th Small Firms' Policy and Research Conference, November.

Bolton, J.E. (1971) *Small Firms – Report of the Committee of Inquiry on Small Firms*. London: HMSO.

Briggs, A. (ed) (1989) *The Longman Encyclopaedia*. London: Longman.

Cantillon, R. (1755) 'Essai sur la nature du commerce en general', reproduced by H. Higgs, London: Macmillan (1931).

Casson, M. (1982) *The Entrepreneur: An Economic Theory*. Totowa: Barnes and Noble.

Chell, E., Haworth, J. and Brearley, S. (1991) *The Entrepreneurial Personality*. London: Routledge.

Christensen, R.C. and Scott, B.R. (1964) *Review of Course Activities*. Lausanne: IMEDE.

Churchill, N.C. and Lewis, V.L. (1983) 'The five stages of small business growth', *Harvard Business Review*, May–June.

Cromie, S. and Birley, S. (1990) 'Entrepreneurial networks: some concepts and empirical evidence'. Paper presented at the 13th Small Firms' Policy and Research Conference, November.

Dodge, R.H. and Robbins, J.E. (1992) 'An empirical investigation of the organisational life cycle model for small business development and survival', *Journal of Small Business*, January.

Dunn, S. (1990) 'Root metaphor in the old and new industrial relations', *British Journal of Industrial Relations*, Vol. 28, No. 1.

Flamholtz, E.G. (1986) *How to Make the Transition from Entrepreneurship to a Professionally Managed Firm*. San Francisco: Jossey-Bass.

French, W.L. and Bell, C.H. (1990) *Organizational Development: Behavioral Science Interventions for Organizational Improvement*. 4th Edition, Englewood Cliffs, NJ: Prentice-Hall.

Gartner, W.B. (1989) '"Who is an entrepreneur?" is the wrong question', *Entrepreneurship Theory and Practice*, Summer.

Gibb, A.A. and Davies, L. (1992) 'Development of a growth model', *The Journal of Entrepreneurship*, Vol. 1, No. 1.

Gill, J. (1985) *Factors Affecting the Survival and Growth of the Smaller Company*. London: Gower.

Greiner, L.E. (1972) 'Evolution and revolution as organizations grow', *Harvard Business Review*, July–August.

Handy, C.B. (1985) *Understanding Organisations*. 3rd Edition, Harmondsworth: Penguin.

Jacobs, R. and Pons, T. (1993) 'Developing a new model of individual and team competence in small business'. Paper presented at the 16th National Small Firms' Policy and Research Conference, November.

Jennings, P.L. and Banfield, P. (1993) 'Improving competence in small firms'. Paper presented at the 16th National Small Firms' Policy and Research Conference, November.

Johannisson, B. and Nielsson, A. (1989) 'Community entrepreneurs: networking for local development', *Entrepreneurship for Regional Development*, Vol. 1.

Kanzanjian, R.K. (1984) 'Operationalizing stage of growth: an empirical assessment of dominant problems', in Hornday, J.A., Tarpley, F., Timmons, J.A. and Vesper, K.H. (eds) *Frontiers of Entrepreneurial Research*. Wellesley, Mass.: Babson College, Center for Entrepreneurial Studies.

Khan, R.L., Wolfe, D.M., Quinn, R.P and Snoek, J.D. (1964) *Organizational Stress: Studies in Role Conflict and Ambiguity*. New York: Wiley.

Kimberley, J.R. (1980) *The Organizational Life Cycle*. Miles & Associates, San Francisco: Jossey-Bass.

Kimberley, J.R. and Miles, R.H. (1980) *The Organizational Life Cycle*. New York: Jossey-Bass.

Kirzner, I.M. (1982) 'The theory of entrepreneurship in economic growth', in Kent, C.A., Sexton, D.L. and Vesper, K.H. (eds) *Encyclopaedia of Entrepreneurship*. Englewood Cliffs, NJ: Prentice-Hall.

Lambshead, C. and Levy, F. (1989) 'Stress and small business management'. Paper presented at the 12th National Small Firms' Policy and Research Conference, November.

Lievegoed, B.C.J. (1973) *The Developing Organization*. Millbrae, CA: Celestial Arts.

McClelland, D.C. (1961) *The Achieving Society*. New York: Van Nostrand.

McGuire, J.W. (1963) *Factors Affecting the Growth of Manufacturing Firms*. Washington: Bureau of Business Research, University of Washington.

Mintzberg, H. (1979) *The Structuring of Organizations*. Englewood Cliffs, NJ: Prentice-Hall.

Mintzberg, H. (1983) *Structure in Fives*. Englewood Cliffs, NJ: Prentice-Hall.

Mitton, D.G. (1989) 'The complete entrepreneur', *Entrepreneurship Theory and Practice*, Spring.

Morgan, G. (1986) *Images of Organization*. Newbury Park, CA: Sage.

Penrose, E.T. (1952) 'Biological analogies in the theory of the firm', *American Economic Review*, Vol. 19.

Reference International (1984) *Family Medical Encyclopedia*. London: Guild Publishing.

Ritchie, J., Eversley, J. and Gibb, A. (1982) 'Aspirations and motivations of would-be entrepreneurs', in Webb, T., Quince, T. and Watkins, D. (eds) *Small Business Research*. London: Gower.

Roberts, M.B.V. (1986) *Biology: A Functional Approach*. London: Nelson.

Rothschild, M.L. (1992) *Bionomics: The Inevitability of Capitalism*. London: Futura.

Rotter, R. (1966) 'Generalised expectations for internal versus external control of reinforcement', *Psychological Monographs*, No. 609.

Say, J.B. (1964) *A Treatise on Political Economy, or the Production, Distribution and Consumption of Wealth*. New York: Augustus Kelley.

Scase, R. and Goffee, R. (1980) *The Real World of the Small Business Owner*. Chelmsford: Croom Helm.

Schumpeter, J.A. (1934) *The Theory of Economic Development* (translated by R. Opie). Cambridge, Mass.: Harvard University Press.

Sombart, W. (1950) *The Quintessence of Capitalism: A Study of the History and Psychology of the Modern Business Man* (translated by M. Epstein). London: Fisher and Unwin.

Stanworth, J. and Curran, J. (1986) 'Growth and the small firm', in Curran, J., Stanworth, J. and Watkins, D. (eds) *The Survival of the Small Firm: Vol. 2*. London: Gower.

Stanworth, J. and Gray, C. (1991) *Bolton 20 Years On: The Small Firm in the 1990s*. London: Paul Chapman.

Steinmetz, L.L. (1969) 'Critical stages of small business growth', *Business Horizons*, Vol. 12, No. 1.

Stevenson, H.H. and Sahlman, W.A. (1989) 'The entrepreneurial process', in Burns, P. and Dewhurst, J. (eds) *Small Business and Entrepreneurship*. London: Macmillan.

Vyakarnham, S. and Jacobs, R. (1993) 'Teamstart – overcoming the blockages to small business growth'. Paper presented at the 16th National Small Firms' Policy and Research Conference, November.

FURTHER READING

General

Metaphors

Lakoff, G. and Johnson, M. (1980) *Metaphors We Live By*. Chicago: University of Chicago Press.

Ortony, A. (1975) 'Why metaphors are necessary and not just nice', *Educational Theory*, Vol. 25, No. 1.

Ortony, A. (ed) (1993) *Metaphor and Thought*. 2nd Edition, Cambridge: Cambridge University Press.

Sacks, S. (ed) (1979) *On Metaphor*. Chicago: University of Chicago Press.

Organisation Development

Bennis, W.G. (1969) *Organization Development: Its Nature, Origins, and Prospects*. Reading, Mass.: Addison-Wesley.

Cummings, T.G. and Worley, C.G. (1993) *Organization Development and Change*. 5th Edition, St Paul: West Publishing.

French, W.L. and Bell, C.H. (1990) *Organization Development: Behavioural Science Interventions for Organizational Improvement*. 4th Edition, London: Prentice-Hall.

Harvey, D.F. and Brown, D.R. (1992) *An Experiential Approach to Organisation Development*. 4th Edition, London: Prentice-Hall.

McLean, A.J., Sims, D.B.P., Mangham, I.L. and Tuffield, D. (1982) *Organization Development in Transition: Evidence of an Evolving Profession*. Chichester: Wiley.

Part I Metaphors and Organisational Analysis

Alvesson, M. (1993) 'The play of metaphors', in Hassard, J. and Parker, M. (eds) *Postmodernism and Organizations*. London: Sage.

Morgan, G. (1980) 'Paradigms, metaphors and puzzle solving in organization theory', *Administrative Science Quarterly*, Vol. 25.

Morgan, G. (1983) 'More on metaphor: why we cannot control tropes in administrative science', *Administrative Science Quarterly*, Vol. 28.

Morgan, G. (1986) *Images of Organization*. Newbury Park, CA: Sage.

Pinder, C.C. and Bourgeois, V.W. (1982) 'Controlling tropes in administrative science', *Administrative Science Quarterly*, Vol. 27.

Pondy, L.R., Frost, P.J., Morgan, G. and Dandridge, T. (eds) (1988) *Organizational Symbolism*. Greenwich: JAI Press.

Tsoukas, H. (1991) 'The missing link: a transformational view of metaphors in organizational science', *Academy of Management Review*, Vol. 16, No. 3.

Tsoukas, H. (1993) 'Analogical reasoning and knowledge generation in organization theory', *Organization Studies*, Vol. 14, No. 3.

Turner, B.A. (ed) (1990) *Organizational Symbolism*. Berlin: Walter de Gruyter.

Part II Organisational Culture and Change

Organisational Culture

Brown, A. (1995) *Organisational Culture*. London: Pitman.

Deal, T. and Kennedy, A. (1982) *Corporate Cultures*. Reading, Mass.: Addison-Wesley.

Frost, P.J., Moore, L.F., Louis, M.R., Lundberg, C.C. and Martin, J. (eds) (1991) *Reframing Organizational Culture*. California: Sage.

Louis, M.R. (1983) 'Organizations as culture-bearing milieux', in Pondy, L.R., Frost, P.J., Morgan, G. and Dandridge, T. (eds), *Organizational Symbolism*. Greenwich: JAI Press.

Schein, E.H. (1985) *Organizational Culture and Leadership*. San Francisco: Jossey-Bass.

Smircich, L. (1983) 'Studying organizations as cultures', in Morgan, G. (ed) *Beyond Method*. California: Sage.

Organisational Change

Barrett, F.J. and Cooperrider, D.L. (1990) 'Generative metaphor intervention: a new approach for working with systems divided by conflict and caught in defensive perception', *Journal of Applied Behavioral Science*, Vol. 26, No. 2.

Burnes, B. (1992) *Managing Change*. London: Pitman.

Goodman, P.S. and Associates (eds) (1982) *Change in Organizations: New Perspectives on Theory, Research and Practice*. London: Jossey-Bass.

Marshak, R.J. (1993) 'Managing the metaphors of change', *Organisational Dynamics*, Vol. 22, No. 1.

Sackmann, S. (1989) 'The role of metaphors in organisation transformation', *Human Relations*, Vol. 42, No. 6.

Part III The Intervention Process

Argyris, C. (1970) *Intervention Theory and Method*. Reading, Mass.: Addison-Wesley.

Blake, R.R. and Mouton, J.S. (1983) *Consultation: A Handbook for Individual and Organizational Development*. Reading, Mass.: Addison-Wesley.

Buchanan, D. and Boddy, D. (1992) *The Expertise of the Change Agent*. Hemel Hempstead: Prentice-Hall.

Clark, T. (1995) *Managing Consultants*. Buckingham: Open University Press.

Cockman, P., Evans, B. and Reynolds, P. (1992) *Client-Centred Consulting*. London: McGraw-Hill.

Dimock, H.G. (1993) *Intervention and Collaboration: Helping Organizations to Change*. San Diego, CA: Pfeiffer.

Kotter, J.P. (1978) *Organizational Dynamics: Diagnosis and Intervention*. Reading, Mass.: Addison-Wesley.

Lippitt, G.L. and Lippitt, R. (1986) *The Consulting Process in Action*. 2nd Edition, San Diego, CA: University Associates.

Mangham, I.L. (1978) *Interactions and Interventions in Organizations*. Chichester: Wiley.

Part IV Management Strategies and Development

Human Resource Management

Blyton, P. and Turnbull, P. (eds) (1992) *Reassessing Human Resource Management*. London: Sage.

Dunn, S. (1990) 'Root metaphor in the old and new industrial relations', *British Journal of Industrial Relations*, Vol. 28, No. 1.

Storey, J. (ed) (1991) *New Perspectives on Human Resource Management*. London: Routledge.

Outdoor Management Development

Bank, J. (1985) *Outdoor Development for Managers*. Aldershot: Gower.

Bronson, J., Gibson, S., Kichar, R. and Priest, S. (1992) 'Evaluation of team development in a corporate adventure training program', *Journal of Experiential Education*, Vol. 15, No. 2.

Jones, P.J. and Oswick, C. (1993) 'Outcomes of outdoor management development: articles of faith?', *Journal of European Industrial Training*, Vol. 17, No. 3.

Small Business Development

Curran, J.A. and Blackburn, R.A. (1991) *Paths of Enterprise: The Future of the Small Business*. London: Routledge.

Stanworth, J. and Gray, C. (1991) *Bolton 20 Years On: The Small Firm in the 1990s*. London: Paul Chapman.

Storey, D.J. (1994) *Understanding the Small Business Sector*. London: Routledge.

INDEX